Southern Living

home cooking

BASICS

Southern Living®

home cooking

BASICS

a complete illustrated guide to Southern cooking

great food made simple

Oxmoor House®

ISBN-13: 978-0-8487-3515-9
ISBN-10: 0-8487-3515-3
Library of Congress Control Number: 2012937201

Printed in the United States of America
First Printing 2012

Oxmoor House
Editorial Director: Leah McLaughlin
Creative Director: Felicity Keane
Senior Brand Manager: Daniel Fagan
Senior Editor: Rebecca Brennan
Managing Editor: Rebecca Benton

Southern Living Home Cooking Basics
Editor: Ashley T. Strickland
Project Editor: Sarah H. Doss
Senior Designer: Emily Parrish
Assistant Designer: Allison Sperando Potter
Director, Test Kitchen: Elizabeth Tyler Austin
Assistant Directors, Test Kitchen: Julie Christopher, Julie Gunter
Recipe Developers and Testers: Wendy Ball, R.D.; Allison E. Cox; Victoria E. Cox; Stefanie Maloney; Callie Nash; Leah Van Deren
Recipe Editor: Alyson Moreland Haynes
Food Stylists: Margaret Monroe Dickey, Catherine Crowell Steele
Photography Director: Jim Bathie
Senior Photo Stylist: Kay E. Clarke
Photo Stylist: Katherine Eckert Coyne
Assistant Photo Stylist: Mary Louise Menendez
Senior Production Manager: Greg A. Amason

Contributors
Editor: Katherine Cobbs
Project Editor: Georgia Dodge
Copy Editor: Dolores Hydock, Julie Bosché
Proofreaders: Rhonda Lee Lother, Polly Linthicum
Indexer: Mary Ann Laurens
Interns: Erin Bishop; Morgan Bolling; Mackenzie Cogle; Jessica Cox, R.D.; Blair Gillespie; Laura Hoxworth; Maribeth Jones; Susan Kemp; Alicia Lavender; Alison Loughman; Emily Robinson; Lindsay Rozier; Caitlin Watzke; Ashley White
Food Stylists: Ana Price Kelly
Recipe Developers and Testers: Tamara Goldis, Erica Hopper, Tonya Johnson, Kyra Moncrief, Kathleen Royal Phillips,
Photo Stylists: Mindi Shapiro Levine, Anna Pollock

Time Home Entertainment Inc.
Publisher: Jim Childs
VP, Strategy & Business Development: Steven Sandonato
Executive Director, Marketing Services: Carol Pittard
Executive Director, Retail & Special Sales: Tom Mifsud
Director, Bookazine Development & Marketing: Laura Adam
Executive Publishing Director: Joy Butts
Finance Director: Glenn Buonocore
Associate General Counsel: Helen Wan

Southern Living®
Editor: M. Lindsay Bierman
Creative Director: Robert Perino
Managing Editor: Candace Higginbotham
Art Director: Chris Hoke
Associate Art Director: Erynn Hedrick Hassinger
Executive Editors: Rachel Hardage Barrett, Jessica S. Thuston
Food Director: Shannon Sliter Satterwhite
Test Kitchen Director: Rebecca Kracke Gordon
Senior Writer: Donna Florio
Senior Food Editor: Mary Allen Perry
Recipe Editor: JoAnn Weatherly
Assistant Recipe Editor: Ashley Arthur
Test Kitchen Specialist/Food Styling: Vanessa McNeil Rocchio
Test Kitchen Professionals: Norman King, Pam Lolley, Angela Sellers
Directors of Photography: Julie Claire, Mark Sandlin
Style Director: Heather Chadduck
Senior Photographers: Ralph Lee Anderson, Gary Clark, Art Meripol
Photographers: Robbie Caponetto, Laurey W. Glenn
Senior Photo Stylist: Buffy Hargett
Studio Assistant: Caroline Murphy Cunningham
Editorial Assistant: Pat York
Office Manager: Nellah Bailey McGough

For more than 45 years, *Southern Living* has provided millions of readers with delicious, fool-proof recipes that we've perfected in our test kitchen. If you love reading about great Southern food but lack confidence in your own kitchen, *Home Cooking Basics* is the book for you.

These pages will give you all the inspiration and information you need to prepare memorable meals just like momma did. From the best knives to must-have baking equipment, we've researched all the essentials. You'll learn how to stock your spice cabinet, how to select in-season produce, and how to determine the best cut of meat to use in your recipe. Step-by-step photographs demonstrate good-to-know techniques such as deveining shrimp and cutting a mango. You'll even become a whiz at boiling, braising, grilling, and sautéing, so you can easily apply what you've learned to the over 375 recipes included in the book!

Best of all, *Home Cooking Basics* proves that "basic" should never mean boring. We'll transform you into an everday gourmet who entertains with ease—so let go of your trepidations, toss your take-out menus, and let's get cooking!

Lindsay

M. Lindsay Bierman
Editor, *Southern Living* Magazine

Watermelon Salsa,
page 382

Contents

the SETUP

The tools and equipment that make cooking a pleasure

COOKWARE

When equipping your kitchen, the first place to start is cookware. The quality of the cooking vessels you have can greatly affect the end result of a recipe. Stock your kitchen with varying sizes and shapes of these, and you'll be armed and ready to tackle any dish.

1. Stockpot This is perfect for tackling heavy-duty jobs such as making large batches of chili or steaming lobsters. Thick-bottomed pots are ideal to prevent scorching.

2. Dutch Oven This versatile pot is a must-have. It's made for stovetop and oven use, and, while ideal for making soups, it's also perfect for frying and braising.

3. Tongs This tool is oftentimes a chef's favorite, allowing you to grab hot items with ease.

4. Steamer Basket You'll find this is great for steaming veggies, dumplings or even fish. Look for collapsible models with a center rod that allows for easy removal from your pot.

5. Skillet The shallow sides of this pan allow for searing and quick reduction of sauces. Nonstick skillets are perfect for cooking delicate foods such as omelets and make cleanup a breeze.

6. Saucepan A kitchen staple, saucepans come in many sizes and are perfect for just about every stovetop task. Look for pans with tight-fitting lids and rounded corners so your whisk and spoon can easily reach every nook and cranny.

7. Cast-Iron Skillet The beauty of cast iron is that it heats up slowly but retains heat well. It's fairly inexpensive and lasts forever. Be sure to keep it well seasoned, and it'll be your go-to "nonstick" skillet for everything.

8. Grill Pan This pan offers all the benefits that a grill does, such as caramelizing ridges for grill marks.

9. Cutting Board Buy this in a variety of shapes, sizes, and materials for versatility. Butcher blocks are the most durable, as they're made of wood. Plastic and rubber boards are more convenient, especially when they fit into a dishwasher.

10. Roasting Pan A necessity for holiday feasts, this pan with low sides promises even brownness for meats and veggies with maximum exposure to the oven's heat.

BAKEWARE

Whether you're a serious baker or a beginner, these pans, utensils, and bowls will help guarantee recipe success. They're all relatively inexpensive and can make everyday tasks a little easier. As with cookware, quality is key —so don't skimp.

1. Mixing Bowl It's a good idea to have both stainless steel and ceramic mixing bowls in various sizes. Ceramic bowls are microwave-safe, and stainless steel bowls are ideal for whipping egg whites.

2. Whisk Be sure to have several different shapes and sizes of this tool to best perform the job at hand. Balloon whisks have long, thin wires in a wide "balloon" shape to beat cream to perfect fluffiness and egg whites to stiff peaks. Skinny whisks are ideal for making sauces, because they reach into tight spaces.

3. Loaf Pan If you love to bake, you'll definitely need a couple of these. It's a good idea to have a pair of the same size in case your recipe makes 2 loaves of bread.

4. Oven Mitt This is a necessity to grab hot pans from the oven or stovetop. Mitts that are machine washable are the most practical.

5. Bundt Pan This specialty pan is what you need for pound cakes and coffee cakes. Be sure to buy heavy-weight cast aluminum with clearly defined ridges for easy release and a capacity of 12 cups for use with most recipes.

6. Pie Plate This glass dish is useful for more than just pies. It's also great for quiches, for dredging meats into flour, and so much more. The most common size is 9-inch, but you can also buy deep-dish and 10-inch dishes.

7. Tart Pan The bottom of this pan is removable so you don't destroy delicate crusts. A 9-inch pan is the most versatile size.

8. Springform Pan The removable sides of this pan make it ideal for cheesecakes. You can remove the cake from the pan without destroying its creamy texture. It's a good idea to have at least 2 different sizes on hand, and be sure that there is a tight seal between the band and the bottom of the pan so batter won't escape during baking.

9. Cake Pan Choose round or square varieties. It's a good idea to have a pair of the same size so that you can make layer cakes. Look for pans with high, straight sides and a nonstick finish.

10. Rubber Scraper This tool is especially important when scraping batter from bowls. Make sure yours is heatproof so that it doesn't melt when stirring hot mixtures.

11. Muffin Tin The traditional $1/2$-cup capacity is a best bet for making perfect muffins and cupcakes. Look for pans with a dark nonstick surface to ensure even browning during baking.

12. Spatula This tool is handy when flipping fried eggs or hamburgers. Make sure you have a few that are heatproof and some that are non-metal for when you're cooking on nonstick surfaces.

13. Baking Sheet Rimmed baking sheets wear many hats in the kitchen—they can bake up your favorite batch of cookies or sub as a roasting pan for veggies. Buy those with light-colored surfaces and heavy thicknesses for even baking.

14. Baking Dish/Pan This pan is used for everything from baking casseroles and roasting vegetables to baking sheet cakes. A 13- x 9-inch pan is the most commonly used size, but you may also want to have a smaller 11- x 7-inch, a square baking dish, and some round 2- and 3-quart dishes. The same is true for baking pans.

15. Cooling Rack Meant for holding hot pans straight out of the oven, this tool can double as a rack for a roasting pan. Be sure to buy racks with tightly woven, heavy-duty metal bars.

16. Silicone Mat Once found only in professional kitchens, these handy baking mats take away the need for parchment, wax paper, oil, or grease for baking pans. They are safe to heat up to oven temperatures of 475°.

KNIVES

It is virtually impossible to get around the kitchen without a good knife. So be sure to choose knives made of high-quality carbon steel, which won't rust or corrode. For strength and balance, look for knives with full tangs, where the metal of the blade extends the entire length of the handle and is anchored with rivets. Handles can be made of wood, resin, plastic, rubber, or metal. While knives can be purchased in sets, selecting each individually allows you to gauge how they feel and fit your hand. After all, the most important feature of a good knife is comfort.

1. Paring Knife Like a chef's knife in miniature, the tapered blade of a paring knife ranges from 3 to 4 inches in length and is most often used for peeling and slicing fruits and vegetables. It comes in handy when precision cutting is required, such as hulling strawberries, peeling potatoes, or cutting pastry embellishments.

2. Chef's Knife This large-bladed knife is the workhorse of the kitchen. Its slightly curved, broad blade and heft make it extremely versatile. Use it in a rocking fashion to chop, dice, and mince and in a sweeping fashion to slice or fillet. Use the broad side of the knife to crush garlic or pit olives. It comes in a range of sizes, but an 8-inch blade is good for most cooks.

3. Meat Cleaver This hefty knife looks like a hatchet and is ideal for cutting through bones or chopping big slabs of meat. It also works well when crushing garlic.

4. Boning Knife With a flexible, modestly curved blade of 5 to 7 inches, this knife is an excellent choice for separating cooked and uncooked meats from the bone or peeling fruits and vegetables.

5. Utility Knife Like a paring knife, only larger, the utility knife's slightly curved blade comes in handy for carving small cuts of meat.

6. Carving Knife Its blade can be rigid or flexible and range from 8 to 15 inches. Rigid blades are used for slicing roasted meats, while flexible blades are ideal for filleting large fish or carving a bird. It comes with either a smooth or granton edge.

7. Serrated Knife Its tooth-like blade makes it the ideal choice for slicing through soft or crusty breads; cakes and other baked goods; thick-skinned fruts such as citrus; and tender-skinned ingredients, such as tomatoes, which often burst under the pressure of a non-serrated knife.

8. Santoku The loose translation of the name of this knife of Japanese origin is "three virtues," and it holds true to the claim. It is ideal for mincing, dicing, and slicing. The handle is in line with the top of the blade, while the tip of the knife curves down to meet the sharp edge, creating a balanced knife. This knife often comes with a "granton" or scalloped edge that helps food release after cutting.

kitchen secret:

Keep your investment in top form by washing and drying knives by hand immediately after use and always storing them in a knife block or a drawer insert to protect the blades.

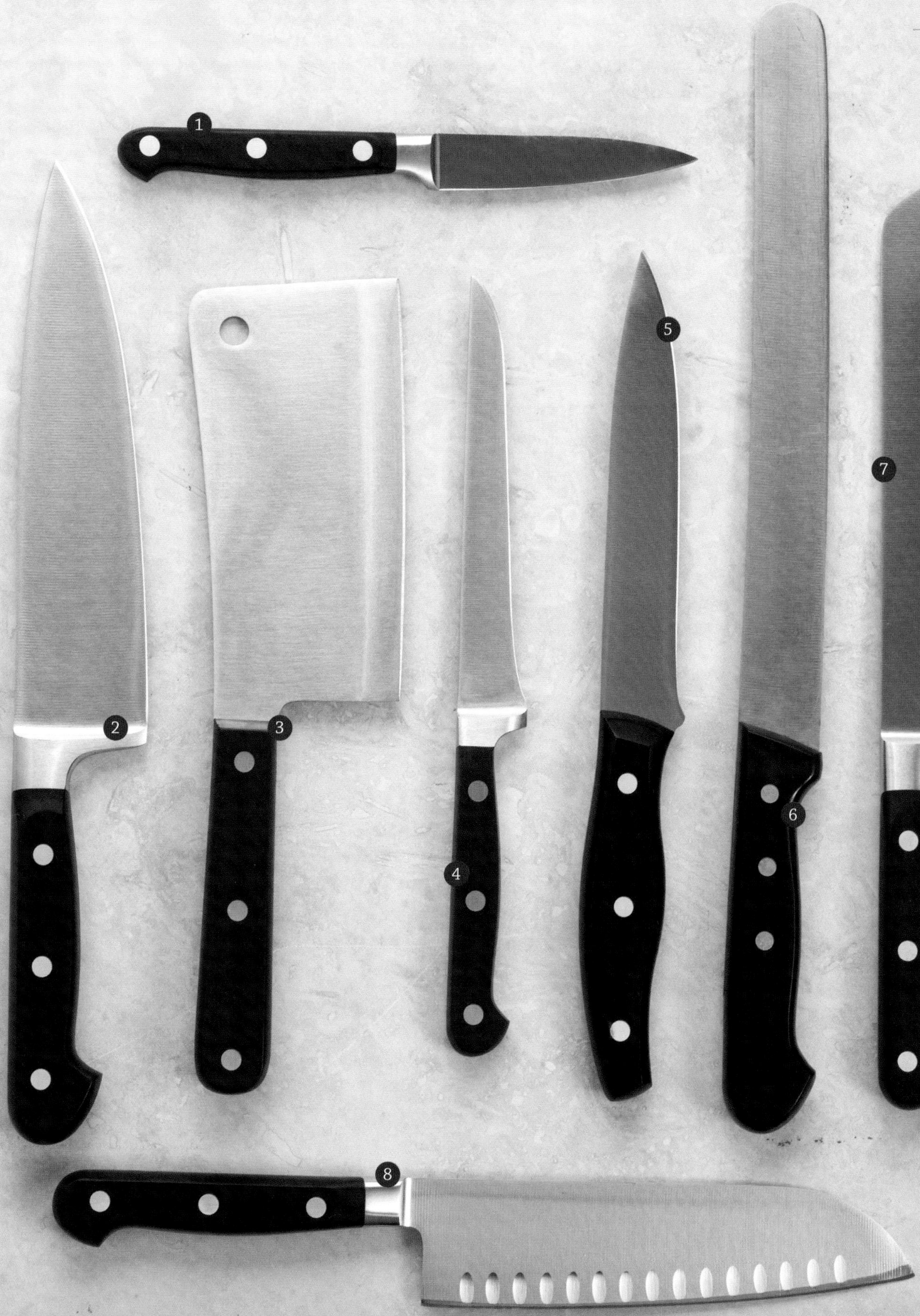
1
2
3
4
5
6
7
8

how to:
sharpen kitchen knives

While sharpening steels are included in many knife sets, they won't actually sharpen a knife. They do maintain a blade's alignment and extend the life of the sharp edge. Sharpening stones, called benchstones or whetstones, and ceramic knife sharpeners or V sharpeners are your best bet for home sharpening.

To use a sharpening steel: Hold the tip of the steel down on a sturdy surface. Grasp the knife handle, holding the blade at a 20-degree angle and, with the wide end of the blade at the top of the steel, draw the blade down along the steel, curving slightly so that you draw the entire edge over the steel; repeat the procedure for the other side of the blade using the opposite side of the steel. Repeat the movement 5 to 10 times, alternating sides.

To use a stone: Moisten the stone with water or mineral oil to reduce friction. Place the damp stone on a damp towel placed at the edge of a sturdy work surface. If using the fine-grain side of the stone, position the wide end of the knife blade against the upper corner of the stone and tilt the blade at a 20-degree angle; use a 25- to 35-degree angle for the coarse-grain side. Carefully pull the blade toward you in a slight arc over the stone, beginning with the wide end and ending with the tip. Repeat several times, alternating sides of the knife.

To use a ceramic sharpener: Grip the handle firmly, holding the sharpener steady against the work surface. Carefully draw the blade from the wide end to point through the slit, which contains rods or spheres often coated with diamond dust of varying grits. This tool does a good job of sharpening and honing for general knife maintenance at home.

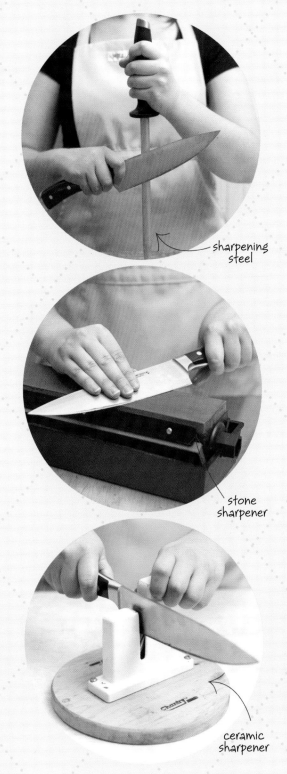

sharpening steel

stone sharpener

ceramic sharpener

TOOLS

With so many kitchen gadgets on the market, it's hard to determine which ones are absolutely necessary. Depending on the task at hand, these tools can make the job easier and have your recipe ready in no time.

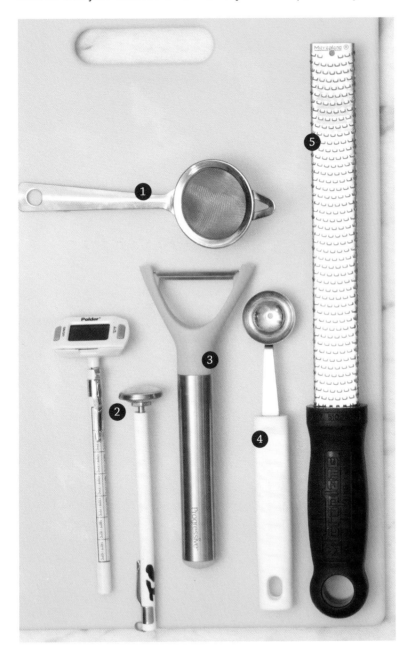

1. Sifter This small gadget is just what you need to sift powdered sugar or cocoa onto your baked goodies. It also works well as a loose-leaf tea strainer for hot tea.

2. Thermometer This tool is essential to take the guesswork out of determining when foods are done. Digital thermometers, as opposed to analog, are easiest to use because you can take a quick glance and know the temperature. Look for models with long stems that will reach the very center of the food.

3. Vegetable Peeler This little tool removes unwanted peelings from potatoes, carrots, and more. Be sure to buy a model with a comfortable handle and a sharp, swiveling blade.

4. Melon Baller If you're tired of cubing your fruit, this tool scoops melon into cute bite-size balls. It also works great as an apple and pear corer.

5. Rasp When you want to grate a little zest from a lemon or top your pasta with some fresh cheese, this handheld tool will do the trick. Be sure to buy a model with sharp teeth and a handle that fits nicely in your hand.

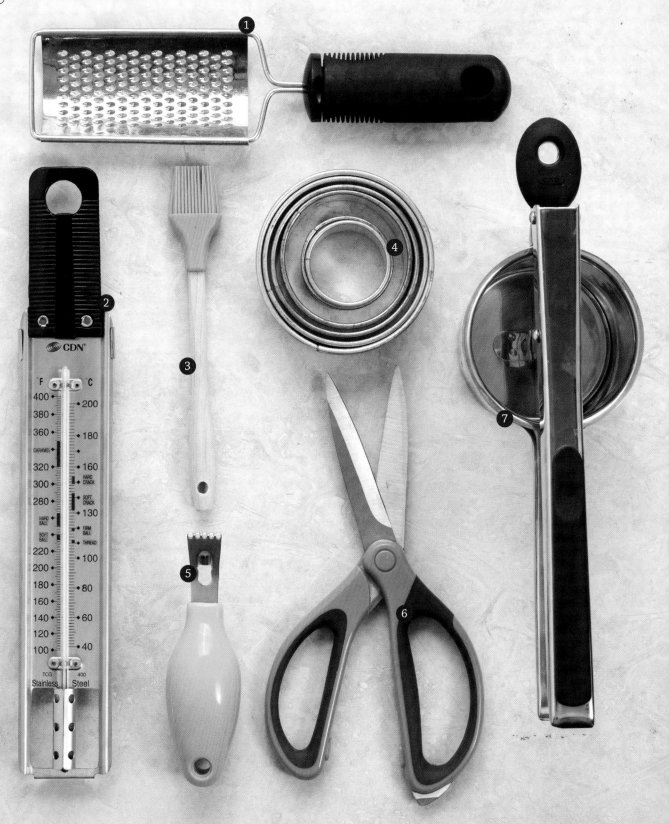

1. Handheld Grater This easy-to-use tool is great for grating hard food items such as Parmesan cheese and chocolate.

2. Candy Thermometer This thermometer is designed to measure precise high temperatures of foods, such as caramel. Be sure to buy one that is easy to read and has a clip attachment so you don't have to hold it in place while you stir.

3. Pastry Brush This is ideal for brushing on butter, an egg wash, basting meats with marinades and sauces, and so much more. The new silicone varieties last much longer than traditional pastry brushes, and they are a snap to clean.

4. Biscuit Cutters These round cutters are perfect for cutting dough into biscuits or cookies. Look for a set with sharp edges and many different sizes. Cutters with a storage container and lid are also handy.

5. Zester Extract bold citrus flavor from the peel of oranges, lemons, and limes easily with this tool. The small, round prongs also turn the skin of the fruit into beautiful curls perfect for garnishing cakes and cookies.

6. Kitchen Shears A pair of shears makes a tedious job such as chopping herbs and canned tomatoes a breeze. They're also great to have on hand for cutting kitchen twine and noodles and opening stubborn packaging. Models that can easily be taken apart are ideal, because you can throw them in the dishwasher with other kitchen utensils.

7. Potato Ricer This tool makes mashed potatoes ultra-creamy. The handheld crank pushes the cooked potatoes through the grate, and you're left with small flakes. Just add some butter, milk, salt, and pepper, and you're good to go.

kitchen secret:

Not everyone is lucky enough to have a lot of storage space. If you've got a small kitchen, this list of tools will get the job done without overloading your cabinets with equipment:

- **Skillets:** a large skillet, at least 12 inches in diameter, a nonstick skillet, and a cast-iron skillet
- A Dutch oven
- A saucepan, at least 3 quarts
- Baking sheets, rimmed and unrimmed
- Baking dishes, a 13- x 9-inch and 8-inch square
- **Power tools:** food processor, mixer, and blender
- A box grater
- Cutting boards
- **Gadgets:** colander, heatproof spatulas, kitchen shears, measuring cups and spoons, whisks, vegetable peeler, and an instant-read thermometer
- **Knives:** chef's knife, paring knife, and a serrated knife

1. Stainless, Silicone, and Wooden Spoons Keep a large supply of varying sizes and shapes on hand. If you're using nonstick cookware, don't forget to use wooden or rubber spoons.

2. Rolling Pin When it comes to this tool, wooden cylinders with tapered ends make it easy to roll dough to an even thickness.

3. Potato Masher Soft cooked potatoes and other vegetables become creamy in no time with this tool. Look for models with sturdy, comfortable handles.

4. Box Grater This metal gadget shreds and grates cheeses, carrots, and other foods into a variety of sizes. Be sure to buy one with sharp teeth and a sturdy handle.

5. Fine-Mesh Strainer Separate solids from liquids quickly. The woven design traps any unwanted particles.

6. Mortar and Pestle This duo is used to grind and crush whole spices and herbs.

7. Colander The perforated design of this bowl allows for easy draining of pasta and rice. Be sure to buy models with small enough holes so that your food won't escape and end up down the drain.

8. Juicer Use this tool to extract juice from citrus fruits. A citrus reamer also works well.

9. Kitchen Timer This gadget is essential for all cooks. It ensures precision, especially for baking.

10. Measuring Spoons These are a must, especially when it comes to baking. Look for spoons with a flat top and long handle so that ingredients can be leveled easily.

11. Pastry Tips These metal tips come in a variety of shapes and sizes and fit on the ends of pastry bags to pipe frostings and fillings into decorative designs.

12. Pastry Blender This handheld gadget is used to work butter and shortening into flour for baking. The metal wires prevent the fat from melting while cutting it into smaller pieces. If you don't have a pastry blender, a fork works as a nice substitute.

13. Ladle Serve up soups and stews without creating a mess.

14. Measuring Cups Be sure to have both dry and liquid measuring cups. Straight-sided cups that are sturdy and long-handled are ideal to make leveling dry ingredients a snap. Cups with a pouring spout and easy-to-read measures are intended for liquids.

15. Custard Cups Also known as ramekins, these little bowls are made for baked custards but also work well to hold prepped food.

POWER TOOLS

These appliances will last for years if you stay away from cheap models. Some may seem like luxury items, but when you consider all the blending, chopping, and shredding that can be done, they become valuable everyday tools.

1. Food Processor This tool makes tedious tasks like chopping, slicing, and shredding a snap. Look for a machine with a large feed tube and sturdy, sharp blades.

2. Blender This is the only kitchen tool that will blend hot and cold foods into a smooth texture. Look for one with a tall jar, short blades and a variety of settings.

3. Handheld Mixer Beat eggs and mix batters with this affordable, lightweight baking essential.

4. Immersion Blender This is a great lightweight tool to use when pureeing soups or other liquefied dishes because you can blend in the pot you've already gotten dirty.

5. Coffee Grinder When you're looking for the freshest tasting coffee, grind your own beans. But it's not only for coffee—it wears another hat as a spice grinder.

6. Stand Mixer If you're a serious baker or cook, a heavy-duty stand mixer is a tool you won't be able to live without. It allows for hands-off mixing, usually comes with a variety of attachments, and is great for heavy-duty jobs such as making bread dough. Look for a model that is easy to operate, has a powerful motor, and has large-capacity bowls.

TABLE SETTINGS

Traditional table settings can be easy to navigate, once you understand the uses for each serving piece. The end result of a perfectly adorned table sets the stage for a wonderful meal.

Traditional Place Setting:

1. Butter Knife This small knife is placed on the individual bread plate at each setting.

2. Bread Plate This individual plate is placed to the upper left of the dinner plate.

3. Salad Fork Diners use this fork for the salad course before dinner. It can also be used for desserts, appetizers, or other small foods.

4. Dinner Fork This is used for the main dinner course.

5. Dessert Fork Always placed above the dinner plate, this fork is intended for eating cakes, pies, and pastries that follow the main course. It looks a lot like a salad fork.

6. Dinner Knife This knife is used for the main dinner course but may also be used for spreading butter and/or condiments.

7. Place Spoon Also known as a tablespoon, this versatile utensil may be used for soup, dessert, or cereal. It can even double as a serving spoon.

8. Teaspoon This spoon is used for stirring coffee and tea and can also be used for dessert, soup, and cereal.

9. Wine Glasses Place these to the upper right of the dinner plate.

Serving Pieces:

10. Meat Fork Use this fork for serving meats, cheeses, and even some types of vegetables.

11. Sugar Shell This shell-shaped spoon is commonly used with a sugar bowl.

12. Table Serving Spoon This large spoon is used for serving vegetables.

13. Slotted Serving Spoon This spoon is very similar to a table serving spoon but offers holes in the bowl of the spoon to serve vegetables that need to be drained.

14. Butter Knife This is used to serve pats of butter from a butter dish to the individual bread plate.

15. Pierced Table Spoon An alternative to a slotted serving spoon, the pierced edges of this spoon allow spearing of vegetables such as asparagus and green beans.

16. Gravy/Sauce Ladle Commonly 6 to 8 inches long, this ladle is used to serve sauces and gravies.

17. Pie/Cake Server This utensil is used to cut and serve pie and cake slices neatly and evenly.

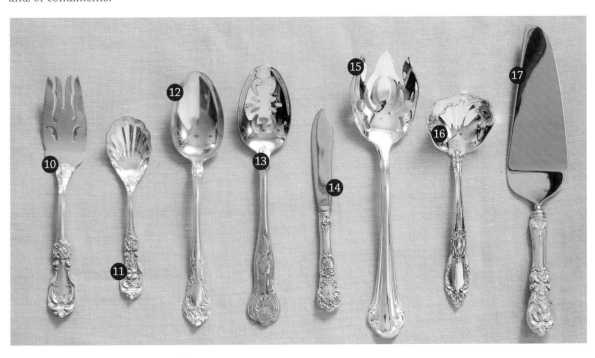

BARWARE

There's more to stocking your bar than liquor, beer, and wine. Having a varied supply of glasses allows you to entertain in style.

1. Cocktail Shaker This is a nifty way to mix various types of liquors and juices. The mixture is shaken with ice to cool it down and then strained into a serving glass.

2. Coffee Glass This glass is perfect for Irish coffee or hot chocolate.

3. Pilsner Glass Used for pale lagers, pilsners, and light beers, the tall shape of this glass reveals the beer's color and carbonation.

4. Beer Stein This traditional mug from Germany is made of silver, pewter, or stoneware and has an open top or lid with a thumb lever.

5. Margarita Glass This glass is a variation of the Champagne coupe and is used for margaritas served on the rocks or frozen.

6. Martini Glass Also known as a cocktail glass, its long stem allows you to hold it without affecting the cocktail's temperature, and the wide bowl offers a large surface area to release the drink's aroma.

7. Iced Tea/Water Glass This flat-bottomed, tall tumbler is used for cold drinks such as iced tea or water.

8. Shooter Glass This double shot glass measures liquor for extra-potent drinks or "shots" and can also be used for certain food items, such as soups or desserts.

9. Old-Fashioned Glass This type of short tumbler was originally designed to hold its namesake, a cocktail of muddled bitters, whiskey, and a twist of citrus. It can be used for any alcoholic beverage.

10. Shot Glass This glass is designed to hold or measure liquor that is drunk straight from the glass or poured into a mixed drink.

1. Red Wine Glass This glass is characterized by a wide, round bowl to increase oxidation. Tall, broader bowled glasses are intended for full-bodied wines.

2. White Wine Glass This glass comes in a variety of sizes but is often smaller and slimmer than a red wine glass to reduce oxidation and maintain crisp, clean flavors.

3. Champagne Flute Tall with a narrow bowl on top, this glass is designed to hold sparkling wines. The height of the glass allows the wine to stay cold longer.

4. Champagne Coupe This traditional Champagne glass has a shallow bowl and is most commonly used for weddings or formal occasions.

5. Cordial Glass This glass is used for serving small sips of after-dinner drinks.

6. Sherry/Port Glass This small glass is designed for serving sherry and other aromatic liqueurs.

the INGREDIENTS

A guide to purchasing and storing wholesome food

SPICES

Stock your cabinet with these common spices and you'll be prepared for most any recipe. For best results, be sure to store them in a cool, dark place for no longer than 6 months.

1. Star Anise This star-shaped pod is native to China and has a slightly bitter licorice flavor. It is commonly used in Asian cuisines and is one of the spices used in Chinese five-spice powder.

2. Red Pepper A general name given to a variety of hot red chile peppers, red peppers are usually dried and are available whole, flaked, or ground. Cayenne pepper, a powder made from the various ground dried hot chiles, has a bright orange-red color and is often referred to as ground red pepper.

3. Curry Powder This blend of up to 20 spices includes ground cardamom, cinnamon, cloves, coriander, cumin, fennel, nutmeg, pepper, and turmeric. It is commonly used in Indian cooking.

4. Cumin This aromatic dried seed has a nutty flavor and is available ground or unground.

5. Cloves This spice can be bought whole, as shown here, or ground and is used in a variety of dishes from savory to sweet. Whole cloves are the unopened bud of the clove tree.

6. Pickling Spice This mixture of spices is used for pickling cucumbers and other canned vegetables. It typically contains a mix of whole allspice, crushed bay leaf, coriander seeds, mustard seeds, peppercorns, and cloves.

7. Celery Seed This pungent spice is the seed of the wild celery plant, called lovage. It should be used in small quantities and is most often found in potato salad and other salad recipes as well as soup and meat recipes.

8. Ground Ginger This dried and ground form of the gingerroot has a peppery-sweet flavor. While it is not a good substitute for fresh ginger, it is great when used for gingerbread, curries, and other savory dishes.

9. Turmeric This bright yellow spice is what gives curry powder and prepared mustard their vibrant color. It is used to pump up flavor and color in a variety of dishes.

10. Cardamom This pod, native to Asia and South America, is a member of the ginger family and has a sweet and spicy flavor. It can be purchased ground or in pod form.

11. Cinnamon The inner bark of a tropical evergreen tree is what we have come to know as cinnamon. There are two varieties: Ceylon and cassia. Ceylon cinnamon is lighter in color and has a mild, sweet flavor. Cassia cinnamon is the most common type sold in the U.S. and has a darker color and slight bittersweet flavor.

12. Chili Powder This combination of ground spices includes ground chiles, cloves, coriander, garlic, cumin, and oregano.

13. Saffron Luckily, a little bit of this pricey spice goes a long way. It is the stigma from a crocus plant, hand-picked, dried, and used to flavor dishes such as paella and bouillabaisse.

14. Peppercorns This hot spice is the berry of the pepper plant. Black peppercorns come whole, cracked, and ground.

15. Mace This spice is the red membrane that covers the nutmeg seed but is stronger in flavor than nutmeg. Once the membrane is removed and dried, it is ground into a bright yellow powder.

16. Nutmeg This ancient seed is native to the Spice Islands. It is sold whole or ground, but whole is preferred for freshness. Nutmeg graters or metal rasps work well for grating.

17. Ground Mustard This potent spice is made from finely ground mustard seeds. The two major types of mustard seeds are white (or yellow) and brown. Brown seeds are smaller and more pungent than white seeds.

18. Allspice Indigenous to South America and the West Indies, these berries taste like a combination of nutmeg, cinnamon, and cloves and are sold either ground or whole.

19. Paprika This vibrant red spice is made from several grindings of sweet red pepper pods. Most common commerical varieties come from Spain, Hungary, South America, and California. From mild to hot, this spice can be used as a garnish or as a seasoning.

SUGARS & SALTS

This go-to guide makes it easy to determine how to add a little sweet or salty flavor to a dish.

1. Smoked Sea Salt Smoked over a wood fire, this salt ranges from light grey to dark brown in color. Naturally smoked sea salt is extremely versatile, adding distinctive smoky aroma and flavor to a variety of main and side dishes.

2. Kosher Salt This salt gets its name from its ability to "kosher" meat by removing the surface blood. It is ideal for using in spice blends as well as for blending with other flavors during cooking and contains fewer additives than ordinary table salt.

3. Table Salt This salt is mined from underground salt deposits and contains an anti-caking agent not found in sea salt as well as the essential nutrient iodine. Due to its fine grain, there is more salt in a teaspoon of table salt than in a tablespoon of kosher or sea salt.

4. Hickory Smoked Salt Used since the Viking Age, this salt lends natural smoky flavor without the fire. For strong flavor, add it to fish and poultry dishes.

5. Granulated Sugar Also known as white sugar, this is the most common sugar used in the U.S. It is made from sugar cane or sugar beets and has a white, grainy appearance.

6. Turbinado Sugar This sugar, also known as cane sugar or raw sugar, resembles brown sugar and is less processed than other sugars. Like brown sugar, turbinado sugar should be kept in an airtight container to maintain freshness.

7. Powdered Sugar Also known as confectioners' sugar, powdered sugar is granulated sugar that has been crushed into a fine powder and supplemented with cornstarch to prevent clumping. Because it is quick to dissolve, this sugar is best used in icings or frostings or dusted over desserts.

8. Fleur de Sel This hand-harvested sea salt maintains its crystallized structure when sprinkled on moist foods but dissolves faster than table salt when used for cooking. It is best served sprinkled over a dish just before serving.

9. Sanding Sugar Often called decorating sugar or pearl sugar, sanding sugar consists of large crystals that do not dissolve when heated. This sugar is the ideal topping to make cookies and baked goods sparkle.

10. Brown Sugar With the two most common types being light and dark, brown sugar is actually white sugar combined with molasses. The darker the color of this sugar, the stronger its flavor.

fix it!

Problem: Even though the brown sugar was sealed in a bag, it's now as hard as a rock.

Solution: Brown sugar often becomes hard when the moisture has evaporated. To soften it, place half of a cut apple inside the bag with the brown sugar. Seal the bag and let it stand for a day or 2. Once the sugar has softened again, remove the apple and reseal the bag.

VINEGARS

Whether used in dressings, as a condiment, or to make your windows streak-free, this acidic ingredient is one of the most versatile to keep on hand.

1. Red Wine Vinegar As with the wine from which it's derived, red wine vinegar gets better with age. Most can mature for up to 2 years.

2. White Wine Vinegar This moderately tangy vinegar made from white wine is often used to make hollandaise and béarnaise sauces.

3. Sherry Vinegar This vinegar, made from sherry, is produced in Spain and adds immense flavor to many dishes. It can be aged anywhere from 6 months to 10 years.

4. Distilled White Vinegar This vinegar is the least expensive, most versatile, and most commonly used vinegar. It is made from grain alcohol and can be infused with herbs for added flavor. It's also a great natural cleaning agent.

5. Cider Vinegar Also known as apple cider vinegar, this inexpensive vinegar works well for pickling and adds tangy fruit flavor to marinades and dressings.

6. Balsamic Vinegar Originating from Italy, this vinegar is made from trebbiano grape juice and acquires its dark color from aging in barrels. It has a rich aroma and sweet flavor and serves as the perfect base for dressings and sauces.

7. Herb Vinegar This vinegar is made by allowing herbs to steep in vinegar for several days. Tarragon, dill, and rosemary are several herbs that make great flavorings for vinegar.

8. Rice Vinegar Often found in Asian dishes, this vinegar is made from fermented rice. It provides delicate, sweet flavor and is less acidic than regular vinegar.

9. Fruit-Infused Vinegar This type of vinegar is flavored with fruits such as figs, raspberries, and pears. It's mostly used in dressings or sauces.

10. Malt Vinegar This British favorite is made by malting barley into ale. Its high acidity lends strong flavor, and it is often used as a pickling agent or as a condiment to sprinkle onto foods.

FATS & OILS

Fats and oils are the flavor carriers for recipes. They also affect the texture of cakes, breads, and other baked goods.

1. Sesame Oil This oil, extracted from sesame seeds, is used to enhance the flavor of many Asian dishes. It has a high smoke point and is available as light or dark.

2. Vegetable Oil This oil has mild flavor and a high smoke point, making it ideal for deep-frying.

3. Stick Butter This preferred fat for baking burns at a lower temperature than oil while adding the most flavor. It is available as salted or unsalted and contains at least 80% milk fat.

4. European-Style Butter Richer than its American counterparts, this butter is cultured and has a higher butterfat content.

5. Whipped Butter This butter has had air whipped into it and is the ideal spread for breads and rolls. It is not recommended for cooking.

6. Olive Oil This prized oil comes in a variety of grades and flavors and can be used as a condiment, for sautéing, and for salad dressings and sauces.

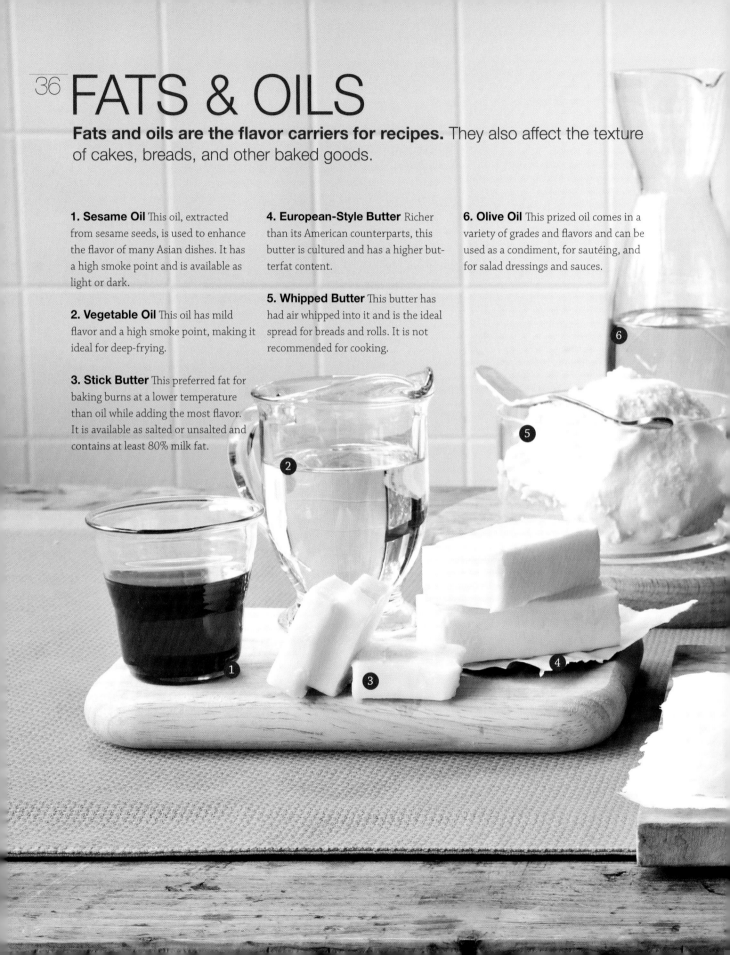

7. Extra Virgin Olive Oil This cold-pressed oil is the highest grade of olive oil because it is made from the first pressing of the olives. It can range in color from Champagne to dark green.

8. Flavored Oil Used to boost the flavor of both sweet and savory dishes, flavored oils can be added to a recipe or brushed atop meats and vegetables.

9. Grapeseed Oil With a relatively high smoke point, this oil is ideal for cooking over higher heat. Due to its mild flavor, grapeseed oil is also great for salad dressings.

10. Shortening This fat is solid at room temperature and is made from vegetable oils. It is often used to grease baking pans and to give flakiness to doughs. It can also be used as an alternative to frying with oil.

11. Lard The quality of this cooking fat depends on the area of the pig from which it was taken. Lard produces little smoke when heated and lends its distinctive taste when combined with other foods.

RICE

This ancient grain is a staple in diets across the world. Its versatility and relatively low price make it a favorite for many.

1. Wild Rice Blend This combination of rice often includes several varieties such as black wild rice, brown rice, rust wild rice, and long-grain rice. The multiple colors and textures are both pleasing to the eye and to the palate.

2. Basmati Rice Originating from India, basmati has longer grains than most other types of rice and can usually be identified by its light, nutty flavor. This fluffy rice does not stick together when cooked.

3. Pearl Rice Short-grained and sticky, this glutinous variety is ideal for making sushi or rice pudding. Available in white and brown forms, look for kernels that are intact with no signs of scratches or damage.

4. Arborio Rice Commonly used to prepare classic Italian risotto, arborio rice lends a creamy texture to dishes. It has a pearly white exterior and is ready when it becomes "al dente," or slightly firm when cooked.

5. Wild Rice Also known as Indian rice, this native grain of North America is high in protein and fiber and low in fat. It's actually a long-grain marsh grass instead of rice and should be rinsed thoroughly before cooking.

6. Black Rice Also known as forbidden or purple rice, black rice has a mild, nutty flavor similar to that of brown rice but contains greater amounts of vitamins and antioxidants.

7. Medium-Grain Rice Shorter but slightly wider than long-grain rice, this grain is often used in casseroles, breads, and stir-fry recipes and remains moist and tender when cooked.

8. Jasmine Rice With its naturally occurring floral scent, jasmine rice is commonly used in Asian and Thai dishes and has a light, fluffy texture and mellow, nutty flavor. It's often compared in flavor and texture to basmati rice.

9. Red Cargo Rice This unpolished type of long-grain rice is non-glutinous and has a chewier texture than standard white rice. It should be soaked in water 30 minutes before cooking to ensure a soft texture.

10. Mochi Rice This variety of rice has short, fat grains and has a higher starch content. Because of its sweetness, it's commonly used to make rice cakes and confections.

OTHER GRAINS

These rice-alternative grains are inexpensive and an excellent source of protein and healthy carbohydrates.

1. Oats Though harvested in the fall, this cereal grain is available year-round and is best prepared by adding cold water and then simmering until cooked. Rolled oats usually require less cook time than the steel-cut variety and are also available in quick-cooking form.

2. Kasha One of the oldest known dishes in Eastern European Slavic cuisine, these buckwheat groats with a nutty flavor can be used in soups or stews or as a hearty side dish.

3. Barley A member of the grass family, this cereal grain, with its nutty flavor and chewy texture, is often used in soups but can also be used in place of rice in many dishes. It is often sold in varying sizes labeled "pearl barley."

4. Farro This type of whole grain wheat releases starch as it cooks while maintaining a chewy texture. It is full of fiber and can be used in soups, salads, and breads.

5. Quinoa Grown for its edible seeds, this "mother grain" has a slightly mild, nutty flavor and cooks fairly quickly. It is very high in protein, vitamins, and minerals and can stand in for rice in almost any dish.

6. Bulgur Wheat This cereal grain is made from steamed, dried, and crushed wheat kernels. It has a chewy texture, and because it is precooked, it requires minimal cook time in dishes, often as little as 10 minutes.

CORN

From grits to cornbread, corn products are a staple in Southern cooking and are great to keep in the pantry for quick weeknight meals or special family dinners.

1. Dried Polenta This golden-yellow Italian cornmeal is made from dried corn and can be ground coarse or fine. It is used in dishes similarly to grits.

2. Fresh White Corn White corn is a sweet corn variety, and both the kernels and the milk of white corn are creamy white in color. White corn kernels tend to be smaller than other varieties.

3. Cornstarch Derived from the endosperm of the kernel, this gluten-free powder adds structure to baked goods while increasing tenderness. It's also used as a thickener for gravies, desserts, and sauces. Cornstarch should be dissolved in cold water or another cold liquid before adding as a thickener; otherwise it'll form lumps.

4. Corn Syrup This sweet syrup, often used when making candy and found in many processed commercial products, is made by processing cornstarch with enzymes. Light corn syrup has been clarified while dark corn syrup (shown here) has caramel and coloring added to lend a molasses flavor to recipes.

5. Fresh Yellow Corn This is the most widely grown grain crop in the Americas. It can be cooked either with or without its husk and can be enjoyed on or off the cob. When purchasing fresh corn, be sure that the kernels are plump and tightly arranged in rows.

6. Dried Yellow Corn One cup of dried yellow corn yields about 2 cups of cooked corn. Dried corn can conveniently be stored in airtight containers.

7. Corn Flour Available in yellow and white varieties, corn flour can be used as a breading or in combination with other flours in baked goods. It is ground cornmeal from the whole kernel of corn. Masa harina is a well-known corn flour used in Latin cooking.

8. Stone-Ground Grits A popular breakfast staple in the South, stone-ground grits are made in a traditional stone mill, which allows them to retain the natural oil of corn. Grits can be enjoyed on their own with seasonings or as an ingredient in casseroles and other dishes.

9. Cornmeal Cornmeal is made from dried corn kernels ground into a flour-like powder. There are three textures available—fine, medium, and coarse. The color of the meal is dependent upon the color of the corn. With its sweet flavor and hearty texture, blue cornmeal (shown here) is often used in making tortillas or tortilla chips.

10. Refrigerated Polenta This popular dish in European and Italian cuisines is now available precooked and refrigerated. It can be reconstituted into a creamy dish by mashing, adding broth or cream, and heating over low heat, or it can be grilled or baked.

11. Corn Oil Extracted from the germ of corn, corn oil has a high smoke point, making it ideal for frying. It is also less expensive than other types of oils.

NUTS & SEEDS

Full of healthy fats as well as protein and fiber, nuts and seeds serve as a great addition to many dishes and can also be enjoyed on their own as a satisfying snack.

1. Soy Nuts These nuts are made from soaked soybeans that have been baked until crispy. They have a similar taste and texture to peanuts but contain less fat and more protein.

2. Macadamia Nuts Due to their high fat content, these buttery-rich nuts should be properly stored to avoid rancidity. Unopened nuts can be stored in the refrigerator for up to 6 months or frozen for up to 1 year.

3. Pine Nuts This esssential ingredient in pesto comes from several varieties of pine trees. Pine nuts can be toasted in the oven to bring out their natural flavor. Like macadamia nuts, they have a high fat content and should be stored in an airtight container.

4. Pistachios These popular green-colored nuts are available in many forms—roasted, salted, shelled, and unshelled. When purchasing unshelled pistachios, be sure that the shells are slightly opened, indicating that they are mature. They can be stored for up to 3 months in the refrigerator and can be toasted in the oven to restore crispness.

5. Walnuts The two most common varieties of this tree nut are the English walnut and the black walnut. They are available year-round and come in three sizes: large, medium, and baby. Unshelled nuts may be stored in a cool, dry place, while shelled nuts should be stored in the refrigerator in an airtight container for up to 6 months.

6. Pecans These native nuts can be found year-round, with their peak season in autumn. They are widely grown throughout the South, and whether chopped, halved, or whole, they add rich, buttery flavor to both sweet and savory dishes.

7. Almonds These versatile nuts, rich in vitamin E, add delicate flavor and crunch to a variety of dishes and can be found throughout the year. Their sweet flavor is also highlighted in almond extract and almond paste.

8. Hazelnuts Full of smoky, sweet flavor, hazelnuts are the key ingredient in nutty spreads and can also be enjoyed roasted in their whole form. They are also called filberts and are grown in temperate climates. To easily remove the skins, bake them for 10 to 15 minutes at 350° and then rub them vigorously with a towel.

9. Pepitas Also known as pumpkin seeds, this favorite fall snack can be roasted at home and enhanced with sweet or salty flavor. After scooping the seeds from the pumpkin, make sure to boil them for 10 minutes before toasting in the oven. This will further remove any pumpkin membrane still attached. You may also purchase them hulled at many supermarkets year-round.

10. Sunflower Seeds These seeds, rich in polyunsaturated oils and iron, are encased by a hard black and white shell and are harvested from the bold black centers of the sunflower. They can be eaten alone or as an ingredient in many savory dishes. While they are best stored in the refrigerator, they should not be frozen, as it will affect their flavor.

11. Peanuts These common nuts are actually legumes and are widely grown throughout the South. About half of the crop is used to produce peanut butter. The most common varieties are Virginia peanuts and Spanish peanuts. Raw peanuts can be boiled in the shell, or shelled nuts can be roasted and salted. Shelled peanuts should not be chopped until right before consumption to guarantee freshness.

12. Cashews These kidney-shaped nuts come from the bottom of a cashew apple. They are sweet in flavor and have a high fat content. Because of large amounts of oleic acid, cashews will last longer than other nuts but are best kept in a tightly sealed container in the refrigerator to prevent rancidity.

FRESH CHEESES

Varying from spreadable creams to sliceable blocks, this group of unripened, rindless cheeses can be served as a topping to salads, as an accompaniment to crackers, or as a flavor-enhancer to many dishes.

1. Ricotta Literally meaning "recooked," this cheese is made by heating the whey from cheeses such as mozzarella and provolone. It is slightly grainy in texture and has a mild, sweet flavor. Ricotta is most commonly used in Italian dishes such as lasagna and manicotti.

2. Chèvre Also known as goat cheese, this tangy cheese varies in texture from creamy to semi-firm. The goat's milk is sometimes blended with cow's milk, and the cheese comes in different shapes such as logs or rounds. This cheese should be stored wrapped tightly in plastic wrap in the refrigerator for up to 2 weeks.

3. Feta A traditional Greek cheese, feta is made from sheep's or goat's milk and has a salty flavor. It is packed into a square block and is typically stored in its own whey brine. It has a crumbly texture and is great as a topping for chicken, fish, and salads.

4. Cream Cheese This mild, spreadable cow's-milk cheese, most commonly used for cheesecake, was developed in 1872. By law, it must contain at least 33% milk fat and less than 55% moisture. Light and fat-free cream cheese is also available. Cream cheese comes in block or tub form and should be used within 1 week after opening.

5. Fresh Mozzarella This mild, soft, Italian-style cheese is typically made from whole milk and stored in water or whey. Buffalo mozzarella, also a fresh mozzarella, is made of a combination of water buffalo milk and cow's milk.

6. Spreadable Cheese This processed cheese is often mixed with herbs or other seasonings and makes a great spread for crackers. It comes in many forms, from small wedges to tub-style cheese.

7. Fromage Blanc Similar to sour cream, this very soft and smooth cheese is usually eaten as a dessert with fresh fruit.

8. Mascarpone This slightly sweet and spoonable cream is best known for its use in tiramisù. It is made from the addition of citric acid to cream and has a high fat content, making it decadently rich and creamy.

9. Queso Fresco This fresh, Mexican-style cheese is pleasantly salty and crumbly. It's available in rounds or tubs and can be found in Latin markets and many grocery stores.

10. Crème Fraîche With a tangy and nutty flavor, this cream can range in thickness and is a great secret cooking ingredient because it doesn't curdle when boiled.

11. Farmer's Cheese This type of cottage cheese has had the liquid removed from it and typically comes in a round or square cake. It can be sliced or crumbled and has a tangy flavor.

12. Cottage Cheese This fresh cow's-milk cheese is very creamy and comes in several curd sizes. It should be kept in the coldest part of the refrigerator and consumed within 10 days after the stamped date on the carton.

kitchen secret:

Prevent dehydration and the growth of mold by storing fresh cheeses properly. Store cheeses in their original containers (in their original liquid, if applicable). Keep them tightly covered with plastic wrap and chill in the coldest area of the refrigerator. Also, every time you use the cheese, be sure to wrap it in new plastic wrap. Follow these tips, and fresh cheeses should last a few days.

BLUE CHEESES

Characterized by its blue-and-green veined appearance, this group of cheeses also tends to have a pungent aroma, giving a lot of bang for your buck when it comes to flavor.

1. Humboldt Fog This goat's-milk cheese is made in Humboldt County, California, and is named for the ocean fog that commonly rolls into the area. It is a soft-ripened cheese, meaning it ages from the outside-in, with a line of edible ash running through the center. As the cheese ripens, its crumbly center is transformed into a creamy texture.

2. Soft-Ripened Blue Vein This blue cheese starts as a firm and chalky cheese, but after the exterior is exposed to mold, and as it is aged, the interior becomes creamy, runny, and more intensely flavored. Holes are poked into the surface of the cheese, exposing the interior to the mold and creating the blue and green streaks common to blue cheeses.

3. Roquefort Characterized by being pungent, creamy, and salty, this blue cheese is one of the most well-known and is aged for at least 3 months in limestone caves in southwest France. Authentic Roquefort has a red sheep on the wrapper and is sold in short cylindrical packages.

4. Gorgonzola This Italian blue cheese is named for the town where it was originally made. It is made from cow's milk and is creamy with a strong flavor. It is wonderful served with apples and pears and comes in foil-wrapped wedges.

SOFT CHEESES

Silky-smooth centers make this group of cheeses a perfect pairing with a cracker or a piece of fruit.

1. Raclette This Swiss cheese is very similar to Gruyère. It is semi-firm in texture with very small holes and has a mild, nutty flavor.

2. Telème Similar to Brie, the high fat content of this cheese makes it very creamy, and as it ages, it becomes runny and more potent in flavor.

3. Brie One of the most well-known French cheeses, Brie is characterized by an edible white rind and creamy, buttery-soft interior. It is great spread on crackers, apples, and pears. Look for rounds that are plump and white in color.

MELTING CHEESES

Whether you're craving the perfect grilled cheese sandwich or silky cheese fondue, this repertoire of cheeses will fit the bill for any recipe.

1. Fontina The creamy texture and nutty flavor of this semi-firm cow's-milk cheese hails from the Val d'Aosta region of Italy and melts very smoothly.

2. Edam This mild yellow cheese from Holland is made from part-skim milk and is a great all-purpose melting cheese. It is often packaged in a red waxy coating.

3. Havarti This semi-soft Danish cheese is often sold in loaves. It has small holes and is pale yellow in color. Longer-aged Havartis tend to be stronger in flavor.

4. Jarlsberg Semi-firm in texture, this Norwegian Swiss-style cheese has large holes and often has a yellow paraffin coating. Its richness and mildly sweet flavor make it a great all-around cheese for cooking.

5. Cheddar This versatile cow's-milk cheese originates from the village of Cheddar in England. It can vary in sharpness and is commonly shredded and used in casseroles.

6. Monterey Jack Hailing from Monterey, California, this buttery, mild cow's-milk cheese has a high moisture content, making it an ideal melting cheese. It's often flavored with herbs and jalapeños.

7. Low-Moisture, Part-Skim Mozzarella This factory-produced cheese is best loved for its excellent melting properties. It can be found in low-fat and fat-free versions, in blocks, and in pre-shredded form.

8. Provolone This white cow's-milk cheese was originally produced in Italy, but is now made in the U.S., too. It's typically aged for 2 to 3 months, and its mild, smoky flavor increases over time.

9. Gruyère This cow's-milk cheese is characterized by its nutty flavor. It's produced in Switzerland and France and is aged for at least 10 months.

10. White Cheddar This version of Cheddar has not been dyed by annatto, a seed of the achiote tree often used as food coloring. It can vary in sharpness based upon how long it is aged.

11. Gouda Holland's most famous cheese, Gouda is yellow in color and has small holes. It has a similar nutty flavor to Edam, but it's silkier in texture due to a higher fat content.

kitchen secret:

Cheese sauces often have the habit of breaking or curdling. To prevent this from happening, grate the cheese as finely as possible and try adding a starch to it, such as flour or cornstarch, before stirring into a warm liquid. Also be sure to cook the sauce over very low heat. Heat that's too high can cause it to curdle.

GRILLING CHEESES

Due to high melting points, these three cheeses are perfect on the grill, making them a great addition to salads and crostini.

1. Queso Blanco An unaged white Spanish cheese, Queso Blanco is similar to Queso Fresco and is a mild cow's-milk cheese. When heated, it only softens instead of melting completely, making it a great grilling cheese.

2. Scamorza This firm Italian cheese was originally made from buffalo milk but is now most commonly made from whole cow's milk. It's often smoked and is similar in flavor to fresh mozzarella.

3. Halloumi This firm, white cheese hailing from Cypress is similar in flavor and texture to fresh mozzarella and is very popular in the Middle East. Its high melting point allows it to be fried or grilled without melting completely.

GRATING CHEESES

This group of firm cheeses adds a punch of flavor when grated over pasta dishes, casseroles, soups, and salads.

1. Asiago This nutty-flavored Italian cow's-milk cheese is aged for at least a year to become a hard grating cheese. It is often used similarly to Parmesan.

2. Parmigiano-Reggiano One of the most well-known Italian cheeses, Parmigiano-Reggiano is made in Parma and towns close by, and is aged at least 2 years or more. It has a light yellow color and grainy texture and is often served grated over pasta dishes.

3. Manchego Spain's most famous cheese, Manchego gets its name from the sheep's milk used to make it. Its golden color and mild flavor make it a great addition to many dishes. The longer it's aged, the more the flavor intensifies and the firmer the cheese becomes.

4. Dry Jack When Monterey Jack is aged, the moisture content decreases, creating a nice, dry cheese with a firm texture and a sharp flavor similar to Cheddar.

5. Cotija This hard cow's-milk cheese from Mexico originates from the region of the same name. It is produced from July through October when the cows eat the grasses that only grow during those months in the rainy season.

6. Romano This cheese from Rome is used mostly for grating. Pecorino Romano, a sheep's-milk cheese, is the most well-known Romano, especially for its sharpness. Other Romano cheeses are made from a combination of cow's milk and sheep's milk.

DRIED BEANS

This inexpensive pantry staple is great to keep on hand to add protein to vegetarian dishes or to create a comforting stew. Just be sure to rinse well and soak before cooking.

Lima Beans There are two types of this bean: the large Fordhook lima (shown here) and the smaller baby lima. These beans are often called butterbeans in the South because of their rich, creamy texture.

Cranberry Beans Red-streaked white or beige, these beans have a mild, chestnut-like flavor and should be washed thoroughly before cooking.

Navy Beans These mild-flavored white beans got their name from the fact that they were a staple in meals served in the U.S. Navy. They are wonderful in soups and are the bean of choice for Boston baked beans.

Pinto Beans These legumes are pale pink with reddish-brown streaks and are often used in chilis and stews. They are also used to make refried beans.

Black Beans These popular beans are characterized by a dark black skin and creamy white flesh and are commonly used in Latin, Caribbean, and Mexican cuisines.

Great Northern Beans These large white beans are similar to lima beans in shape but have a more delicate flavor. They absorb flavor well and are a nice substitute for navy or cannellini beans.

Black-Eyed Peas Characterized by its black "eye" in the inner curve, this small pea is thought to bring luck on New Year's Day in Hoppin' John.

Red Kidney Beans These dark red-skinned, bold-flavored beans are used in chilis and for red beans and rice. Their white counterpart, cannellini beans, have a milder flavor.

Garbanzo Beans Also known as chickpeas, these round legumes are found in a variety of Mediterranean dishes, such as hummus and falafel. They have a round, irregular shape, nutty flavor, and can be stored in an airtight container for up to a year.

FRESH BEANS

During warm months, a plethora of this fresh vegetable can be found at farmers' markets across the country. Fresh beans are quick and easy to prepare, making them a perfect addition to any meal.

1. Bush Beans Also known as string beans, bush beans have an edible pea and pod. When purchasing these beans, look for ones that are bright green and free of dark spots.

2. Snow Peas Not to be confused with snap peas, snow peas have flat, translucent pods with tiny sweet seeds. These edible pods are best enjoyed within 2 days of purchase.

3. Crowder Peas A subcategory of field peas, these peas are known for their dark juices and strong flavor. They are similar in appearance to black-eyed peas but have more flavor and should not be overcooked.

4. Butterbeans These lima beans are soft and creamy and are the bean of choice for succotash. Fresh beans are usually sold in their pods and should be shelled just before cooking.

5. Pole Beans These green beans grow taller than bush beans and often have a thicker pod. They also often have a thick string that runs down the center.

6. Edamame These soybeans are bright to dark green in color and contain firm green peas. While the pod is not edible, the beans can be enjoyed hot or cold after being squeezed from the pod.

7. Sugar Snap Peas These edible pods and peas are a cross between the English pea and the snow pea. Their crisp texture and sweet flavor can be enjoyed raw or cooked to deliver a snap of flavor.

8. Pink-Eyed Peas Also known as purple hull peas, these field peas are common in the South and are characterized by a pink "eye" and pale green skin. These peas are ready to shell when the pod reaches a deep purple color.

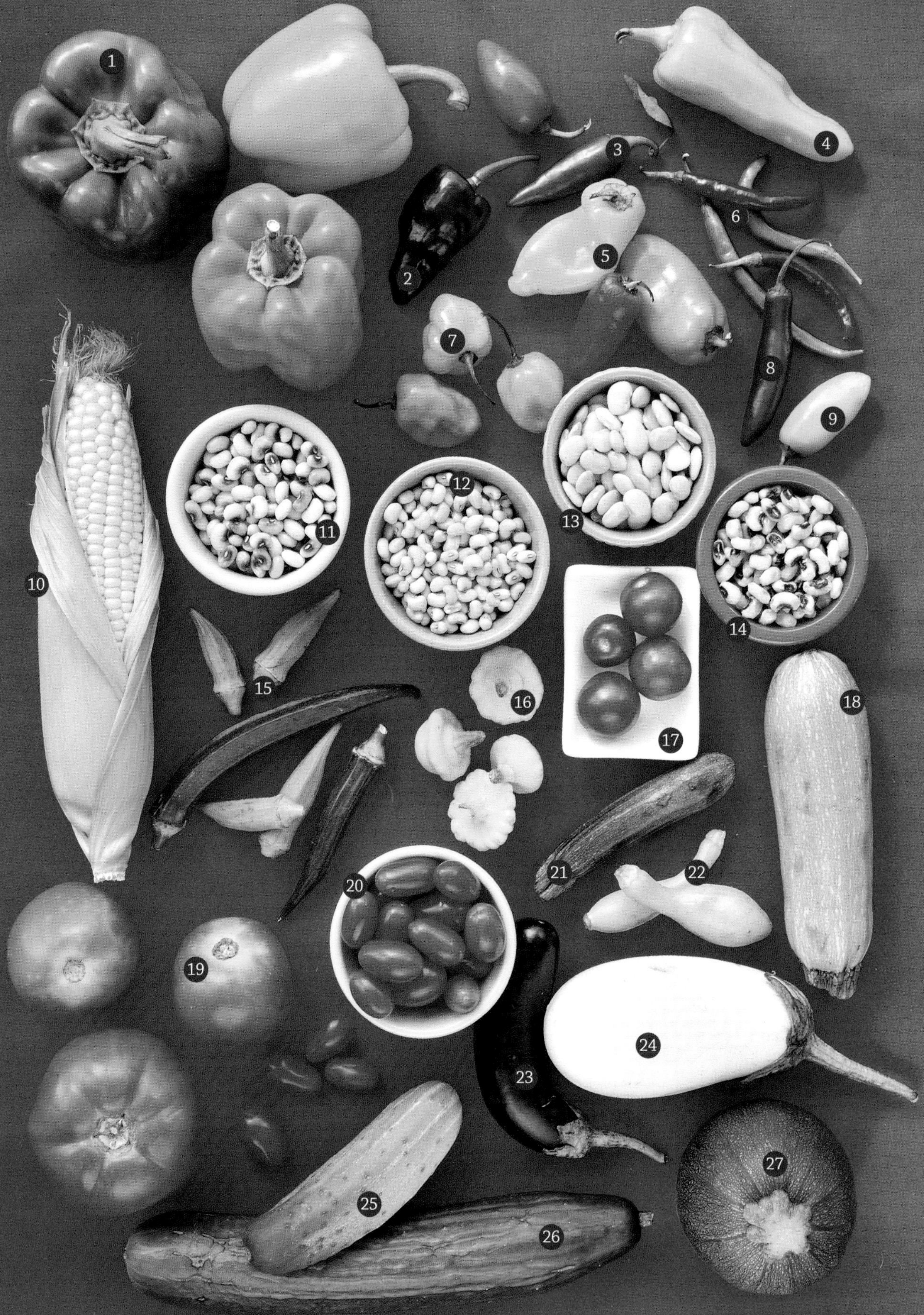
1
2
3
4
5
6
7
8
9
10
11
12
13
14
15
16
17
18
19
20
21
22
23
24
25
26
27

VEGETABLES (WARM SEASON)

These veggies require warm soil and high temperatures for steady growth and are best enjoyed during hot summer months.

1. Bell Peppers These crisp peppers are available in a variety of colors and become sweeter and milder in flavor as they age.

2. Poblano Pepper This dark green chile ranges in spiciness and is often stuffed with cheese or rice. Dried poblanos, also called ancho chiles, as well as canned poblanos are also available.

3. Jalapeño Pepper This chile is dark green or red when ripe and ranges in spiciness from hot to very hot. To reduce heat, remove the veins and seeds.

4. Anaheim Pepper A mild chile, this pepper is light to medium green in color and has a long, narrow pod.

5. Piquillo Pepper This sweet variety of chile is traditionally grown in Spain. It ranges in color from yellow to red.

6. Thai Chile This 1^1/$_2$-inch long chile packs a hot punch and is used in Southeast Asian cooking. It ranges in color from green to red.

7. Habanero Pepper This extremely hot chile is small and ranges in color from light green to orange.

8. Serrano Pepper This small, pointed chile pepper is very hot. As it ripens, the color changes from bright green to vibrant red and then to yellow.

9. Banana Pepper This sweet, long, and light yellow-green pepper has a mild flavor and is often pickled.

10. Corn (see page 41)

11. Pink-Eyed Peas (see page 53)

12. Field Peas Most commonly harvested to be dried, these peas are also available fresh in the summer.

13. Butterbeans (see page 53)

14. Black-Eyed Peas (see page 52)

15. Okra This fuzzy green pod is best in summer months and should be firm upon purchase. When cooked, okra emits a viscous substance that works as a thickener for dishes such as gumbo.

16. Pattypan Squash Noted for its small, round shape with scalloped edges, this squash can be yellow, green, or white and is most tender when young.

17. Cherry Tomatoes These 1-inch tomatoes are the perfect way to top off a summer salad or deliver a burst of juicy, sweet flavor to savory dishes.

18. Cousa Squash This summer squash is pale green in color and similar in shape to zucchini. When purchasing, look for cousa squash that is small to medium and heavy for its size.

19. Tomatoes A juicy favorite of the summer months, tomatoes are available in many varieties, offering a range of colors, tastes, and textures. They should be stored at room temperature and out of direct sunlight.

20. Grape Tomatoes These tomatoes are half the size of cherry tomatoes, are noticeably sweeter, and are available when other varieties are out of season.

21. Zucchini This cylindrical summer squash ranges in color from dark to light green. Small zucchini tend to be more tender. They are best sautéed, grilled, steamed, or baked.

22. Crookneck Squash A yellow summer squash, Crooknecks have a watery flesh with a mildly sweet flavor. Choose firm squash with no discoloration.

23. Japanese Eggplant This eggplant variety has a slender, oblong shape and mild, sweet flavor. It has a more delicate skin than common eggplants and should be used soon after purchase.

24. Eggplant A fruit belonging to the nightshade family, eggplants range in color from dark purple to white and in size from small to large. The most common is the pear-shaped eggplant with glossy skin. Choose those that are firm and show no signs of dark spots. Fresh eggplant should be used within a few days of purchase to avoid bitterness.

25. Kirby Cucumber This short and plump cucumber is perfect for pickling and is best purchased in late spring and early fall.

26. English Cucumber Also known as a hothouse cucumber, this seedless cucumber is typically 12 to 15 inches long and is sold in plastic wrap. While it's more expensive than the slicing variety, this cucumber generally has a sweeter, less bitter flavor.

27. Eight-Ball Zucchini This sweet, softball-size squash is round and ideal for stuffing.

VEGETABLES (COOL SEASON)

These cold weather-loving veggies are harvested during winter months and can be enjoyed in a variety of dishes.

1. Fennel This sweet, anise-flavored veggie has an edible bulb, stalk, leaves, and seeds. It is often used raw in salads or sautéed or braised in savory dishes.

2. Broccoli Rabe A member of the mustard family, broccoli rabe has a bitter flavor, and both the leaves and the broccoli-like stems are edible.

3. Green Onions Also known as scallions, these premature onions have a less intense flavor than large bulb onions and are often used in raw form.

4. White Mushrooms These cultivated mushrooms vary in size from button to jumbo and deliver better flavor when sautéed or grilled. To clean mushrooms, don't soak them in water. Instead, wipe them with a damp paper towel.

5. Cremini Mushrooms These baby portobellos have an earthy flavor and are a terrific accompaniment to beef and vegetable dishes.

6. Brussels Sprouts These small cabbages range from 1 to 1¹/₂ inches in diameter. Choose sprouts that are bright green.

7. Purple Potatoes These pretty potatoes are dense in texture and can be prepared the same as white potatoes.

8. Baking Potatoes Also known as Russet potatoes, these large spuds are great for baking and making french fries.

9. Porcini Mushrooms These highly prized Italian mushrooms have a meaty texture and nutty flavor.

10. Shiitake Mushrooms Popular in Asian cuisine, these mushrooms have a meaty texture. The stems can be tough and are often removed.

11. Red Potatoes These firm and round potatoes have a waxy flesh and less starch than baking potatoes, so they hold their shape when cooked.

12. Yukon Gold Potatoes These buttery-fleshed potatoes are ideal for making mashed potatoes.

13. Sugar Snap Peas (see page 53)

14. Beets These jewel-toned root vegetables range in color from garnet red to vibrant yellow. Wear gloves when cutting beets, as the juice can stain.

15. Bush Beans (see page 53)

16. Garlic This bulb adds onion-like flavor and healthful nutrition to many savory dishes. Purchase bulbs that are plump and firm and make sure that the skin is unbroken.

17. Cauliflower This member of the cabbage family ranges in color from white to green to purple and is available in florets or as a large head.

18. Broccoli This cruciferous veggie has tight clusters and edible stems. It can be bought as pre-cut florets or as a large head.

19. Onions These roots are popular for cooking in most any dish and are available in several varieties. Vidalia onions are the sweetest, while the white

and Spanish varieties offer a more pungent taste. Red onions are often eaten raw because they can lose their bright color during cooking.

20. Radish This root vegetable from a mustard plant ranges in color from white to red to purple. It has a crisp texture and peppery flavor and can be used in salads or as crudités for dips.

21. Turnip This white-fleshed root vegetable is ideal for soups and is at its peak from October to March. Small turnips have a sweeter, more delicate flavor than larger ones.

22. Rutabaga This veggie looks like a large turnip and has a pale yellow flesh and sweeter flavor than turnips.

23. Artichoke Also known as the bud of the thistle plant, artichokes have tough leaves but a soft flesh and tender heart after being cooked. Fresh artichokes should be dark green with closed heads.

24. Asparagus This popular vegetable is grown in sandy soil. When purchasing, look for stalks that are firm and bright green. Fatter stalks usually yield a more tender cooked product.

25. Carrot This vitamin A all-star is delightful raw or cooked. Choose carrots that are firm and smooth and show no signs of cracks.

26. Leek This member of the onion family has a mild flavor and is often used to flavor soups. Look for leeks with white necks and dark green leaves and be sure to wash them thoroughly to remove sand.

VEGETABLES (COOL SEASON)

Winter squash are harvested in the mature fruit stage, when the outer skins have developed into tough rinds. They are ideal for many hearty stews and side dishes.

1. Butternut Squash This sweet squash is pear-shaped and typically weighs 2 to 3 pounds. It has a smooth tan skin and bright orange flesh and will keep for months in a cool, dry place. It can be baked, steamed, or sautéed.

2. Cushaw Squash An heirloom winter squash, also known as a sweet potato squash, cushaw is often used similarly to pumpkin in cooking. It's commonly used in Creole and Cajun cuisine.

3. Buttercup Squash This turban squash is characterized by bumps and a "turban" on the blossom end of the squash. It comes in a range of sizes and is typically used for ornamental purposes, but it may be baked, steamed, or sautéed.

4. Pumpkin This symbol of Halloween and pie staple for several holiday tables has many varieties. A small white pumpkin is shown here. Smaller pumpkins tend to have more tender flesh. Pureed pumpkin is available year-round in canned form.

5. Sweet Potato This sweet spud comes in two main varieties. The pale yellow-fleshed sweet potato is not as sweet as the darker-fleshed and has a dry texture when cooked. The darker, orange-fleshed variety is very moist in texture. Canned sweet potatoes are also available. Store fresh potatoes 3 to 4 weeks in a dark, dry area.

6. Acorn Squash This sweet and buttery oval-shaped winter squash is dark green and has yellow flesh. It can be baked or boiled, and enjoyed in soups or stand alone as a fiber-filled side dish.

7. Ambercup Squash This relative of the butternut squash resembles a small pumpkin with its bright orange skin and flesh. It has a sweet flavor and is available from June to November.

8. Spaghetti Squash The flesh of this oblong yellow squash separates into spaghetti-like strands when cooked. It is low in calories and high in vitamins and can be served with sauce as a healthy substitute to pasta.

kitchen secret:

Many recipes call for peeled, cubed squash. Winter squash has a tough skin that is often difficult to cut through. Pierce the squash a few times with a fork and microwave on HIGH at 2-minute intervals until the squash is easy to cut. You can then safely cut the squash into the shape you need.

GREENS

From salads to stir-fries, follow this trusty guide when trying to add a little green to your diet.

1. Bok Choy With a white crunchy stem and dark green, spinach-like leaves, this versatile veggie is often stir-fried or eaten raw in salads. Choose bunches with firm stalks and unwilted green leaves.

2. Baby Spinach Slighty bolder in flavor than large varieties, baby spinach is an excellent addition to salads or can be enjoyed cooked into your favorite dish. When purchasing spinach, choose crisp leaves that are bright green and show no yellow spots. Store in a plastic bag in the refrigerator for up to 3 days.

3. Radicchio This reddish-purple Italian chicory plant has a slightly bitter flavor but nicely accents other greens when used in salads. It can also be grilled or sautéed. When purchasing radicchio, choose heads that have bright-colored leaves and show no signs of browning.

4. Kale This non-heading member of the cabbage family can withstand the winter chill and is thought to be a winter green, although it is available year-round. Its curly leaves can be simmered to perfection or quickly cooked in olive oil and are often added to soups, stews, or pasta. It's important to remove the center stem, however, because it can be tough.

5. Mâche Also known as "lamb's lettuce" and corn salad, this green has a nutty, sweet flavor and velvety texture and can be paired with a variety of dressings. It can also be steamed and served as a vegetable. Store mâche in a plastic bag in the refrigerator for up to 3 days.

6. Watercress This member of the mustard family has small green leaves and a peppery flavor. It is often used in soups, salads, and sandwich recipes as well as entrées.

7. Iceberg Lettuce This variety of crisp-head lettuce has a tightly packed head with pale green leaves. It's very crunchy and has a neutral flavor, making it a popular choice for mixed green salads.

8. Arugula An aromatic salad green, arugula has elongated, dark green leaves and a peppery mustard flavor. It can be used in salads or cooked in soups and other vegetable dishes.

9. Belgian Endive This cigar-shaped green is grown in complete darkness to achieve its white, slightly bitter-flavored leaves. Its peak season is in colder months, from November to April, and it is best served in a salad or braised. Choose crisp, tightly closed heads with pale green tips and store in the refrigerator for up to 1 day.

10. Kohlrabi This member of the turnip family is available from mid-spring to mid-fall. Its sweet, turnip-like bulb and uniquely shaped leaves can both be eaten. It is best steamed, but is also popular in stir-fries and soups.

11. Leaf Lettuce This antioxidant-rich lettuce has a loose bunch of crisp leaves and ranges in color from medium to dark green. Red leaf lettuce (shown here) has burgundy-tinted tips. When purchasing, choose leaf lettuce that is crisp and firm with no signs of wilting.

12. Romaine Lettuce As the star of the Caesar salad, this lettuce has an elongated head and crisp leaves. The outer leaves are darker green than the pale green center.

13. Escarole This broader, less bitter variety of endive thrives in the months from June to October. This green is great in salads or sautéed for vegetable dishes and soups.

14. Mustard Greens These peppery greens, second in popularity only to collards, can range from mildly spicy to jalapeño hot, depending on where they are harvested. They are in season from December to March and are also available frozen or canned. When purchasing fresh greens, choose young leaves that are deep green in color.

15. Chard Also known as Swiss chard, this tall, leafy green vegetable is a member of the beet family and peaks in the summer. Ruby chard has a bright red stalk and red-tinged leaf. When purchasing, choose greens that are vividly green in color and have nice crisp stalks.

16. Napa Cabbage This Chinese cabbage is a common ingredient in Asian stir-fries. The crinkly, thin leaves provide a milder flavor than green cabbage and should be stored tightly wrapped in the refrigerator for up to 3 days.

17. Cabbage This cruciferous vegetable contains hefty amounts of vitamins C and A. It is enjoyed by boiling its leafy head or shredding raw to use in slaws. Red cabbage is deep purple in color and lends a burst of brightness.

HERBS

Whether grown in your garden or purchased in markets, fresh herbs enhance dishes with bright flavors and beautiful garnishes. For best results, use them within 1 week of purchasing or clipping.

1. Lemongrass This herb, also known as citronella, is popular in Thai cuisine and similar in shape to green onions. It's available in fresh and dried forms and is used mostly for flavoring soups and Asian dishes.

2. Sage Native to the Mediterranean, this herb has a mint-like flavor. It's often used to flavor turkey and dressing, but is also great in many other meat and poultry dishes. Store in the refrigerator for up to 2 days.

3. Rosemary This hearty herb is a member of the mint family. It can be potent, so you get a lot of bang for your buck. Rosemary is wonderful to flavor a variety of dishes, including meats, stews, and vegetables. In addition to being a nice shrub for your garden, its strong stems can double as skewers for grilled kabobs.

4. Oregano This pungent herb is a member of the mint family and is native to the Mediterranean and Mexico. It is similar in flavor to marjoram but is a bit stronger. Look for bunches with bright-green leaves and store in the refrigerator for up to 3 days.

5. Curly Parsley This fresh-flavored herb can be found year-round in just about every grocery store. Look for crisp leaves without any signs of yellowing.

6. Chives This mild, onion-flavored herb is widely available in most markets. It has long, hollow stems that can be snipped with kitchen shears. Store chives in the refrigerator for up to 1 week.

7. Thyme This perennial herb is a member of the mint family. Its tiny leaves are very versatile and can be used to flavor meats, soups, sauces, and vegetables.

8. Basil There are many varieties of this well-loved summer herb from the mint family. It's characterized as having tender leaves and a spicy flavor. Thai basil, purple basil, and lemon basil are a few of the varieties available. Store fresh basil wrapped in damp paper towels in a plastic bag in the refrigerator for 3 to 4 days.

9. Mint Peppermint and spearmint are the most common varieties of this aromatic herb, and both lend a sweet flavor to both savory and dessert dishes. Choose evenly colored leaves and store refrigerated in a small cup of water.

10. Marjoram This herb is similar in flavor to oregano but is milder. Sweet marjoram is what is sold in stores, and it is commonly used to flavor meats and vegetables.

11. Chervil This delicate herb is a member of the parsley family and has small leaves with a slight licorice flavor. It can be used in place of parsley, but it should be added towards the end of cooking to protect its flavor.

12. Italian Flat-Leaf Parsley This stronger-flavored parsley is used for garnishing as well as adding a freshness to dishes. Choose bunches with no signs of wilting and be sure to wash thoroughly to remove any particles of soil.

13. Lavender The fragrant flowers of this herb are commonly used to scent soaps and lotions and are often dried for sachets. Small amounts may also be used to flavor cookies, dressings, and teas.

14. Cilantro This herb is the leaf of the coriander plant. It's commonly used in Latin and Asian cuisines and has a unique, bright flavor. Look for bunches with no signs of wilting and store in a plastic bag in the refrigerator for up to 1 week.

15. Tarragon Often used in French cuisine, this herb is characterized by long, pointy leaves and a licorice flavor. It adds distinct flavor to bèarnaise sauce and is also a great flavoring for vegetables.

MELONS

Known for their sweet, juicy flavor, melons belong to the same gourd family as squash and cucumbers but have a thicker skin.

1. Temptation Melon This melon is actually a hybrid of cantaloupe and honeydew. It has a smooth, light-green skin like a honeydew and a peachy-orange center like a cantaloupe. It is most similar in flavor to honeydew.

2. Canary Melon This sweet melon with a smooth, yellow skin and pale green to yellow flesh has a flavor similar to honeydew but is more tangy.

3. Cantaloupe Also known as a muskmelon, this low-calorie melon was named for a castle in Italy. It has a sweet, musky aroma and a soft, juicy flesh. Ripe and cut melons should be stored in the refrigerator wrapped tightly with plastic wrap to prevent absorption of odors.

4. Honeydew This pale green-fleshed variety of muskmelon is very sweet and has better flavor if left unrefrigerated for several days. Ripe honeydew should have a waxy surface and be heavy for its size.

5. Crenshaw Melon This teardrop-shaped hybrid muskmelon has a tender, peach-colored flesh with sweet and slightly spicy flavor. Crenshaw melon is best purchased in the fall and should have a golden-green skin.

6. Watermelon A summertime favorite, watermelon is in season from May through August. This crunchy melon is available in several varieties, ranging from a large oval shape to small and round. It also comes seedless or with seeds. Select those that are symmetrical in shape, and wait to refrigerate until after cutting.

7. Casaba Melon Closely related to cantaloupe and honeydew, casaba melon has a bright yellow skin, pale green flesh, and tastes like a cucumber. Though not as sweet as other melons, casaba has a longer storage life than most.

STONE FRUIT

Often harvested when underripe, these fruits don't reach their optimal sweetness until after they are picked. They are best in the summer and have a juicy flesh and a single, hard seed.

1. Nectarines These close relatives to the peach are sweeter and more nutritious and don't have the fuzz. For best taste, nectarines should be allowed to ripen at room temperature for several days.

2. Apricots More than 90 percent of this sweet summer fruit is produced in California, with its peak season from May to August. Apricots are similar to peaches but are smaller and have a smooth skin.

3. Plums These deep purple-colored fruits are juicier than other stone fruits and have an extended growing season. They come in sweet and acidic varieties. When purchasing plums, be sure that they don't have any soft spots. Dried plums are also known as prunes.

4. Cherries These small fruits are divided into two groups: sweet and sour. Heart-shaped sweet cherries are delicious by themselves or pitted and cooked into pies. Sour cherries are smaller and rounder. When purchasing, select brightly colored and plump cherries.

5. Peaches These juicy fruits reach their peak during the summer months. Peaches come in both clingstone and freestone varieties and can be enjoyed alone or as the star in pies and cobblers. White peaches are also available and tend to be sweeter than yellow peaches.

TROPICAL FRUIT

These warm weather-loving fruits are available year-round and are great eaten alone or used as an ingredient in both sweet and savory dishes.

1. Grapefruit Usually eaten by scooping out the flesh, grapefruit can also be peeled similar to an orange. This citrus fruit gets its name from the fact that it grows in clusters, like grapes. Grapefruit varieties can be seeded or seedless and can have pink, ruby red, or white-colored flesh.

2. Lemon This versatile citrus fruit can be used for cooking as well as non-culinary purposes. Its high acidity is ideal for balancing salad dressings and bringing brightness to many dishes. Its juice also makes the popular and refreshing lemonade.

3. Lime This well-known small green citrus fruit is available in two main varieties: Persian limes (the most widely available) and Key limes (from Florida). Key limes are smaller and have a slightly sweeter flavor. Limes can be refrigerated for up to 10 days and can be used for cooking or as a garnish.

4. Tangerine This easy-to-peel Mandarin orange has a thin skin and sweet flesh. It can be kept in the refrigerator for up to 2 weeks.

5. Orange This citrus fruit, popular for its juice and its flesh, comes in three basic types: sweet oranges, bitter oranges, and loose-skinned oranges. The most popular sweet oranges are the seedless navel, the Valencia, and the juicy red blood orange. Seville and Bergamot oranges are bitter oranges and are most commonly used to make marmalade. Mandarin oranges are a common loose-skinned orange, named as such because they are very easy to peel and their segments divide easily.

6. Banana A potassium-rich favorite, bananas are nature's perfect prepackaged fruit. They are picked green and ripen over time. If purchased while still green, they can be ripened at home by placing them in a paper bag. Bananas are also affected by oxygen in that the flesh will turn brown over time. To avoid this, brush sliced bananas with lemon juice.

7. Kiwifruit Weighing just about 4 oz. each, kiwifruit is a furry, brown-skinned fruit containing vibrant green flesh. It contains a significant amount of vitamin C, and ripened kiwifruit can be stored at room temperature or in the refrigerator.

8. Coconut This fruit of the coconut palm tree is in season from October to December and has several layers to protect the inner coconut meat and coconut juice. Whole coconuts will store at room temperature for up to 6 months.

9. Pineapple This pinecone-shaped fruit originally hailing from Central and South America is one of the sweetest tropical fruits. To determine ripeness, pull out one of the center leaves of the crown—it should come out easily. Fresh pineapple can be peeled and cored using a knife to cut off the base and crown. The cut fruit will retain nutrients for up to 9 days if chilled.

10. Mango One of the world's most popular fruits, the mango is firm with a fruity scent when ripe. It comes in a variety of shapes and sizes and is characterized by a large flat seed running down the entire center of the fruit. Ripe mangoes are very juicy and sweet.

11. Star Fruit This fruit, also known as carambola, has a 5-pointed shape, is very juicy, and ranges in flavor from sweet to tart. It is readily available during winter months and can be enjoyed by itself or in salads and desserts.

12. Passion Fruit This egg-shaped fruit is typically about 3 inches long and has a deep purple skin. The tender flesh is sweet and has a fruity fragrance.

13. Papaya Native to Central America, papaya contains the enzyme papain, which helps digest proteins. This fruit can be eaten by scooping the flesh with a spoon. The large center of this brilliant orange-fleshed fruit contains peppery light black seeds that are edible but often discarded.

BERRIES

Celebrate the bounty of these handheld fruits in pies and cobblers, and on top of salads and cereals.

1. Raspberries These scarlet berries are also available in golden and black varieties. Their small individual drupelets are connected to form juicy red fruits. When purchasing, choose berries that are brightly colored and plump. Because they are so delicate, don't wash them until just before serving.

2. Cranberries Grown in large bogs, these tart red gems are harvested from late September to October. They're mostly sold in bags and can be used immediately or frozen.

3. Blueberries These small, sweet berries are perfect for muffins and cobblers, or as a topping for cereals and salads. Harvest season is from May to October. When purchasing, choose berries that are firm and plump, and don't wash them until just before you're ready to serve.

4. Grapes This wine-making fruit is also available as a commercial table grape variety. Grapes are smooth-skinned and come with seeds or are seedless. White grapes should be light green in color and black grapes should be light red to purple. Choose bunches where the grapes are firmly attached to the stems, and be sure to thoroughly wash them before consuming.

5. Blackberries These berries grow on thorny bushes and are the largest in size of the wild berry group. Look for darker-colored berries, as they indicate sweetness. Redder berries tend to be tart.

6. Strawberries Ripe in late spring and early summer, these berries are actually members of the rose family. Choose bright red berries with vibrant green stems, and don't wash them until ready to use.

fake it!

Are the berries called for in your recipe out of season? No need to worry! Frozen berries are a great substitute when fresh are unavailable or out of season. They are flash-frozen at the peak of ripeness, and the same amount can be used in place of fresh. When purchasing frozen berries, just be sure that no extra sugar or flavorings have been added.

POULTRY

The versatility of chicken makes it easy to cook. To save money, purchase a whole chicken and cut it into smaller pieces. Experiment with other game birds for something different.

Leg This dark meat cut has a higher fat content than the white meat. It's great grilled, fried, or stewed and is perfect for little hands to hold.

Thigh A dark meat cut, chicken thighs are flavorful and tender. They're great grilled or stewed, and boneless, skinless thighs are readily available in many grocery stores. Chicken quarters are thighs with legs attached.

Breast This popular cut is very lean and versatile. Cooking with bone-in breasts tends to yield a juicier product, but boneless, skinless breasts are also available. Keep in mind that when a recipe calls for chopped cooked chicken breast, one breast yields about $1\frac{1}{2}$ cups.

Wing This white chicken cut is great to use for appetizers. Typically the tip is removed and the two sections, drumette and flat, are separated. They are great grilled or fried.

Back This cut is not eaten but is great to use when making homemade chicken stock.

Duck This domesticated bird is a descendant of either mallard or muscovy ducks, with Long Island ducks and Peking ducks being two of the most popular. It is rich in flavor and has dark meat. The skin is high in fat, which yields wonderful richness and moisture to the meat.

Cornish Hen This small bird weighs about $2\frac{1}{2}$ lb. with a small meat-to-bone ratio. It is best roasted or grilled, and due to the small meat content, one bird will be enough for one serving.

Quail Sometimes referred to as a partridge, this small, white-meat bird is best served grilled, broiled, or roasted. It is mostly sold "dressed" and is available in the freezer section of most grocery stores.

PORK

This Southern favorite can be found on tables for breakfast, lunch, and dinner.

1. Ham Hock Typically cured or smoked, a ham hock consists of the lower hind leg of the hog and is often used to add smoky flavor to soups and stews.

2. Bacon This breakfast favorite is the side pork that has been cured and smoked. It's available in many forms. Sliced bacon can be found as applewood smoked, center-cut, lower-sodium, and thick-cut. Packaged sliced bacon can be kept unopened in the refrigerator for up to 1 week past its sell-by date and frozen for up to 1 month.

3. Salt Pork This salt-cured layer of fat with streaks of lean is cut from the pig's belly and sides and is most often used for flavoring. It's different from fatback in that it is unsalted and may be blanched to remove excess salt.

4. Ham Cut from the thigh of the pig, ham can be aged, cured, smoked, or cooked. Ham tends to be higher in sodium than other meats and is often added to vegetables or other dishes during cooking to add flavor. Hams are sold in various forms, including boneless, bone-in, and partially boned. It is also sold fully-cooked (heated to an internal temperature of 148° or above), partially cooked (heated to at least 137°), and uncooked. Partially cooked and uncooked hams must be cooked before eating.

5. Spareribs Taken from the lower portion of the ribs and breastbone, spareribs are a long, narrow cut of meat that contains a significant amount of fat. They are most often barbecued after being marinated.

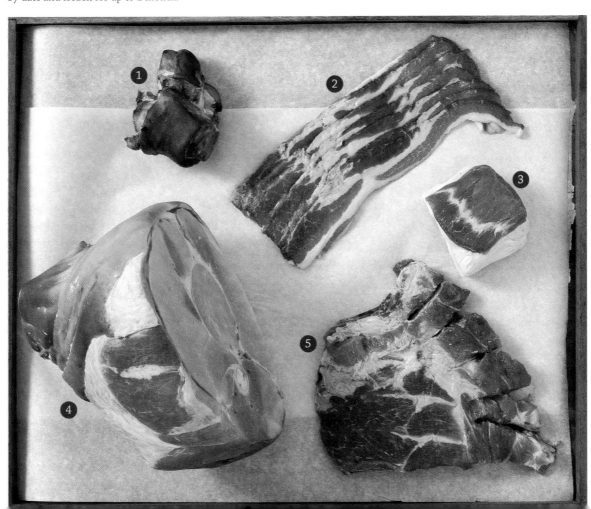

FISH & SHELLFISH

From flounder and salmon to shrimp, lobster, and crab, these fruits of the sea are not only healthful, they're tasty, too!

1. Scallops These bivalves are available in two species groups. Bay scallops are harvested on the East Coast and are much smaller than sea scallops (shown here). Sea scallops are around 1½ inches in diameter and should have a creamy beige to pink flesh and be virtually odorless or have a slightly sweet scent.

2. Trout This white-fleshed fish is mostly found in fresh water, but some saltwater species are common as well. It is similar to salmon and is simple to prepare. Trout can be found filleted or whole and can be grilled, broiled, and baked.

3. Oysters These popular bivalves can be consumed cooked or raw and are best enjoyed from fall to early spring. In the U.S., the three most commonly harvested species are Olympia oysters (from Puget Sound), Pacific oysters, and Atlantic oysters. When purchasing oysters in the shell, be sure that the shells are tightly closed (indicating that the oysters are still alive). Shucked oysters should be plump in size and stored in clear, uncloudy oyster liquor.

4. Flounder A mild-flavored and white-fleshed flatfish, flounder can be found on the sandy bottoms of the Atlantic and Pacific Oceans. It can be baked, sautéed, poached, or broiled. When purchasing this fish, remember that Pacific flounder is the most sustainable choice.

5. Cobia This tropical and subtropical saltwater fish has firm white flesh and a delicate flavor when cooked. It's fished by recreational fishermen and is best grilled or poached.

6. Red Snapper This reddish, pink-skinned fish is firm, mild-flavored, and very lean. It is one of the few fish whose skin is enjoyed, and it can be cooked several ways. Markets typically sell snapper ranging from 2- to 8-lb. in size.

7. Shrimp A favorite crustacean available year-round, shrimp has many species. They can be sold fresh or frozen, peeled or unpeeled, and in the following size categories: colossal (10 or fewer per lb.), jumbo (11 to 15 per lb.), extra-large (16 to 20 per lb.), large (21 to 30 per lb.), medium (31 to 35 per lb.). When purchasing, choose shrimp that smell like the sea and have no hint of ammonia.

8. Tuna This member of the mackerel family is popular all over the world. Yellowfin tuna (shown here) is also known as ahi tuna and is best served cooked rare or raw in sushi. Albacore tuna is lighter colored in flesh and often used for canned tuna. Bluefin tuna is the largest of the species and can weigh up to 1,000 or more pounds.

9. Salmon This fish is anadromous, meaning that it migrates from saltwater to fresh water every year to spawn. It has a red-orange flesh and a high fat content, making it rich in omega-3s. Some popular Pacific salmon choices are king salmon and sockeye salmon. Atlantic salmon stocks have diminished over time but tend to be lighter in color than Pacific salmon. This fish is sold in fillets or steaks and is available year-round. It can be grilled, sautéed, broiled, or baked and is also widely available canned and smoked.

10. Mussels These black or dark-blue mollusks should have tightly closed shells when purchased. They have a slightly sweet flavor and range from 2 to 3 inches in length. Their "beards" should be removed before cooking, and be sure to discard any mussels whose shells remain unopened after they've been steamed or sautéed.

11. Crab This sweet and succulant crustacean is sold whole cooked or live and in cooked form, lump (body meat) or flaked (claw and body meat). The most commonly caught Pacific Coast crabs are Dungeness and king crab. Along the Atlantic and Gulf coasts, blue crab and stone crab are the most common. Soft-shell crabs are those that have shed their hard shells.

12. Grouper A member of the sea bass family, this fish is firm and white-fleshed and retains moisture better than other fish. It hails from the waters of the Atlantic and Gulf of Mexico and is sold whole, as fillets, and as steaks. The skin is strongly flavored, so it should be removed before cooking.

13. Clams These bivalves are available in either hard-shelled or soft-shelled varieties. Hard-shelled clams include littleneck clams, cherrystone clams, chowder clams, and pismo clams. Soft-shelled clams have thin, brittle shells. The most common are steamer clams, razor clams, and geoduck clams. Clams are sold year-round, fresh or frozen-shucked, and should be cooked before consuming. Before cooking fresh clams, discard any whose shells are opened.

STEAK CUTS

Whether you're firing up the grill or cooking indoors, you can enjoy these steaks any time of year.

1. Flank This flat, large cut comes from the hindquarters and is best marinated and grilled. For optimum tenderness, cut into thin strips across the grain.

2. Flat-Iron Cut from the shoulder and also labeled as "top blade," this steak is well-marbled and fairly inexpensive, making it a great value for the amount of flavor it yields.

3. T-Bone Characterized by a T-shaped bone, this steak includes the tenderloin on one side and the New York strip, or top loin, on the other. A porterhouse steak is a type of T-bone with a larger portion of the tenderloin.

4. New York Strip This popular tender steak is also known as shell steak, Delmonico steak, and Kansas City strip. It's best grilled.

5. Filet Mignon This steak is the most expensive and comes from the tenderloin. It is very tender but tends to lack some flavor due to the lower fat content.

6. Rib-eye This tender steak comes from the section between the chuck and the loin. Its higher fat content, or marbling, gives this steak a ton of flavor.

7. Round Also known as eye of round, bottom round, and top round, this steak has a lower fat content and is best when braised or cooked low and slow.

WINES

From light-bodied whites to full-bodied reds, these wines pair well with many dishes.

1. Sparkling These wines can range in flavor from dry (brut) to sweet (sec). Sweeter wines labeled demi-sec or doux are considered dessert wines. Champagne, from that region in France, as well as Prosecco from Italy, are some of the most popular types of sparkling wine.

2. Pinot Noir This grape is used mostly in Burgundy wines and produces a variety of tasting notes, from flowery to spicy. These wines tend to be light- to medium-bodied.

3. Malbec The high tannin content of the grape used in this wine lends a bold and juicy flavor. The Malbec grape is one of the 6 varieties used in Bordeaux wines.

4. Sauvignon Blanc This light-bodied, bright, and herbaceous wine is made using the grape with the same name. It's commonly produced in California, Italy, France, Chile, and Australia.

5. Rosé This wine is made from red grapes, but the skins are removed within 3 days of processing, which gives it a light pink color. Rosés tend to be light in body and slightly sweet and should be served chilled.

6. Riesling Hailing from Germany, this sweet and fruity wine has a delicate flavor that makes it pair perfectly with seafood and poultry dishes.

the
PREP

Everything from mincing garlic to deveining shrimp

It is important to know chop from mince and slice from julienne, as these cuts are the action words of most recipes. Chopping and mincing require less precision than most cuts, but mastering them is equally important to the finished dish.

1. Chop To cut food into small, irregular pieces with a chef's knife or cleaver. A food processor may also be "pulsed" to chop food. Cutting boards and sharp knives are crucial for speed and ease of manual chopping.

2. Cube To cut into uniform pieces $1/2$ inch or larger on each side. Food that has been cut into cubes is generally larger than diced (see below).

3. Julienne Food cut into thin matchstick-size strips ($1/8$ x $1/8$ x $1^1/2$ inches). Vegetables cut in this manner are often used in stir-fry recipes or as a garnish.

4. Baton A larger cut than julienne, batons are $1/4$-inch x $1^1/2$-inch matchsticks and are used for vegetables that need a uniform cut to cook evenly or for easy-to-pick-up vegetable sticks for snacking.

5. Dice To cut food with a knife into large ($1/2$-inch), medium ($1/4$-inch), or small ($1/8$-inch) cubes.

$1/2$-inch dice $1/4$-inch dice

¹⁄₈-inch dice

6. Mince To very finely cut food into irregular pieces that are smaller than ¹⁄₈ inch. Something that has been minced is cut into smaller pieces than something that has been chopped.

7. Diagonal slice Food that has been sliced on the bias or at an angle into uniformly thick pieces. This cut is often used for garnishes and accents.

8. Slice To cut across a piece of food with a knife to get uniformly thick pieces, as with a loaf of bread or a tomato.

9. Lardon A matchstick of fat or thick-cut rasher of bacon to be crisped for use in dishes or as a garnish.

10. Chiffonade Finely sliced or shredded herbs or leafy greens that are most often used as a garnish. This is done by stacking the leaves, rolling them like a cigar, and slicing them crosswise.

Southern foodlore

Master these cuts and you can make your own "piccalilli," as cooked vegetables and relishes were called when preserved in jars.

how to:
prepare an apple

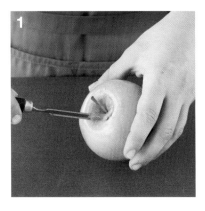

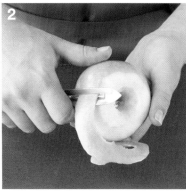

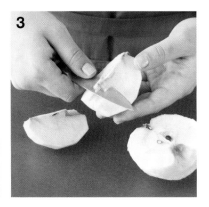

1. Insert a peeler near the stem end of the apple and rotate, prying out the loosened core.

2. Rotate the apple against a nonswivel peeler blade. Immediately rub with a lemon half to keep it from turning dark.

3. Cut the apple in half and then into wedges, cutting the core and seeds out of the center of each wedge.

how to:
prepare an artichoke

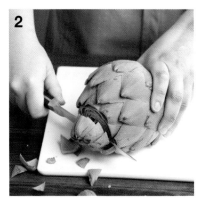

1. Cut off stem ends. With scissors, trim about one-fourth off the top of each outer leaf and rub top and edges of leaves with a lemon wedge to prevent discoloration.

2. Trim about $1/2$ inch from top of each artichoke. Remove any loose bottom leaves.

3. Halve the artichoke and scoop out the fuzzy choke and prickly red leaves from the center.

4. Place cut artichoke halves in a large bowl with water to cover. Squeeze lemon juice into the bowl to prevent browning.

how to:
peel an avocado

1. Slice all the way around the pit and through both ends of the fruit with a chef's knife.

2. Twist the halves in opposite directions and pull them apart.

3. Tap the pit sharply with the knife and twist the blade to lift the pit.

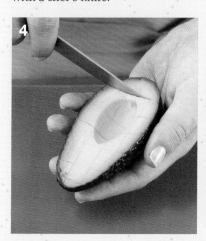

4. With a paring knife, score each avocado half by cutting parallel lines down to the peel and then cutting another set perpendicular to the first ones.

5. Use a large spoon to scoop the avocado pieces into a bowl. Since avocado flesh quickly turns brown when exposed to air, sprinkle with a little fresh lemon juice to slow discoloration.

kitchen secret:

Grocery stores are notorious for selling rock-hard avocadoes. To ripen them quickly, place them in a paper bag with a banana, apple, or other ripe fruit. The avocado will be ripe when the stem easily presses into the fruit.

how to:
peel a bell pepper

1. Place the pepper directly over a gas burner, on a grill, or under a broiler. Char the pepper, turning occasionally, until completely blackened.

2. Place the pepper in a glass bowl; cover with plastic wrap and let stand 10 minutes to loosen skin.

3. Or, place the pepper in a heavy-duty zip-top plastic bag and let stand 10 minutes to loosen skin.

4. Peel off the skin with your fingers or by grasping the skin between your thumb and a paring knife.

how to:
seed a bell pepper

1. Slice the pepper downward from stem to tip, following the shape of the pepper to slice the sides off the core.

2. Using your fingers or a paring knife, trim any strips of white membrane from the interior and discard the core and seeds.

how to:
freeze berries

1. Wash berries and remove stems.

2. Place berries, flat sides down, in a single layer on a baking sheet; place in freezer until solid.

3. Quickly transfer to a plastic freezer bag or container and keep in the freezer for up to 9 months.

how to:
prepare quick bread

1. Lightly spoon flour into a dry measuring cup and level with the back of a knife or other flat surfaced-utensil.

2. Combine flour with other dry ingredients in a bowl and make a well in the center.

3. Slowly pour liquid into the center of the well.

4. Stir liquid into dry ingredients just until combined. Over-mixing will cause the bread to become tough.

how to:
prepare Brussels sprouts

1. Remove discolored leaves from whole Brussels sprouts.

2. Cut off a small piece at the end of the stem.

3. Cut a shallow X into the bottom of each stem to allow the sprouts to cook evenly.

how to:
shred Brussels sprouts

1. Cut Brussels sprouts in half lengthwise through stem end.

2. Cut Brussels sprout halves crosswise into thin slices.

Southern foodlore

Brussels sprouts were first brought to and cultivated in the United States in the 1700s when the French settled in Louisiana.

how to:
clarify butter

1. Melt whole butter over low heat in a stainless steel saucepan.

2. When milk solids sink to the bottom, skim off the froth that rises to the top.

3. Strain off the clear, yellow butter into a jar, without adding the sediment of milk solids.

how to:
make compound butter

1. Mix softened butter and fresh or dried herbs in a bowl.

2. Place the softened butter on a sheet of wax paper and fold 1 edge of the paper over the butter. Wrap the edge of the paper under the butter and smooth it into a log by sliding both hands along the wax paper and rolling the log up in the paper.

3. Twist the ends of the wax paper in opposite directions to seal. Chill the butter for at least 1 hour in the refrigerator.

how to:
core and shred cabbage

1. Cut the cabbage into quarters through the center of the core.

2. Cut the core out of each quarter.

3. If using a chef's knife, place the cabbage, cut side down, onto a cutting board. Slice cabbage thinly.

4. If using a mandoline, cut the cabbage into small squares to fit the width of the slicing surface. Select desired blade. Press the hand piece of the mandoline into the cabbage and slide the cabbage up and down the mandoline, pressing gently.

how to:
cut a chicken

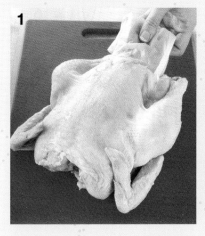

1. Remove gizzards and innards; set aside.

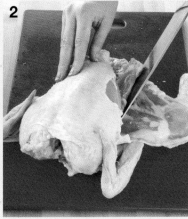

2. Remove leg quarters.

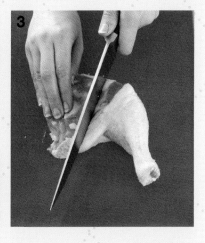

3. Separate thigh and drumstick.

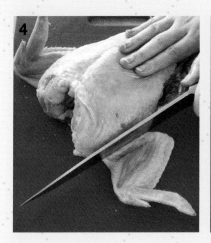

4. Remove wings.

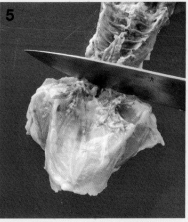

5. Cut carcass in half from tail to neck; cut through ribs on either side of backbone. Use a chef's knife or kitchen shears to remove backbone.

6. Remove the breast by cutting down through shoulder blades. Cut breast in half.

how to:
section citrus fruit

1. Cut the ends off an orange or other citrus fruit just far enough to expose the flesh.

2. Place the orange on a cutting board and carefully cut away the peel with a knife. Remove as little flesh with the peel as possible by following the orange's shape.

3. Using a knife, cut along the inside of the membranes to separate the wedges, working over a bowl to catch the juices and letting the sections fall into the bowl.

how to:
prepare fresh corn

1. Cut off the tip of the cob.

2. Holding onto the stem, rest the cut tip end on the bottom of a pie plate or large bowl. Using a chef's knife, cut through the kernels about three-quarters from the top of the kernel, avoiding the tough cob.

how to:
seed a cucumber

1. Cut the cucumber in half lengthwise.

2. Scrape out the seeds with a spoon.

3. Place the seeded cucumber half hollow side down on a cutting board. Cut horizontally along the length of the cucumber to form half moon–shaped slices.

how to:
beat egg whites to stiff peaks

1. Beat egg whites with a pinch of cream of tartar using a whisk in a copper bowl until soft peaks form.

2. Continue beating until egg whites hold a point to form stiff peaks. Don't overbeat, or they'll become dry.

kitchen secret:

To guarantee that egg whites are beaten to stiff peaks, make sure that there is no egg yolk or oily residue in the bowl. The fat will prevent the whites from forming peaks.

how to:
separate eggs

1. Tap the egg on a hard surface and hold it over a bowl. Pull the halves apart, holding one half like a cup to cradle the yolk, and let the white flow into the bowl underneath. Rock the yolk back and forth between the 2 shells until all of the white has dripped into the bowl.

2. Or, toss the shells and cup the yolk with your hand, passing the yolk back and forth until all of the white has dripped into the bowl.

how to:
temper eggs

1. Slowly stir a little hot liquid into a bowl of beaten eggs while whisking in order to gradually cook the eggs without causing them to curdle.

how to:
make a bouquet garni

1. Determine the size of the bouquet garni by the amount of liquid it will be simmered in. A small amount of sauce will require a bunch the thickness of your thumb. A large stockpot will require a bunch the size of your forearm. Tie together at the stems.

kitchen secret:

A bouquet garni is a bundle of fresh herbs tied together with kitchen string and is used to flavor stocks, soups, and sauces. Or, if you'd rather, you can place the herbs in a cheesecloth bag.

how to:
prepare garlic

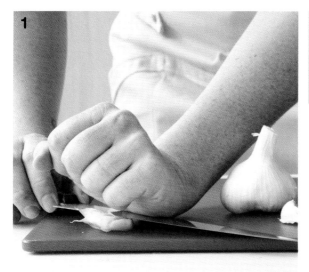

1. Press the garlic clove with the side of a chef's knife to gently loosen skin.

2. Remove skin.

3. Mince garlic with a chef's knife or slice finely.

4. You can also prepare garlic with a garlic press, pushing cloves through a perforated grid to extract the pulp and juice. Or, rub a peeled clove over a rasp grater.

how to:
prepare leeks

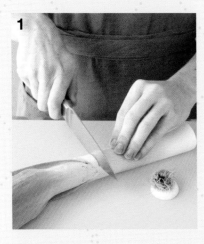

1. Trim off the roots and the tough tops of the green leaves.

2. Cut the leek stalk in half.

3. Rinse trimmed leeks in a colander.

4. Rinse again under cold running water, gently separating the layers and rubbing the leaves to remove trapped dirt and sand.

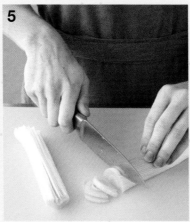

5. Place leek halves cut side down on a cutting board, and slice into thin half moons.

6. Rinse sliced leeks in a colander.

how to:
zest a lemon

1. Rub the fruit against a rasp grater, only removing the colored skin and not the white pith, which tends to be very bitter.

2. Or, you can also use a citrus zester, which, like a citrus stripper, cuts strips from the rind of citrus fruits. The zester has a cutting edge with holes which, when pulled across the surface of citrus fruit, makes various sized strips of zest, depending on the size of the holes.

how to:
prepare a mango

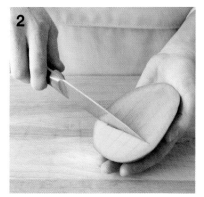

1. Stand mango up on its narrow side on a cutting board with the stem end facing away from you. Using a chef's knife, cut down the length of the fruit, about 1 inch from the stem and just grazing the pit. Repeat on the other side.

2. Place one mango half, cut side up, on the board. Using a paring knife, make 1/2-inch cuts in a criss-cross pattern in the flesh, stopping short of the skin.

3. With both hands, hold the scored mango half from its skin side and push up to expose cubes of mango flesh.

4. Using a knife, carefully cut across the base of the cubes to free them, letting them fall into a bowl.

how to:
make mayonnaise by hand

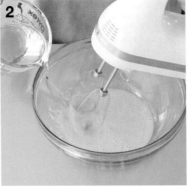

1. Combine egg yolks, mustard, and lemon juice or vinegar in a small bowl and beat until smooth.

2. Slowly pour 1 tsp. of oil at a time down the side of the bowl and beat into the egg mixture.

3. When the mayonnaise stiffens slightly, add the oil more quickly, about 1 Tbsp. at a time. Continue until mayonnaise is stiff.

how to:
make mayonnaise with a blender

kitchen secret:

For about 2¼ cups mayonnaise, use 3 pasteurized egg yolks, 1 Tbsp. Dijon mustard, 2 Tbsp. lemon juice, and 2¼ cups olive oil.

1. Combine egg yolks, mustard, and lemon juice in a blender.

2. With the blender on the lowest speed, pour the oil in a slow but steady stream through opening in the top, blending until the mixture stiffens.

how to:
correct separated mayonnaise

1. Pour the mayonnaise and any remaining oil into a measuring cup.

2. Put an egg yolk into a clean bowl and add 1 Tbsp. of the broken mayonnaise. Using an electric mixer, beat until the two are just combined.

3. By carefully controlling the rate at which you combine the broken mayonnaise and fresh yolk, it can be re-emulsified. Taste and adjust seasonings as needed.

how to:
grind meat for hamburgers

1. Cube meat into 1½-inch pieces.

2. Process in 8 oz. batches, pulsing 8 to 10 times or until finely chopped. Use a light touch to combine ground meat and seasonings.

3. Gently shape into burgers.

how to:
prepare a melon

1. Place the melon on its side on a cutting board and put a hand on one end to secure it. Carefully but firmly cut the melon in half crosswise with a chef's knife.

2. Use a large spoon to scoop out the seeds from the center of the melon and discard the seeds.

3. Stand the melon hollow side up, and cut it in half. Repeat with remaining half to yield 4 wedges.

how to:
shuck oysters

1. Hold the oyster in the palm of your hand with an oven mitt to prevent cutting yourself, positioning the oyster so that the curved side of the shell faces down and the flat side faces up. Insert a paring or oyster knife between the shells, near the hinge. Twist the knife to detach the muscle.

2. Remove the top shell and use the knife to take the oyster meat out of the bottom shell.

Southern foodlore

It has long been believed that you should only consume oysters in the months that have the letter "r" in them. However, it is safe to consume them in non-"r" months if they are harvested from cold water environments.

how to:
chop an onion

1. Use a sharp knife to cut through the stem end of the onion and peel back the papery skin.

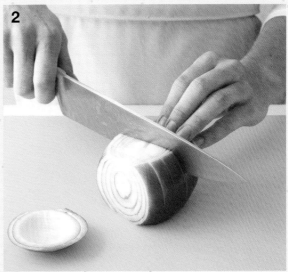

2. Remove the root end to create an even base. Place the peeled onion on the cut root end. Make several parallel vertical cuts through the onion layers.

3. Rotate the onion 90° and make several parallel vertical cuts.

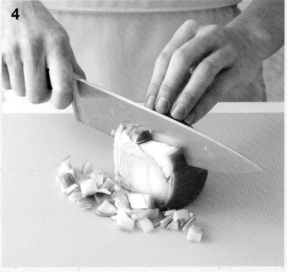

4. Cut across the grain to make chopped pieces.

how to:
prepare a pineapple

1. Slice off the green top.

3. Stand the pineapple on one cut end and slice off the skin, cutting just below the surface, in wide vertical strips, leaving the small brown eyes. The eyes can be removed by carefully cutting diagonally around the fruit, following the pattern of the eyes and making shallow, narrow furrows, cutting away as little of the flesh as possible.

2. Slice off the bottom stem.

4. Cut the pineapple into slices, chunks, or rings, and use a cookie cutter or knife to remove the center core.

how to:
dice a potato (or any vegetable)

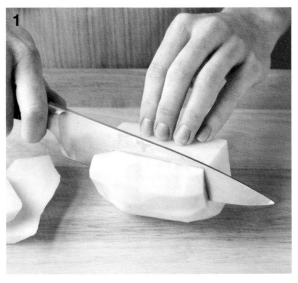

1. Slice off the sides of the peeled vegetable to form a cube. Reserve curved sides for another use, or use them in Steps 3 and 4.

2. Slice the cube, making sure slices are all the same thickness.

3. Holding the slices together with your fingers, slice them again so that you end up with sticks.

4. Holding the sticks together, cut them into a dice.

how to:
remove silver skin

1. Place the tip of your knife under one end of the silver skin, pointing the blade up so as not to cut off too much meat.

2. Slide the knife down the piece of meat, holding onto the end of the silver skin and pulling up as you slice, being careful not to remove any meat.

kitchen secret:

Silver skin is the layer of connective tissue found on pork, beef, and a variety of meats. The rubbery texture is unpleasant to eat, so be sure to remove it before cooking. Many butchers will remove it for you, if you'd like.

how to:
butterfly shrimp

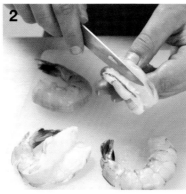

1. Shell the shrimp without removing tail.

2. Insert a knife about three-quarters of the way into shrimp near the head and cut nearly all the way down the center of the shrimp's back to the tail. Remove the vein with the tip of your knife.

3. Using your hands, open the flesh of the shrimp until it lies flat.

how to:
peel stone fruit

1. Use a paring knife to cut a shallow X on the bottom of the fruit.

2. Use a slotted spoon to lower the fruit into a pot of boiling water. Let it sit until the skin loosens, 15 to 30 seconds, depending on ripeness.

3. Immediately transfer to ice water to cool and stop the cooking process.

4. When the fruit cools, find the X from step 1, grasp a corner of loose skin between your thumb and a paring knife, and pull off the skin, repeating to remove all of the skin.

how to:
pit stone fruit

1. Using a paring knife, cut the fruit in half lengthwise, cutting carefully around the pit. Rotate the halves in opposite directions to separate them.

2. Use the tip of the knife to gently dig under the pit and ease it out, trying from different angles.

kitchen secret:

If available, look for freestone peaches. This variety of peaches makes slicing and pitting a piece of cake. Cling peaches are those where the pits "cling" to the fruit and are harder to remove.

how to:
blanch vegetables

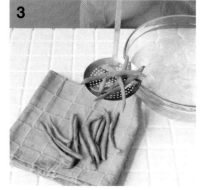

1. Plunge trimmed vegetables into rapidly boiling, generously salted water and cook until crisp-tender.

2. Transfer vegetables to an ice-water bath to cool rapidly.

3. Spread cooled, blanched vegetables on a clean kitchen towel to remove excess liquid.

how to:
peel and seed a tomato

1. Use a paring knife to carefully cut the stem end out of the tomato.

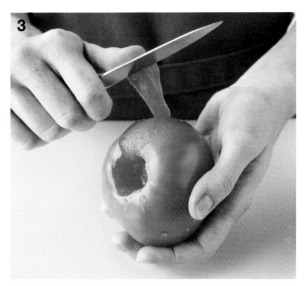

2. Plunge the tomato into boiling water for 15 seconds if ripe, 30 seconds if underripe. Drain the tomato in a colander and place immediately in an ice bath.

3. Peel back the skin in strips by pinching it between your thumb and a paring knife.

4. Cut tomato in half crosswise. Hold half in your hand and gently squeeze, removing the seeds with your fingers or a spoon.

the METHODS

Everything you want to know about cooking Southern

NO
COOK

When the weather is warm or you're short on time, there's no need to turn on the oven or stand over a hot stove for hours. Assemble a crowd-pleasing appetizer with fresh ingredients from the store, toss together a crisp salad with a homemade vinaigrette, let the food processor make easy work of creating a delicious soup, or freeze a creamy custard pie for dessert.

Simple Antipasto Platter

Hands-on Time: 10 min.
Total Time: 10 min.
Makes: 8 servings

- 1 (5-oz.) goat cheese log
- 2 Tbsp. chopped fresh parsley
- 1 (16-oz.) jar pickled okra, drained
- 1 (8-oz.) jar kalamata olives, drained and rinsed
- 1 (7-oz.) jar roasted red bell peppers, drained and cut into pieces
- 4 oz. sliced salami
- 4 oz. prosciutto

Breadsticks and assorted crackers

1. Roll goat cheese log in parsley; place on a serving platter.
2. Halve okra lengthwise. Arrange okra and next 3 ingredients on platter with goat cheese.
3. Cut prosciutto into 1-inch-thick strips; wrap around breadsticks. Arrange on platter with remaining antipasto; serve with additional assorted crackers.

how to:
assemble a simple antipasto platter

1. Gather varieties of deli meats, cheeses, and pickled vegetables. Drain olives and vegetables.

2. Roll goat cheese in chopped fresh herbs until thoroughly coated.

3. Slice pickled okra and other vegetables into bite-size pieces.

4. Slice prosciutto into thin strips and wrap around grissini (thin breadsticks) before serving.

kitchen secret:

Add even more variety to your antipasto platter with prepared hummus found in the deli and baked pita chips.

Caribbean Crab Sandwiches

Hands-on Time: 22 min.
Total Time: 22 min.
Makes: 6 servings

- 2 limes
- 1 lb. fresh crabmeat, drained
- ¼ cup chopped fresh cilantro
- 6 hoagie rolls, split
- 1 mango, peeled and chopped
- 1 avocado, peeled and chopped

1. Grate zest from 1 lime to equal ½ tsp. Squeeze juice from limes to equal 6 Tbsp. Gently combine zest, lime juice, crabmeat, and cilantro.
2. Spoon crabmeat mixture into rolls; sprinkle with mango and avocado. Serve immediately.

how to:
make caribbean crab sandwiches

1. Pick through crabmeat to remove any shells. Add fresh lime zest to crabmeat.

2. Gently combine lime zest, juice, and cilantro.

3. Spoon crabmeat mixture into halved hoagies. Top with mango and avocado; serve immediately. (The avocado will darken if it's exposed to oxygen.)

Tomato-Cucumber Bread Salad

Hands-on Time: 25 min.
Total Time: 40 min.
Makes: 6 servings

- 3 crusty artisan sourdough bread slices
- 3 cups mixed salad greens
- 1 cup halved grape tomatoes
- 1 medium cucumber, peeled, seeded, and chopped
- ½ cup loosely packed fresh basil leaves, cut into chiffonade (see page 79)
- ½ cup thinly sliced red onions

Red Wine Vinaigrette

1. Preheat oven to 425°. Cut bread into 1-inch cubes (about 2½ cups), and place on a jelly-roll pan. Bake 5 to 7 minutes or until lightly toasted. Transfer bread to a wire rack; cool completely (about 10 minutes).
2. Toss bread cubes with salad greens and next 4 ingredients. Serve with Red Wine Vinaigrette.

Marinated Tomato-Cucumber Bread Salad: Omit salad greens. Increase bread slices to 6, and toast as directed in Step 1. Increase grape tomatoes to 1 pt., halved. Toss together 4 medium-size ripe tomatoes, chopped; grape tomato halves; and next 3 ingredients in a large bowl. Toss in ⅓ cup Red Wine Vinaigrette. Let stand 10 minutes. Toss in bread cubes. Let stand 15 minutes.

Red Wine Vinaigrette

Hands-on Time: 5 min.
Total Time: 5 min.
Makes: about ⅔ cup

Store in an airtight container in refrigerator for up to 1 week.

- ¼ cup red wine vinegar
- ½ tsp. salt
- ½ tsp. freshly ground pepper
- ⅓ cup olive oil

1. Whisk together first 3 ingredients in a small bowl. Add oil in a slow, steady stream, whisking constantly until smooth.
2. Use immediately, or store in an airtight container in refrigerator for up to 1 week. If chilled, let stand at room temperature 15 minutes, and whisk before serving.

how to:
assemble tomato-cucumber bread salad

1. Combine salad components except for vinaigrette in a serving bowl. If you'd like to assemble ahead of time, reserve croutons until just before serving; store in refrigerator.

2. Gently toss dry salad to combine ingredients.

3. To make vinaigrette, combine vinegar, salt, and pepper; slowly pour in oil in a steady stream, whisking constantly until smooth.

4. Just before serving, drizzle vinaigrette over salad. Toss gently until greens are well coated.

Creamy Cucumber Soup

Hands-on Time: 20 min.
Total Time: 4 hr., 20 min.
Makes: about 2 qt.

English, or hothouse, cucumbers have thin skins, few seeds, and mild flavor. English cucumbers are sold wrapped in plastic, rather than coated in wax.

- ¾ cup chicken broth
- 3 green onions
- 2 Tbsp. white vinegar
- ½ tsp. salt
- ¼ tsp. pepper
- 3 large English cucumbers (about 2½ lb.), peeled, seeded, chopped, and divided
- 3 cups fat-free Greek yogurt
- Salt to taste
- Garnishes: toasted slivered almonds, freshly ground pepper, chopped red bell pepper

1. Process chicken broth, green onions, vinegar, salt, pepper, and half of chopped cucumbers in a food processor until smooth, stopping to scrape down sides.
2. Add yogurt, and pulse until blended. Pour into a large bowl; stir in remaining chopped cucumbers. Cover and chill 4 to 24 hours. Season with salt to taste just before serving. Garnish, if desired.

kitchen secret:

If you'd like, substitute plain low-fat yogurt for the Greek yogurt. Plain yogurt is not as thick as Greek yogurt, so decrease broth to ½ cup in order not to affect the consistency of the soup.

how to:
make creamy cucumber soup

1. Place all ingredients except half of cucumbers, yogurt, and garnishes in bowl of food processor. Process until smooth, stopping to scrape down sides as needed.

2. Add yogurt to pureed soup. Pulse until blended.

3. Stir in remaining cucumbers and chill until ready to serve. Season with salt to taste and garnish just before serving.

Green Goddess Dipping Sauce

Hands-on Time: 10 min.
Total Time: 1 hr., 10 min.
Makes: 1½ cups

No need for lots of chopping; let the food processor do all the work in this delicious herb-packed sauce. Serve with steamed shrimp as an appetizer.

¾ cup sour cream
½ cup firmly packed fresh parsley leaves
½ cup mayonnaise
1 green onion, chopped
1 Tbsp. firmly packed fresh dill leaves
1 Tbsp. firmly packed fresh tarragon leaves
2 tsp. lemon zest
1 Tbsp. lemon juice
1 garlic clove
½ tsp. salt
¼ tsp. pepper
  Garnish: fresh dill sprigs

1. Process first 11 ingredients in a blender or food processor 30 seconds or until smooth, stopping to scrape down sides as needed. Cover and chill 1 hour before serving. Garnish, if desired. Store in the refrigerator up to 1 week.

fix it!

Problem: The fresh dill you bought in the clamshell container is limp.

Solution: Changes in refrigerator temperature can affect fresh herbs. Diagonally snip the ends of the dill under running water and place in a 1-cup glass measure with about 1 inch of water. Add a cube or 2 of ice and let stand for 30 minutes to 1 hour.

how to:
make green goddess dipping sauce

1. Place all ingredients except garnish in bowl of food processor.
2. Process until smooth, stopping to scrape down sides as needed.

No-Cook Peach Ice Cream

Hands-on Time: 8 min.
Total Time: 1 hr., plus overnight for freezing
Makes: 1¹⁄₂ qt.

- 1 (14-oz.) can sweetened condensed milk
- 1 (5-oz.) can evaporated milk
- 1¼ cups whole milk
- 4 medium-size fresh ripe peaches, peeled and sliced, or 1 (15.25-oz.) can peaches in light syrup, drained
- 2 Tbsp. sugar
- ¼ cup fresh lemon juice
- ¼ tsp. salt
- ¾ cup peach nectar
- Garnishes: fresh peach slices, fresh mint

1. Whisk first 3 ingredients in a 2-qt. pitcher or large bowl until blended. Cover and chill 30 minutes.
2. Process peaches with sugar, lemon juice, and salt in a blender or food processor until smooth. Stir into milk mixture with peach nectar.
3. Pour milk mixture into freezer container of an electric ice-cream maker, and freeze according to manufacturer's instructions. (Instructions and times will vary.)
4. Remove container with ice cream from ice-cream maker, and place in freezer 15 minutes. Transfer to a freezer-safe container; cover and freeze 8 hours or overnight until firm. Spoon into bowls and serve with fresh peach slices and mint, if desired.

Note: We tested with a Rival 4-qt. durable plastic bucket ice-cream maker and a Cuisinart automatic Frozen Yogurt-Ice Cream & Sorbet Maker.

how to:
make no-cook peach ice cream

1. Combine sweetened condensed milk, evaporated milk, and whole milk, stirring well with a whisk. Chill 30 minutes.

2. Place peaches, sugar, lemon juice, and salt in bowl of a food processor; pulse until smooth.

3. Combine peach mixture, milk mixture, and nectar. Place into freezer container of an ice-cream maker and freeze according to manufacturer's instructions.

4. Place container in freezer for 15 minutes. Transfer mixture to a freezer-safe container. Cover and freeze overnight until firm.

Lemonade Pie

Hands-on Time: 15 min.
Total Time: 8 hr., 15 min.
Makes: 8 servings

- 1 (12-oz.) can evaporated milk
- 2 (3.4-oz.) packages lemon instant pudding mix
- 1 Tbsp. lemon zest
- 2 (8-oz.) packages cream cheese, softened
- ½ tsp. vanilla extract
- 1 (12-oz.) can frozen lemonade concentrate, thawed
- 1 (9-oz.) ready-made graham cracker piecrust
- Frozen whipped topping, thawed
- Garnish: lemon zest curls

1. Whisk together evaporated milk and next 2 ingredients in a bowl 2 minutes or until mixture is thickened.
2. Beat cream cheese and vanilla at medium speed with an electric mixer until fluffy. Add lemonade concentrate, beating until smooth; add milk mixture, and beat until blended. Pour into crust. Cover and chill 8 hours or until firm. Dollop each slice with whipped topping. Garnish, if desired.

kitchen secret:

For a homemade look, freeze the crust for 5 minutes and then slip it into your favorite pie plate before adding the filling.

how to:
make lemonade pie

1. Whisk together evaporated milk, pudding mix, and 1 Tbsp. lemon zest.
2. Beat cream cheese and vanilla with an electric mixer until fluffy. Slowly add lemonade concentrate, beating until smooth.
3. Add milk mixture to cream cheese mixture; beat until blended.
4. Pour filling into pie crust. Cover and chill 8 hours or until firm.

BAKE

Baking is a cooking method defined by using prolonged dry heat in the oven, while convection baking uses the assistance of fans to cook foods more quickly. A little magic occurs after flour and sugar are combined with butter to yield pillowy-soft sugar cookies or fresh-baked sweet breads. From quick muffins and yeast rolls to cookies and cakes, baked goods are the ultimate comfort food.

Lemon-Coconut Cake

Hands-on Time: 30 min.
Total Time: 1 hr., 45 min.
Makes: 12 servings

- 1   cup butter, softened
- 2   cups sugar
- 4   large eggs, at room temperature and separated
- 3   cups all-purpose flour
- 1   Tbsp. baking powder
- 1   cup milk
- 1   tsp. vanilla extract
- Lemon Filling
- Cream Cheese Frosting
- 2   cups sweetened flaked coconut

1. Preheat oven to 350°. Beat butter at medium speed with an electric mixer until fluffy; gradually add sugar, beating well. Add egg yolks, 1 at a time, beating until blended after each addition.

2. Combine flour and baking powder; add to butter mixture alternately with milk, beginning and ending with flour mixture. Beat at low speed until blended after each addition. Stir in vanilla.

3. Beat egg whites at high speed with electric mixer until stiff peaks form; fold one-third of egg whites into batter. Gently fold in remaining beaten egg whites just until blended. Spoon batter into 3 greased and floured 9-inch round cake pans.

4. Bake at 350° for 18 to 20 minutes or until a wooden pick inserted in center comes out clean. Cool in pans on wire racks 10 minutes; remove from pans, and cool completely on wire racks.

5. Spread Lemon Filling between layers. Spread Cream Cheese Frosting on top and sides of cake. Sprinkle top with coconut.

Lemon Filling

Hands-on Time: 10 min.
Total Time: 15 min.
Makes: about 1²/₃ cups

- 1   cup sugar
- ¼   cup cornstarch
- 1   cup boiling water
- 4   egg yolks, lightly beaten
- 2   tsp. grated lemon zest
- ⅓   cup fresh lemon juice
- 2   Tbsp. butter

1. Combine sugar and cornstarch in a medium sauce-pan; whisk in 1 cup boiling water. Cook over medium heat, whisking constantly, until sugar and cornstarch dissolve (about 2 minutes). Gradually whisk about one-fourth of hot sugar mixture into egg yolks; add to remaining hot sugar mixture in pan, whisking constantly. Whisk in lemon zest and juice.

2. Cook, whisking constantly, until mixture is thickened (about 2 to 3 minutes). Remove from heat. Whisk in butter, and let cool completely, stirring occasionally.

kitchen secret:

A rasp grater, available in kitchen shops for $12 and up, makes grating the lemon zest super easy. It only takes a minute to squeeze fresh lemon juice, and the taste is worth it.

Cream Cheese Frosting

Hands-on Time: 10 min.
Total Time: 10 min.
Makes: about 3 cups

½ cup butter, softened
1 (8-oz.) package cream cheese, softened
1 (16-oz.) package powdered sugar
1 tsp. vanilla extract

1. Beat butter and cream cheese at medium speed with an electric mixer until creamy. Gradually add powdered sugar, beating at low speed until blended; stir in vanilla.

how to:
make lemon-coconut cake

1. Place eggs in a bowl of water to bring to room temperature. Make sure butter is correctly softened. If you press your index finger into the butter and it doesn't make an indentation, the butter is too hard. If you press your index finger into the butter and it doesn't hold its shape, it's too soft.

2. Beat butter and sugar with an electric mixer until fluffy. Add egg yolks 1 at a time and beat until blended after each addition.

3. Add milk alternately with flour mixture, beginning and ending with flour mixture.

fix it!

Problem: The butter is over-softened.

Solution: Refrigerate for 5 to 10 minutes, depending on softness. Butter is perfectly softened when you gently press your index finger into the butter and it still holds its shape.

4. Beat egg whites until stiff peaks form. (When the whisk is lifted from the bowl, the pointy ridges don't droop or fall over.)

5. Gently fold egg whites into batter, just until incorporated. Over-beating will decrease the amount of air in the batter, which creates a less-tender cake.

6. Grease cake pans with shortening. Be sure to cover all sides and bottom.

7. Sprinkle flour over shortening and shake to completely coat. Shake out excess flour.

8. After cake has baked and cooled, spread filling between layers. Be sure to spread all the way to the edges.

9. Spread frosting on sides and top of cake.

10. Sprinkle cake with coconut.

bake it!

Short on time? Substitute store-bought lemon curd for the lemon filling. Since lemon curds differ in texture, you may need to stir in a little sour cream to create the perfect spreading consistency.

German Chocolate Pie

Hands-on Time: 33 min.
Total Time: 5 hr., 18 min.
Makes: 8 servings

    Basic Pastry for a 10-inch Pie
    1   (4-oz.) package sweet baking chocolate
    ¼   cup butter
    1   (12-oz.) can evaporated milk
  1½   cups sugar
    3   Tbsp. cornstarch
    ⅛   tsp. salt
    2   large eggs
    1   tsp. vanilla extract
    ⅔   cup sweetened flaked coconut
    ⅓   cup chopped pecans
    1   cup sweetened whipped cream
    3   Tbsp. chocolate shavings

1. Preheat oven to 375°. Prepare pastry; place in a 9½-inch deep-dish pie plate. Set aside.
2. Combine baking chocolate and butter in a medium saucepan; cook over low heat, stirring until chocolate melts. Remove from heat, and gradually stir in evaporated milk; set aside.
3. Combine sugar, cornstarch, and salt in a large bowl; add eggs and vanilla, mixing well. Gradually stir in chocolate mixture, using a wire whisk. Pour mixture into unbaked pastry shell, and sprinkle with coconut and chopped pecans.
4. Bake at 375° for 45 minutes. (Pie may appear soft but will become firm after cooling.) Cool at least 4 hours. Top cooled pie with whipped cream and chocolate shavings.

Basic Pastry for a 10-inch Pie

Hands-on Time: 12 min.
Total Time: 12 min.
Makes: 1 pastry

  1½   cups all-purpose flour
    ¾   tsp. salt
    ½   cup shortening
    4   to 5 Tbsp. ice water

1. Combine flour and salt; cut in shortening with a pastry blender until mixture is crumbly. Sprinkle ice water, 1 Tbsp. at a time, evenly over surface; stir with a fork until dry ingredients are moistened. Shape into a disc; cover and chill until ready to use.
2. Roll pastry to ⅛-inch thickness on a lightly floured surface. Place in pie plate; trim off excess pastry along edges. Fold edges under, and crimp. Chill. Proceed as directed.

how to:
make pie crust

1. Combine flour and salt; cut in shortening until mixture is crumbly. Add ice water 1 Tbsp. at a time and combine just until moistened. Don't overmix, or the dough will become tough.

2. Shape the dough into a disc. Cover and refrigerate until ready to use.

Buttermilk Biscuits

This versatile biscuit recipe takes only three ingredients to make.

Hands-on Time: 36 min.
Total Time: 1 hr.
Makes: 2 dozen

½	cup cold butter
2¼	cups self-rising soft-wheat flour
1¼	cups buttermilk
	Self-rising soft-wheat flour
2	Tbsp. melted butter

1. Preheat oven to 450°. Cut ½ cup cold butter with a sharp knife or pastry blender into ¼-inch-thick slices. Sprinkle butter slices over 2¼ cups flour in a large bowl. Toss butter with flour. Cut butter into flour with a pastry blender until crumbly and mixture resembles small peas. Cover and chill 10 minutes. Add buttermilk, stirring just until dry ingredients are moistened.

2. Turn dough out onto a lightly floured surface; knead 3 or 4 times, gradually adding additional flour as needed. With floured hands, press or pat dough into a ¾-inch-thick rectangle (about 9 x 5 inches). Sprinkle top of dough with additional flour. Fold dough over onto itself in 3 sections, starting with 1 short end. (Fold dough rectangle as if folding a letter-size piece of paper.) Repeat entire process 2 more times, beginning with pressing dough into a ¾-inch-thick rectangle (about 9 x 5 inches).

3. Press or pat dough to ½-inch thickness on a lightly floured surface; cut into 2- x 2-inch squares with a pastry cutter, or cut with a 2-inch round cutter, and place, side by side, on a parchment paper-lined or lightly greased jelly-roll pan. (Dough squares or rounds should touch.)

4. Bake at 450° for 13 to 15 minutes or until lightly browned. Remove from oven; brush with 2 Tbsp. melted butter.

Note: We tested with White Lily Unbleached Self-Rising Flour.

how to:
make buttermilk biscuits

1. Cut cold butter slices into flour with a pastry blender until crumbly and mixture resembles small peas.

2. After kneading dough 3 to 4 times, press dough into a rectangle, sprinkling with extra flour as needed. Fold dough over itself in 3 sections (as you would fold a letter). Repeat process 2 times.

3. Press dough to ½-inch thickness and cut into 2-inch squares with a pastry cutter, or use a 2-inch round biscuit cutter. Place biscuits side by side (to increase rising) on a parchment paper-lined or lightly greased baking sheet.

Basic Sweet Muffins

Hands-on Time: 16 min.
Total Time: 36 min.
Makes: 1 dozen

- 1½ cups all-purpose flour
- ½ cup sugar
- 2 tsp. baking powder
- ½ tsp. salt
- 1 large egg
- ½ cup milk
- ¼ cup vegetable oil
- Optional: butter slices

1. Preheat oven to 400°. Stir together first 4 ingredients in a large bowl; make a well in center of mixture. Stir together egg, milk, and oil until blended. Add to dry ingredients, stirring just until moistened.

2. Spoon batter into lightly greased muffin pans, filling two-thirds full.
3. Bake at 400° for 18 to 20 minutes. Remove from pans immediately. Top warm muffins with butter slices, if desired.

Apple Muffins: Add ³/₄ cup peeled, chopped apple; ¹/₄ tsp. ground cinnamon; and ¹/₄ tsp. ground nutmeg to dry ingredients, and proceed as directed.

Blueberry Muffins: Fold ³/₄ cup fresh or frozen blueberries, unthawed, into batter, and proceed as directed.

Date-Nut Muffins: Fold ¹/₂ cup chopped dates and ¹/₂ cup chopped pecans into batter, and proceed as directed.

how to:
make basic sweet muffins

1. Stir dry ingredients together in a large bowl. Make a well in the center of the mixture. (This allows for even consistency and prevents over-mixing.)

2. Combine egg, milk, and oil. Add to dry ingredients, stirring just until moistened. Fold in fruit or nuts, if desired.

3. Spoon batter into muffin cups, filling two-thirds full. An ice cream scoop makes an easy job of dividing the batter evenly.

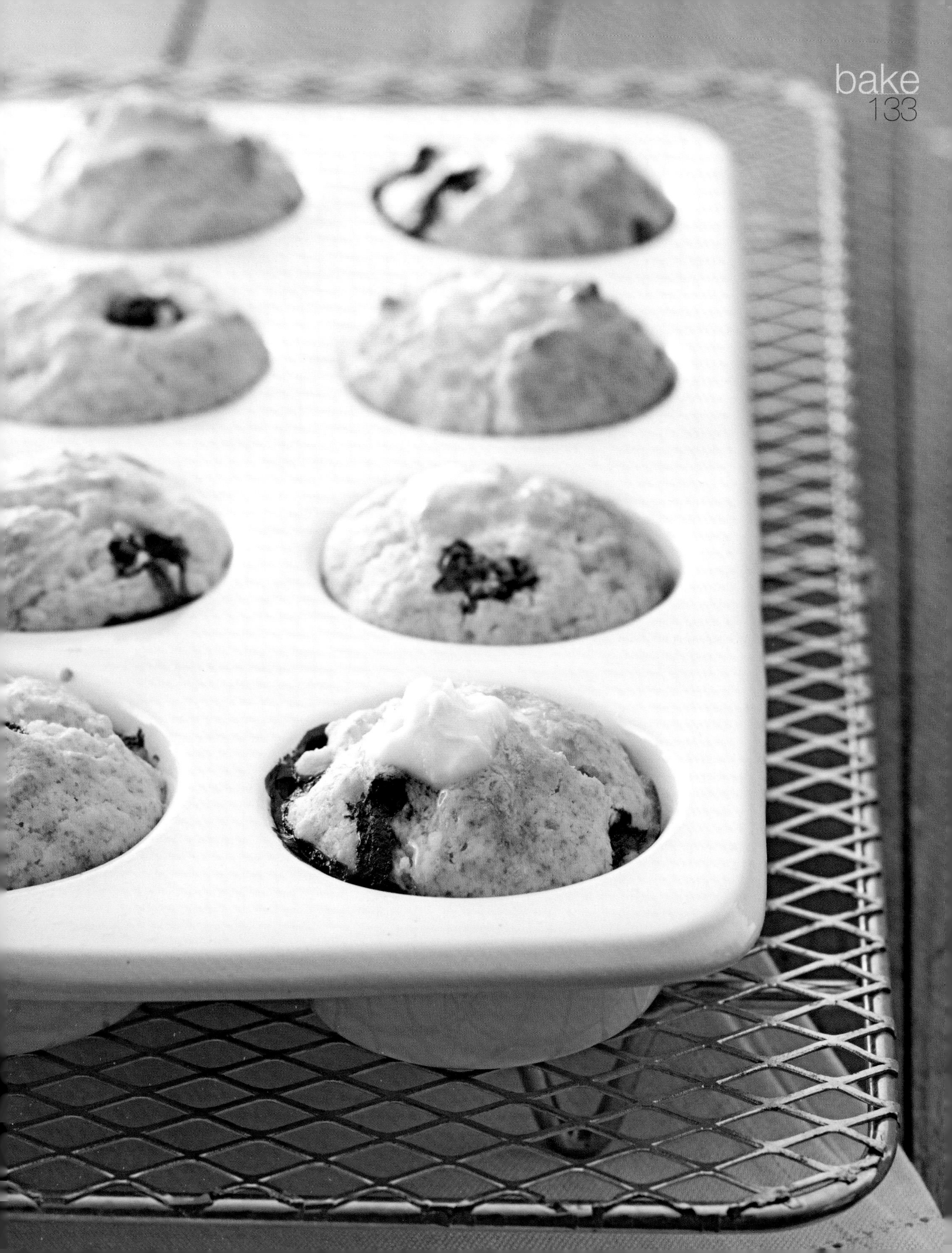

kitchen secret:

When substituting honey for sugar in a recipe, reduce any liquid by ¼ cup and add 1 tsp. of baking soda for each cup of honey used. Also reduce oven temperature by 25° to prevent overbrowning. Coat your measuring cups and spoons with vegetable cooking spray to make it easy for honey to slide out when pouring. Store honey at room temperature. If it crystallizes, remove lid, and place in a container of hot water until crystals dissolve.

Honey Yeast Rolls

Hands-on Time: 35 min.
Total Time: 3 hr., 47 min.
Makes: 28 rolls

¼ cup warm water (100° to 110°)
1 (¼-oz.) envelope active dry yeast
1 tsp. honey
1¾ cups milk
2 large eggs, at room temperature
½ cup butter, melted and cooled
⅓ cup honey
3 tsp. salt
6½ cups all-purpose flour, divided
½ cup butter, softened
¼ cup honey

1. Combine first 3 ingredients in a small bowl, and let stand 5 minutes or until mixture bubbles.
2. Meanwhile, heat milk in a saucepan over medium heat 3 to 5 minutes or until 100° to 110°.
3. Stir together warm milk, eggs, and next 3 ingredients in bowl of a heavy-duty electric stand mixer, blending well. Add yeast mixture, stirring to combine. Gradually add 5 cups flour, beating at medium speed, using paddle attachment. Beat 3 minutes. Cover with plastic wrap, and let stand 1 hour.
4. Uncover dough, and add remaining 1½ cups flour, beating at medium speed 5 minutes. (Dough will be sticky.) Transfer to a lightly greased large mixing bowl. Cover with plastic wrap, and let rise in a warm place (85°), free from drafts, 1 hour or until doubled in bulk.
5. Punch dough down. Turn dough out onto a well-floured surface, and roll into 28 (2½-inch) balls (about ¼ cup dough per ball). Place balls in 4 lightly greased 9-inch pans (7 balls per pan). Cover and let rise in a warm place (85°), free from drafts, 1 hour or until doubled in bulk.
6. Preheat oven to 400°. Stir together ½ cup softened butter and ¼ cup honey.
7. Bake rolls at 400° for 10 to 12 minutes or until golden brown. Brush tops with honey butter. Serve with remaining honey butter.

Note: To freeze, place baked rolls in zip-top plastic freezer bags, and freeze up to 2 months. Let thaw at room temperature. Reheat, if desired.

how to:
make honey yeast rolls

1. Combine warm water, yeast, and honey in a small bowl. Let it stand 5 minutes or until it starts to bubble.
2. Heat milk to 100° to 110°. If it heats to over 110°, let it cool until it is in the desired temperature range so it won't kill the yeast.
3. Combine warm milk, eggs, butter, honey, and salt with an electric mixer; blend well, using the paddle attachment. Add yeast mixture, and beat until combined. Gradually add flour and beat 3 minutes.
4. Transfer dough to a lightly greased large mixing bowl. Cover with plastic wrap and let it rise in a warm place, free from drafts.
5. After dough has risen for about an hour, it should have doubled in bulk.
6. Punch dough down and turn out onto a lightly floured surface. Roll dough into 28 (2½-inch) balls. Place balls on lightly greased pans. Cover and let rise in a warm place, free from drafts, about 1 hour or until doubled in bulk.

Boiling is defined as the **rapid vaporization** of a liquid and occurs when the vapor pressure equals the surrounding environmental pressure. Typically, 212° is the temperature for water to boil. However, **lower air pressure** makes water boil at a lower temperature at high altitudes. Whether bringing water to a boil to cook shrimp or boiling and then reducing to a **simmer** to poach eggs, this cooking technique is one of the most often used in the kitchen.

Perfect Mashed Potatoes

Hands-on Time: 22 min.
Total Time: 43 min.
Makes: about 6 cups

Yukon gold potatoes yield a texture that's just right for holding a pool of flavorful gravy or melted butter.

   3 lb. Yukon gold potatoes
   2 tsp. salt, divided
   ⅓ cup butter
   ⅓ cup half-and-half
   4 oz. cream cheese, softened
   ¾ tsp. coarsely ground pepper
   Butter pats

1. Peel potatoes, and cut into 1-inch pieces. Bring potatoes, 1 tsp. salt, and cold water to cover to a boil in a medium-size Dutch oven over medium-high heat. Reduce heat to medium-low, and cook 16 to 20 minutes or until fork-tender; drain.
2. Return potatoes to Dutch oven. Cook until water evaporates and potatoes look dry. Mound potatoes on one side; add butter, next 3 ingredients, and remaining 1 tsp. salt to opposite side of Dutch oven. Cook 1 to 2 minutes or until butter is melted and mixture boils.
3. Remove from heat; beat at medium speed with a hand-held electric mixer 30 seconds to 1 minute or to desired degree of smoothness. (Do not overbeat.) Top with butter pats. Serve immediately.

how to:
make perfect mashed potatoes

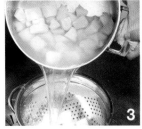

1. Bring cubed potatoes, 1 tsp. salt, and cold water to cover to a boil over medium-high heat. Reduce heat to medium-low.
2. Cook potatoes 16 to 20 minutes or until fork-tender. (A fork is easily inserted through the center of the potato without having to use force.)
3. Drain potatoes. Return potatoes to Dutch oven. Cook until water evaporates and potatoes look dry. Move potatoes to one side of pan. Add butter, half-and-half, cream cheese, pepper, and remaining salt to other side of pan. Cook 1 to 2 minutes or until butter is melted.
4. Mash potatoes with a potato masher or hand-held electric mixer to desired degree of smoothness.
5. If you prefer, you may also use a potato ricer for super creamy mashed potatoes.

Simply Deviled Eggs

Hands-on Time: 25 min.
Total Time: 40 min.
Makes: 2 dozen

- 12 large eggs
- ⅓ cup fat-free Greek yogurt
- 2 oz. ⅓-less-fat cream cheese
- 1 Tbsp. chopped fresh parsley
- 1 tsp. Dijon mustard
- ⅛ tsp. salt

1. Place eggs in a single layer in a stainless steel saucepan. (Do not use nonstick.) Add water to a depth of 3 inches. Bring to a rolling boil; cook 1 minute. Cover, remove from heat, and let stand 10 minutes. Drain.

2. Place eggs under cold running water until just cool enough to handle. Tap eggs on the counter until cracks form; peel.

3. Slice eggs in half lengthwise, and carefully remove yolks. Mash together yolks, yogurt, and next 4 ingredients until smooth using a fork. Spoon yolk mixture into egg white halves. Serve immediately, or cover and chill 1 hour before serving.

kitchen secret:

Try these stir-ins to make your own signature deviled eggs. Prepare recipe as directed, stirring one of the following combos into yolk mixture (Step 3).

1. **Creole Shrimp:** ½ cup finely chopped cooked shrimp, 3 Tbsp. sautéed chopped green bell pepper, 1 minced green onion, ¼ tsp. Creole seasoning, ¼ tsp. hot sauce. Top with cooked shrimp.

2. **Texas Caviar:** 3 Tbsp. chopped roasted red bell pepper, 1 minced green onion, 1 Tbsp. minced pickled jalapeño pepper, 1 Tbsp. chopped fresh cilantro, 1 tsp. Italian dressing mix. Top with canned black-eyed peas and fresh cilantro leaves.

3. **High Society:** ½ cup cooked fresh lump crabmeat, 2 tsp. fresh tarragon, ½ tsp. lemon zest, ¼ tsp. pepper. Top with cooked fresh crabmeat and watercress.

4. **Georgia Peach:** 3 Tbsp. peach preserves, ¼ cup finely chopped country ham, 1 tsp. grated Vidalia onion, ½ tsp. apple cider vinegar, ¼ tsp. pepper. Top with sliced fresh peaches and chopped toasted pecans.

5. **Triple Pickle:** 3 Tbsp. chopped bread-and-butter pickles, 2 Tbsp. chopped capers. Top with pickled okra slices.

fake it!

Short on time? Purchase pre-cooked hard-cooked eggs in the deli section of your local grocery store instead of boiling your own.

how to:
hard-cook eggs

1. Place eggs in a single layer in a stainless steel saucepan. Don't use a nonstick pan because they aren't designed to be heated at high temperatures.

2. Add water to pan to a depth of 3 inches. Bring to a boil; cook 1 minute.

Southern foodlore

No Southern kitchen is complete without a deviled egg plate. These pretty dishes first become popular in the 1940s. Now, they are widely available in glass, ceramic, and even plastic varieties. They may hold as few as a dozen or as many as 30 egg halves.

3. Cover pan; remove from heat. Let stand 10 minutes; drain. Set a timer to be sure eggs aren't overcooked.

4. Place eggs under cold running water until cool enough to handle. Add some ice cubes to speed up the process.

kitchen secret:

Having trouble peeling hard-cooked eggs? Try starting with eggs that have been refrigerated for a few days. Newer eggs are often harder to peel.

5. Tap eggs on the counter until cracks form; peel. (Peeling under cold water is often easiest.)

Shrimp-and-Pasta Salad

Hands-on Time: 10 min.
Total Time: 20 min.
Makes: 4 servings

Light and lemony, this recipe easily doubles for dinner with friends.

- 8 oz. uncooked medium-size shell pasta
- Lemon-Herb Dressing with Mint and Tarragon
- 1 lb. peeled, medium-size cooked shrimp (31/40 count)
- 1 large nectarine, cut into thin wedges
- 1 cup chopped seedless cucumber
- Garnishes: fresh raspberries, arugula

1. Cook pasta according to package directions; drain. Plunge into ice water to stop the cooking process; drain and place in a large bowl. Add $^1/_2$ cup dressing, tossing to coat. Stir in shrimp, nectarine, and cucumber. Serve with remaining $^1/_4$ cup dressing. Garnish, if desired.

Lemon-Herb Dressing with Mint and Tarragon

Hands-on Time: 10 min.
Total Time: 10 min.
Makes: $^3/_4$ cup

- $^1/_3$ cup canola oil
- 3 Tbsp. chopped fresh mint
- 1 Tbsp. chopped fresh tarragon
- 1 Tbsp. honey mustard
- 1 tsp. lemon zest
- $^1/_4$ cup fresh lemon juice
- 1 tsp. salt
- $^1/_2$ tsp. dried crushed red pepper

1. Whisk together all ingredients until well blended.

Lemon-Herb Dressing with Chives and Tarragon:
Substitute chopped fresh chives for mint. Proceed with recipe as directed.

Lemon-Herb Dressing with Basil: Substitute $^1/_3$ cup chopped fresh basil for mint and tarragon. Proceed with recipe as directed. Season with salt to taste.

how to: boil shrimp

1. Bring water to a boil over medium-high heat in a medium saucepan. Add shrimp.

2. Cook shrimp 3 minutes or until done. Shrimp are done when they are pink and no longer translucent.

3. Drain shrimp into a wire-mesh strainer or colander.

4. Place shrimp in colander under cold running water to stop cooking.

Spicy Ham-and-Eggs Benedict with Chive Biscuits

Hands-on Time: 30 min.
Total Time: 55 min.
Makes: 4 servings

- 4 frozen biscuits
- 2 Tbsp. melted butter
- 3 Tbsp. chopped fresh chives, divided
- 1 (0.9-oz.) envelope hollandaise sauce mix
- 1 cup milk
- 1 Tbsp. lemon juice
- ¾ cup chopped lean ham
- ¼ to ½ tsp. ground red pepper
- ½ tsp. white vinegar
- 4 large eggs
- 2 cups loosely packed arugula
- 1 small avocado, sliced
- Pepper to taste

1. Preheat oven to 375°. Bake biscuits according to package directions. Combine melted butter and 1 Tbsp. chives; split biscuits, and brush with butter mixture. Place biscuits, buttered sides up, on a baking sheet, and bake at 375° for 5 minutes or until toasted.

2. Prepare hollandaise sauce mix according to package directions, using 1 cup milk and 1 Tbsp. lemon juice and omitting butter.

3. Cook ham, stirring occasionally, in a medium-size nonstick skillet over medium heat 3 to 4 minutes or until browned. Stir ham and ground red pepper into hollandaise sauce; keep warm.

4. Add water to a depth of 2 inches in a large saucepan. Bring to a boil; reduce heat, and maintain at a light simmer. Add ½ tsp. white vinegar. Break eggs, and slip into water, one at a time, as close as possible to surface of water. Simmer 3 to 5 minutes or to desired degree of doneness. Remove with a slotted spoon. Trim edges, if desired.

5. Place bottom biscuit halves, buttered sides up, on 4 individual serving plates. Top with arugula, avocado, and poached eggs. Spoon hollandaise sauce evenly on top of each egg. Sprinkle with remaining 2 Tbsp. chives and pepper to taste. Top with remaining biscuit halves, and serve immediately.

how to:
poach an egg

1. Bring water and vinegar to a boil in a large skillet. (Vinegar makes the egg whites firm faster.)

2. Reduce heat to a simmer. Break eggs; slip into water one at a time.

3. Cook 3 to 5 minutes. Remove eggs with a slotted spoon. Trim, if desired.

Champagne-Poached Pears

Hands-on Time: 13 min.
Total Time: 33 min.
Makes: 8 servings

For an elegant presentation, serve individually in teacups or bowls.

- 8 Bosc or Bartlett pears
- 1 (750-milliliter) bottle Champagne or sparkling wine
- ½ gal. orange juice
- 1 (3-inch) cinnamon stick
- 5 whole cloves

Garnishes: orange and lemon zest strips, cinnamon sticks

1. Peel and core pears, leaving stems intact. Cut a thin slice from bottom of each pear, forming a base for pears to stand on.

2. Place pears upright in a Dutch oven, and pour Champagne and orange juice over pears. Add cinnamon stick and whole cloves. Bring mixture to a boil; reduce heat, and simmer 15 minutes or until pears are tender. Serve pears warm. Garnish, if desired.

how to:
poach pears

1. Peel pears. Using a paring knife, core pears from the bottom, leaving stems. Cut a small slice from bottom of pear to create an even base for pears to stand upright.

2. Place pears in 1 layer in the bottom of a Dutch oven, standing upright. Pour Champagne and orange juice over pears. Add cinnamon stick and cloves.

3. Bring mixture to a boil; reduce heat and simmer 15 minutes or until tender. Pears are done when the tip of a knife easily inserts into the fruit.

BRAISE

Braising is a cooking method that combines **moist heat with dry heat.** First, the food is typically seared to seal in the juices and create a flavorful crust. Then, a flavorful **braising liquid** is added to finish cooking. This cooking method is ideal for **tough,** inexpensive meats and **imparts immense flavor** to vegetables like greens. It also marries the flavors in hearty soups and stews.

Braised Short Ribs

Hands-on Time: 45 min.
Total Time: 2 hr., 15 min.
Makes: 8 servings

- ¼ cup all-purpose flour
- 1 Tbsp. salt, divided
- ½ tsp. ground black pepper
- ¼ tsp. ground red pepper
- 4½ lb. beef short ribs
- 1 Tbsp. olive oil
- 1 onion, diced
- 1 carrot, diced
- 2 celery ribs, diced
- 2 garlic cloves, minced
- 1 (28-oz.) can crushed tomatoes, undrained
- 2 Tbsp. tomato paste
- 2 Tbsp. lemon juice
- 1 tsp. dried oregano
- 1 bay leaf
- ½ tsp. dried crushed red pepper
- Garnish: chopped fresh parsley

1. Combine flour, 2 tsp. salt, and ground peppers; dredge ribs in flour mixture, and set aside.

2. Brown half of ribs in hot oil over medium-high heat in a Dutch oven. Remove ribs, reserving drippings in skillet. Repeat procedure with remaining ribs.

3. Add remaining 1 tsp. salt, diced onion, and next 3 ingredients to Dutch oven; sauté 10 minutes or until tender. Stir in crushed tomatoes, 1 cup water, and next 5 ingredients. Add ribs, cover, and simmer 1 hour and 30 minutes or until ribs are tender. Remove and discard bay leaf. Skim fat from mixture, and garnish, if desired.

how to:
braise short ribs

1. Place seasoned flour mixture in a shallow dish. Dredge ribs in mixture, and shake off excess. The flour creates a protective crust for the meat and will help to thicken the pan sauce.

2. Brown the ribs, in batches, in a Dutch oven. Remove ribs, and reserve the drippings in the skillet. These "brown bits" are high in flavor and will be deglazed once liquid is added.

3. Add salt and vegetables to Dutch oven, and sauté until tender. Stir in remaining ingredients, except garnish.

4. Return ribs to Dutch oven. Cover and simmer until tender (the meat will start to fall off the bone).

Melt-in-Your-Mouth Braised and Barbecued Chicken

Hands-on Time: 20 min.
Total Time: 1 hr., 5 min.
Makes: 4 servings

- 2 Tbsp. vegetable oil
- 8 bone-in chicken thighs, skinned (about 2 lb.)
- ½ cup orange juice
- ½ cup pineapple juice
- 1 Tbsp. cornstarch
- ⅓ cup soy sauce
- ⅓ cup firmly packed light brown sugar
- 2 Tbsp. minced fresh ginger
- 3 Tbsp. cider vinegar
- 3 Tbsp. ketchup
- ½ tsp. dried crushed red pepper
- 2 garlic cloves, minced
- 2 regular-size bags quick-cooking rice, uncooked
- ¼ cup chopped green onion, green tops only

1. Heat oil in a large skillet over medium-high heat. Add chicken, and sauté 6 minutes, turning once.

2. Combine fruit juices in a large bowl. Stir together cornstarch and 1 Tbsp. juice mixture until smooth; set aside.

3. Stir soy sauce and next 6 ingredients into remaining juice mixture; pour over chicken. Bring mixture to a boil; cover, reduce heat, and simmer 35 minutes, turning chicken after 20 minutes.

4. Prepare rice according to package directions, and keep warm.

5. Uncover chicken, and stir in cornstarch mixture. Cook, stirring constantly, 5 minutes or until sauce thickens.

6. Place chicken onto a serving platter. Sprinkle with chopped green onions. Serve with hot cooked rice.

kitchen secret:

Braising and stewing can be a busy cook's favorite techniques. Both methods call for a bit of attention early in the process and then it is mostly hands-off. When done correctly, the finished dish is always satisfying and flavorful. Considering that the chosen cuts for such long, slow, moist cooking are tougher, inexpensive cuts, braising and stewing are also wonderful preparations for larger gatherings.

how to:
make melt-in-your-mouth braised and barbecued chicken

1. Brown chicken thighs in hot oil in a large skillet.

2. Prepare braising liquid and pour over chicken in pan. Bring mixture to a boil, reduce heat, and cook covered. This locks in the flavor and makes the chicken extra-tender.

3. Turn the chicken about 15 minutes before it's done to guarantee even cooking.

4. Prepare a slurry of equal parts constarch and liquid. Add mixture to braising liquid in pan, and stir to combine. Cook at least 5 minutes to activate the constarch and thicken the sauce.

fix it!

Problem: The sauce isn't thickening.
Solutions:

a. Create a slurry. Combine equal parts cornstarch and cold water (usually 1 Tbsp. of each); stir until smooth. Add mixture to sauce in pan and cook 5 minutes, stirring constantly, until sauce thickens.

b. Sprinkle flour over vegetables in pan. Slowly add broth and whisk to combine. Cook 5 minutes or until sauce thickens.

c. Use equal parts of butter and flour to create a roux. First, melt butter in pan. Add flour; cook, whisking constantly until mixture bubbles and begins to smell nutty. Slowly add liquid and cook, stirring constantly, about 5 minutes or until thickened.

d1. Create a beurre manié by combining equal parts of butter and flour.
d2. Continue kneading the mixture until it forms a dough. Whisk mixture into hot liquid; cook 5 minutes or until sauce thickens.

Italian Pot Roast

Hands-on Time: 18 min.
Total Time: 8 hr., 58 min.
Makes: 6 servings

For an easy side, sauté 2 cups diced zucchini, 1 cup frozen sweet peas, and ½ cup diced onion in 3 Tbsp. olive oil until tender. Toss mixture with 20 oz. hot cooked cheese-and-spinach tortellini, and ½ cup each shredded Parmesan cheese and chopped fresh basil. Season with salt and pepper to taste.

- 1 (8-oz.) package sliced fresh mushrooms
- 1 large sweet onion, cut in half and sliced
- 1 (3- to 4-lb.) boneless chuck roast, trimmed
- 1 tsp. pepper
- 2 Tbsp. olive oil
- 1 (1-oz.) envelope dry onion soup mix
- 1 (14-oz.) can beef broth
- 1 (8-oz.) can tomato sauce
- 3 Tbsp. tomato paste
- 1 tsp. dried Italian seasoning
- 2 Tbsp. cornstarch

1. Place mushrooms and onion in a lightly greased 5- to 6-qt. slow cooker.

2. Sprinkle roast with pepper. Cook roast in hot oil in a large skillet over medium-high heat 2 to 3 minutes on each side or until browned.

3. Place roast on top of mushrooms and onion in slow cooker. Sprinkle onion soup mix over roast; pour beef broth and tomato sauce over roast. Cover and cook on LOW 8 to 10 hours or until meat shreds easily with a fork.

4. Transfer roast to a cutting board. Cut roast into large chunks, removing any large pieces of fat; keep warm.

5. Skim fat from juices in slow cooker; stir in tomato paste and Italian seasoning. Combine cornstarch and 2 Tbsp. water in a small bowl until smooth; add to juices in slow cooker, stirring until blended. Increase slow cooker heat to HIGH. Cover and cook 40 minutes or until mixture is thickened. Stir in roast.

kitchen secret:

Have leftovers? This recipe freezes easily. Place leftover roast in freezer-safe containers and freeze up to 2 months.

how to:
braise in a slow cooker

1. Place mushrooms and onion in a lightly greased 5- to 6-qt. slow cooker.

2. Sprinkle roast with pepper. Brown roast in hot oil in a large skillet on each side. Browning before slow-cooking increases the flavor.

fix it!

Problem: Last time, what you cooked in the slow cooker left behind a big mess.

Solution: To ensure fast and easy cleanup, follow these rules of thumb:

- Be sure to coat the inside of the slow cooker thoroughly with cooking spray before cooking.
- Heavy-duty plastic slow-cooker liners are now readily available. Place the liner inside the slow cooker before adding the recipe ingredients. You can serve the finished dish right out of the slow cooker with the liner still in place. Once the slow cooker has cooled, just throw the liner away.
- If there's still some food stuck on the bottom of the slow cooker, even after it was coated with cooking spray, the best time to clean it is while it's still warm. However, make sure that the insert isn't too hot—pouring cold water into a hot insert can cause it to crack.

3.

4.

3. Place roast over mushrooms and onion in slow cooker. Sprinkle onion soup over roast; pour beef broth and tomato sauce over roast. Cover and cook on LOW 8 to 10 hours.

4. Transfer roast to a cutting board and cut into large chunks. Remove large pieces of fat. Keep warm.

5.

5. Skim fat from juices in slow cooker; stir in tomato paste and Italian seasoning. Combine cornstarch and 2 Tbsp. water; stir into juices in slow cooker. Cover and cook on HIGH 40 minutes or until gravy is thickened. Add chopped roast to slow cooker.

kitchen secrets:

Slow cookers are very convenient, but be sure to follow these safety rules when using them:

- Always fill the slow cooker at least half full but no more than two-thirds full to guarantee even cooking.
- Be sure to defrost any frozen foods called for in a recipe before cooking them in the slow cooker.
- Don't use your slow cooker to reheat leftovers because they won't heat up fast enough, resulting in the possibility of bacterial contamination.

Brunswick Stew

Hands-on Time: 30 min.
Total Time: 6 hr., 30 min.
Makes: 3½ qt.

Brunswick stew is a hearty combination of chicken and vegetables. Bake a batch of cornbread so you can savor every last comforting drop.

1   (3½-lb.) whole chicken, cut up
1   (15-oz.) can baby lima beans, undrained
1   (8-oz.) can baby lima beans, undrained
2   (28-oz.) cans whole tomatoes, undrained
     and chopped
1   (16-oz.) package frozen baby lima beans
3   medium potatoes, peeled and diced
1   large yellow onion, diced
2   (15-oz.) cans cream-style corn
¼   cup sugar
¼   cup butter
1   Tbsp. salt
1   tsp. pepper
2   tsp. hot sauce

1. Bring 2 qt. water and chicken to a boil in a Dutch oven; reduce heat, and simmer 40 minutes or until tender. Remove chicken; set aside. Reserve 3 cups broth in Dutch oven. (Reserve remaining broth for other uses.)
2. Pour canned lima beans and liquid through a wire-mesh strainer into Dutch oven, reserving beans; add tomato to Dutch oven.
3. Bring to a boil over medium-high heat; cook, stirring often, 40 minutes or until liquid is reduced by one-third.
4. Skin, bone, and shred chicken. Mash reserved beans with a potato masher. Add chicken, mashed and frozen beans, potato, and onion to Dutch oven. Cook over low heat, stirring often, 3 hours and 30 minutes.
5. Stir in corn and remaining ingredients; cook over low heat, stirring often, 1 hour.

how to:
prepare brunswick stew

1. Pour canned lima beans and liquid through a wire-mesh strainer into Dutch oven with prepared broth, reserving beans. Add tomatoes.

2. Bring mixture to a boil over medium-high heat. Cook until liquid is reduced by one-third.

3. Mash reserved beans with a potato masher. These beans act as a thickener to the stew. Add chicken, mashed and frozen beans, potato, and onion to Dutch oven. Cook over low heat. About 1 hour before the stew is finished, stir in corn and remaining ingredients. Continue to cook 1 hour, stirring often.

Sweet-and-Tangy Braised Greens with Smoked Turkey

Hands-on Time: 15 min.
Total Time: 1 hr., 15 min.
Makes: 4 servings

- 1 (16-oz.) package fresh collard greens, stems removed
- 1 (0.75-lb.) smoked turkey leg
- 5 garlic cloves, chopped
- 2 Tbsp. oil
- ½ cup cider vinegar
- ⅓ cup low-sodium chicken broth
- ½ tsp. pepper
- 2 Tbsp. maple syrup

1. Thoroughly wash greens. Pat dry with paper towels.
2. Remove skin and meat from turkey leg, discarding skin and bone. Coarsely chop meat.

3. Sauté chopped turkey and garlic in hot oil in a large skillet over medium-high heat 2 to 3 minutes. Add vinegar, chicken broth, and pepper; bring to a boil. Add greens, reduce heat to low, and simmer, stirring occasionally, 25 minutes. Stir in maple syrup; simmer, stirring occasionally, 20 to 30 minutes or until greens are tender. Serve immediately.

Note: For a milder flavor, reduce cider vinegar to ⅓ cup and maple syrup to 1 Tbsp.; increase chicken broth to ½ cup. Proceed with recipe as directed.

Sweet-and-Tangy Braised Kale With Smoked Turkey: Substitute 1 (16-oz.) package fresh kale for collard greens. Prepare recipe as directed.

how to:
skillet-braise greens

1. Thoroughly wash and dry greens. (You may dry them on paper towels or use a salad spinner.) Coarsely chop turkey meat.

2. Sauté turkey and garlic in hot oil in a large skillet. Add vinegar, broth, and pepper. Bring to a boil.

3. Add washed and dried greens to skillet. Reduce heat to low, and simmer 25 minutes, stirring occasionally. Stir in maple syrup. Simmer 20 to 30 more minutes or until tender.

Creamy Pan-Braised Fennel

Hands-on Time: 10 min.
Total Time: 50 min.
Makes: 8 servings

The distinctive flavor of fennel makes a terrific accompaniment to ham, roast beef, or pork.

4	large fennel bulbs
1½	cups whipping cream
½	tsp. salt
½	tsp. pepper
¼	tsp. ground nutmeg
¼	cup fine, dry breadcrumbs
¼	cup (1 oz.) shredded Parmesan cheese
1½	Tbsp. butter

1. Preheat oven to 425°. Trim bases from fennel bulbs; cut into eighths, reserving fronds for another use. Arrange fennel in a lightly greased 11- x 7-inch baking dish.
2. Whisk together whipping cream and next 3 ingredients; pour over fennel slices. Sprinkle fennel slices with breadcrumbs and Parmesan cheese; dot with butter.
3. Bake, covered, at 425° for 20 minutes. Uncover and bake 20 more minutes or until fennel is tender and yields when a knife is inserted into the thickest slices. Serve immediately.

how to:
oven-braise fennel

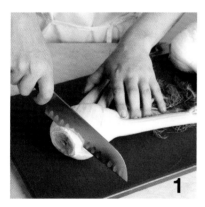  

1. Cut off the root end of the fennel bulb. Trim stems and fronds from bulb and reserve for another use. Cut the bulb into eighths. (Same-size slices allows the fennel to cook evenly.)

2. Arrange fennel in baking dish in an even layer. Combine whipping cream, salt, pepper, and nutmeg. Pour over fennel. Sprinkle breadcrumbs and cheese over fennel; dot with butter.

3. Cover baking dish with foil; bake 20 minutes. Shielding creates a steamy environment to begin to tenderize the fennel. Uncover dish, and bake 20 more minutes or until fennel is tender.

Frying has been popular in the South for generations and involves cooking food in a pan or griddle, especially in **oil or butter.** Deep-fried foods are immersed in enough hot oil to cover and are often characterized by an **extra-crispy skin.** It is important to use a thermometer when deep-frying to help regulate temperature. **Pan-frying** is often used for more fragile types of food, like thin fish fillets or eggs.

Mama's Fried Chicken

Hands-on Time: 30 min.
Total Time: 3 hr.
Makes: 4 to 6 servings

1   (3- to 4-lb.) whole chicken, cut into pieces
1   tsp. salt
1   tsp. pepper
2   cups buttermilk
Self-rising flour
Vegetable oil

1. Sprinkle chicken with salt and pepper. Place chicken in a shallow dish or zip-top plastic freezer bag, and add buttermilk. Cover or seal, and chill at least 2 hours.

2. Remove chicken from buttermilk, discarding buttermilk. Dredge chicken in flour.
3. Pour oil to a depth of 1½ inches in a deep skillet or Dutch oven; heat to 360°. Add chicken, a few pieces at a time; cover and cook 6 minutes. Uncover chicken, and cook 9 minutes. Turn chicken; cover and cook 6 minutes. Uncover and cook 5 to 9 minutes, turning chicken the last 3 minutes for even browning, if necessary. Drain on paper towels.

how to:
fry chicken

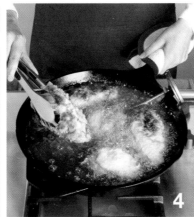

1. Place seasoned chicken in a shallow dish or zip-top plastic freezer bag and add buttermilk. Cover and chill.

2. Dredge chicken in flour; shake off excess. Place chicken on a rimmed baking sheet while oil heats.

3. Heat 1½ inches of oil to 360° in a deep skillet or Dutch oven. (Cast iron is a great conductor of heat.) Add chicken, a few pieces at a time. Cover and cook 6 minutes. Covering helps hold in the heat to cook the chicken evenly. Uncover, and cook 9 minutes.

4. Turn chicken. Cover and cook 6 minutes. Uncover and cook 5 to 9 minutes, turning chicken the last 3 minutes for even browning.

Natalie's Cajun-Seasoned Pan-Fried Tilapia

Hands-on Time: 13 min.
Total Time: 16 min.
Makes: 4 servings

- 4 (4- to 6-oz.) tilapia fillets
- 1½ tsp. Cajun seasoning*, divided
- 3 Tbsp. self-rising flour
- ½ cup plain yellow cornmeal
- 1 Tbsp. butter
- 2 Tbsp. olive oil
- Lemon wedges (optional)
- Garnish: fresh parsley sprig

1. Sprinkle fillets with 1 tsp. seasoning. Combine remaining seasoning, flour, and cornmeal. Dredge fillets in flour mixture, shaking off excess.
2. Melt butter with oil in a large skillet over medium-high heat; add fillets, and cook 3 to 4 minutes on each side or until fish flakes with a fork. Squeeze juice from lemon over fillets, and garnish, if desired. Serve immediately.

*Creole seasoning may be substituted.

Cajun-Seasoned Pan-Fried Chicken Breasts: Substitute 4 (8-oz.) skinned and boned chicken breasts for tilapia. Proceed with recipe as directed, cooking 8 to 10 minutes on each side or until done.

Cajun-Seasoned Pan-Fried Pork Chops: Substitute 4 (8-oz.) bone-in center-cut pork chops for tilapia. Proceed with recipe as directed, cooking 8 to 10 minutes on each side or until done.

how to:
pan-fry fish

1. Sprinkle fish with seasoning. Combine remaining seasoning, self-rising flour, and cornmeal. Dredge fish in mixture, and shake off excess.

2. Melt butter with oil in a large skillet over medium-high heat. (Oil burns at a higher heat than butter, so combining the two prevents the butter from burning.)

3. Add fish to pan. Cook 3 to 4 minutes on each side or until fish flakes with a fork.

Two-Alarm Deep-Fried Turkey

Hands-on Time: 25 min.
Total Time: 1 hr., 25 min.
Makes: 10 to 12 servings

You'll need about 3 to 4 gallons of oil to completely submerge your turkey. Make sure you don't overfill your turkey fryer, and always fry outside.

- 2 Tbsp. kosher salt
- 1 Tbsp. salt-free spicy seasoning blend
- 1 tsp. garlic powder
- 1 tsp. onion powder
- 1 tsp. dried crushed red pepper
- 1 (12- to 14-lb.) whole frozen turkey, thawed
- 2 Tbsp. vegetable oil
- Peanut oil
- Garnishes: sage leaves, apple slices

1. Stir together first 5 ingredients.

2. Remove giblets and neck from turkey, and, if desired, reserve for another use. Rinse turkey with cold water. Drain cavity well; pat dry. Rub turkey evenly with 2 Tbsp. vegetable oil. Loosen and lift skin from turkey breast with fingers without totally detaching skin; spread about one-fourth of salt mixture evenly underneath. Carefully replace skin. Sprinkle additional one-fourth of salt mixture inside cavity; rub into cavity. Sprinkle remaining salt mixture evenly on skin; rub into skin. Place turkey on fryer rod.

3. Pour peanut oil into a deep propane turkey fryer, pouring to 10 to 12 inches below top of fryer. Heat to 300° over a medium-low flame according to manufacturer's instructions. Carefully lower turkey into hot oil with rod attachment.

4. Fry 45 minutes or until a meat thermometer inserted in thickest portion of thigh registers 165°. (Keep oil temperature between 300° to 325°.) Remove turkey from oil; drain and let stand 15 minutes before slicing. Garnish, if desired.

how to:
deep-fry turkey

1. Remove giblets and neck from turkey; rinse turkey with cold water. Drain; pat dry. Rub turkey with oil. Loosen and lift skin from turkey breast without totally detaching the skin. Rub seasoning under the skin, over the skin, and in the cavity.

2. Place turkey, neck side down, on the fryer rod.

3. Pour oil into turkey fryer 10 to 12 inches below top of fryer. Heat oil to 300° according to manufacturer's instructions. Carefully lower turkey into hot oil.

4. Fry turkey 45 minutes or until a meat thermometer inserted in thigh registers 165°. Remove turkey from oil; drain and let stand 15 minutes before carving.

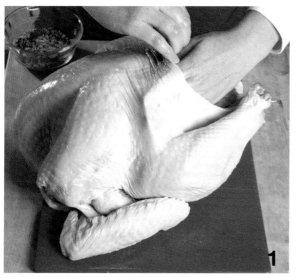

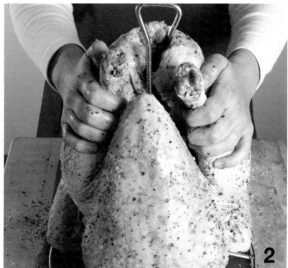

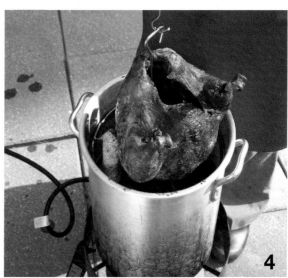

Okra Panzanella

Hands-on Time: 40 min.
Total Time: 40 min.
Makes: 6 to 8 servings

    Buttermilk Fried Okra
  2 cups coarsely chopped fresh tomatoes
  ½ cup diced red onion
  3 Tbsp. chopped fresh basil
  ¼ cup red wine vinaigrette

1. Toss together Buttermilk Fried Okra, coarsely chopped tomatoes, diced red onion, chopped fresh basil, and red wine vinaigrette. Serve immediately.

kitchen secret:

A sprinkling of sugar in the cornmeal coating caramelizes as the okra cooks, creating a crisp, golden crust.

Buttermilk Fried Okra

Hands-on Time: 30 min.
Total Time: 30 min.
Makes: 8 cups

  1 lb. fresh okra, cut into ½-inch-thick slices
  ¾ cup buttermilk
1½ cups self-rising white cornmeal mix
  1 tsp. salt
  1 tsp. sugar
  ¼ tsp. ground red pepper
    Vegetable oil

1. Stir together okra and buttermilk in a large bowl. Stir together cornmeal mix and next 3 ingredients in a separate large bowl. Remove okra from buttermilk, in batches, using a slotted spoon. Dredge in cornmeal mixture, and place in a wire-mesh strainer. Shake off excess.
2. Pour oil to a depth of 1 inch into a large, deep, cast-iron skillet or Dutch oven; heat to 375°. Fry okra, in batches, 4 minutes or until golden, turning once. Drain on paper towels.

how to:
fry okra

1. Combine okra and buttermilk in a large bowl. Combine breading mixture in a pie plate or large bowl. Remove okra from buttermilk with a slotted spoon.
2. Add okra to breading mixture, dredging gently.

3. Place okra in a wire-mesh strainer to shake off excess cornmeal mixture.
4. Fry okra, in batches, in hot oil in a large Dutch oven or deep skillet.

Open-Face Ham-and-Egg Sandwich

Hands-on Time: 25 min.
Total Time: 41 min.
Makes: 4 servings

It's easy to find Italian bread in your grocer's fresh bakery area. Ciabatta is a wonderful toasting bread that you may have to ask for.

- ½ (5-oz.) package arugula
- 1 Tbsp. chopped fresh basil
- 2 Tbsp. balsamic vinaigrette
- 1 Tbsp. melted butter
- 4 (½-inch-thick) crusty Italian bread or ciabatta slices
- 1 Tbsp. butter
- 4 large eggs
- ¼ tsp. salt
- ¼ tsp. freshly ground pepper
- 8 thin slices smoked ham (about ½ lb.)
- 4 thin slices sharp provolone cheese

1. Preheat oven to 350°. Toss together first 3 ingredients in a medium bowl.

2. Brush melted butter on one side of each bread slice. Place bread slices, buttered sides down, on an aluminum foil-lined baking sheet.

3. Bake at 350° for 14 minutes, turning once after 8 minutes. Preheat broiler with oven rack 6 inches from heat.

4. Meanwhile, melt 1 Tbsp. butter in a large nonstick skillet over medium heat. Gently break eggs into hot skillet, and sprinkle with salt and pepper. Cook 2 to 3 minutes or until whites are almost set. Cover, remove from heat, and let stand 1 to 2 minutes or until egg whites are set and yolks are cooked to desired degree of doneness.

5. Top each bread slice with 2 ham slices and 1 cheese slice. Broil 2 minutes or until cheese begins to melt.

6. Top each sandwich with ⅓ to ½ cup arugula mixture and 1 fried egg.

how to:
fry an egg

1. Melt butter in a large nonstick skillet over medium heat.

2. Gently break egg into hot skillet. Sprinkle with salt and pepper. Cook 2 to 3 minutes or until whites are almost set.

3. Cover, remove from heat, and let stand 1 to 2 minutes or until whites are set and yolks are cooked to desired degree of doneness.

Grilling is a favorite cooking method used most often during **warm months.** Meats, seafood, fruit, vegetables, and even breads and desserts are placed over **direct or indirect** heat depending on the type of grilling method used. Whether searing a steak to lock in juiciness or smoking pork to create hickory flavor, grilling is a convenient method to **boost flavor.** And, best of all—cleanup is a breeze!

Summer Vegetable Kabobs

Hands-on Time: 25 min.
Total Time: 1 hr., 55 min.
Makes: 8 servings

We suggest using a Chardonnay in the marinade for the kabobs.

   12-inch-long wooden skewers
  ¼ cup dry white wine
  ¼ cup honey
  3 garlic cloves, minced
  2 Tbsp. balsamic vinegar
  2 Tbsp. olive oil
1½ tsp. pepper
  1 tsp. salt
16 cups assorted cut vegetables

1. Soak skewers in water 1 hour.

2. Whisk together wine and next 6 ingredients until blended; reserve ¼ cup. Combine remaining white wine mixture and vegetables in a large bowl. Cover and chill at least 30 minutes or up to 2 hours. Remove vegetables from marinade, discarding marinade.

3. Preheat grill to 350° to 400° (medium-high). Thread vegetables onto skewers. Grill according to directions in Guidelines and Cook Times for Vegetable Kabobs on facing page.

4. Transfer skewers to a platter. Remove vegetables from skewers, if desired. Serve with reserved ¼ cup white wine mixture.

how to:
grill vegetables

1. Soak wooden skewers in water 1 hour. Soaking the skewers prevents them from burning.

2. Remove vegetables from marinade; discard marinade. Thread vegetables onto skewers. Threading the same vegetable on each skewer allows for even cooking.

3. Grill vegetables over medium-high heat according to instructions (on facing page).

Guidelines and Cook Times for Vegetable Kabobs

Cut vegetables thick so they will stay on skewers as they cook. Thread one type of vegetable onto each skewer, threading so the cut sides lie flat on the cooking grate to ensure even cooking. Grill skewers, covered with grill lid, over 350° to 400° (medium-high) heat according to the times below. Your goal is to achieve tender, slightly charred vegetables.

Zucchini and Squash. Prep: Cut into ³/₄-inch rounds; thread onto skewers. Grill Time: 7 to 10 minutes on each side or until tender.

Okra. Prep: Remove stems, and thread onto skewers. Grill Time: 6 to 8 minutes on each side or until tender.

Eggplant. Prep: Cut Japanese eggplant into ³/₄-inch rounds. Cut Italian eggplant crosswise into quarters; cut into ³/₄-inch slices. Thread onto skewers. Grill Time: 5 to 6 minutes on each side or until tender.

Bell Peppers. Prep: Cut into 1-inch-thick strips; thread onto skewers. Grill Time: 4 to 5 minutes on each side or until tender.

Mushrooms. Prep: Trim stems, and thread onto skewers. Grill Time: 3 to 5 minutes on each side or until tender.

Onions. Prep: Cut into wedges, and thread onto skewers. Grill Time: 3 or 4 minutes on each side or until lightly charred.

Cherry Tomatoes. Prep: Thread onto double skewers. Grill Time: 1 to 3 minutes on each side or just until skins begin to split.

Grilled Peaches Jezebel

Hands-on Time: 6 min.
Total Time: 11 min.
Makes: 6 servings

¼ cup honey
2 tsp. Dijon mustard
1 tsp. horseradish
6 firm, ripe peaches, halved
Vegetable cooking spray

1. Whisk together first 3 ingredients. Brush half of honey mixture evenly over cut sides of peaches.
2. Coat a cold cooking grate with cooking spray, and place on grill over medium heat (300° to 350°). Arrange peach halves, cut sides down, on grate; grill, covered with grill lid, 3 minutes on each side or until tender and golden. Remove from grill, and brush cut sides of peaches evenly with remaining honey mixture.

how to:
grill peaches

1. Brush half of basting mixture over cut sides of peaches.

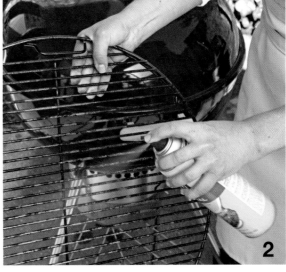

2. Coat a cold cooking grate (to prevent flare ups) with cooking spray. Place on grill over medium heat.

3. Arrange peach halves, cut sides down, on grate; grill, covered, 3 minutes.

4. Turn peaches over; grill 3 more minutes or until tender and golden. Remove from grill and brush cut sides of peaches with remaining basting mixture.

Mexican-Grilled Shrimp

Hands-on Time: 28 min.
Total Time: 33 min.
Makes: 4 servings

If using wooden skewers, be sure to soak them at least 30 minutes before grilling.

- 2 lb. unpeeled, large raw shrimp
- 20 (12-inch) skewers
- ½ cup firmly packed dark brown sugar
- 6 garlic cloves, pressed
- 1 canned chipotle pepper in adobo sauce, minced
- 2 Tbsp. rum
- 1 Tbsp. adobo sauce
- 1 Tbsp. tamarind paste
- ¼ tsp. salt
- 1 Tbsp. olive oil
- Smoky Sweet Sauce

1. Peel shrimp, leaving tails on; devein, if desired. Thread shrimp onto skewers. Set aside.
2. Cook brown sugar in a small heavy saucepan over low heat until melted. Add garlic, 2 Tbsp. water, and next 5 ingredients. Cook 5 minutes or until tamarind paste melts. Remove from heat.
3. Brush shrimp with olive oil. Grill, uncovered, over medium-high heat (350° to 400°) for 4 to 6 minutes or until shrimp turn pink, turning once, and basting with tamarind glaze. Serve with Smoky Sweet Sauce.

kitchen secret:

Tamarind is a tree-grown fruit. Its long pods contain a sweet-and-sour pulp from which a paste is made. Look for tamarind paste in the Mexican or Asian section of your grocery store.

Smoky Sweet Sauce

Hands-on Time: 10 min.
Total Time: 10 min.
Makes: 1¾ cups

- 1 cup low-sodium fat-free chicken broth
- ½ cup chopped refrigerated mango slices
- ¼ cup loosely packed chopped fresh cilantro
- 2 tsp. adobo sauce
- ¾ tsp. salt
- ⅓ cup whipping cream
- 2½ Tbsp. butter

1. Process first 5 ingredients in a blender 1 minute. Pour mixture into a saucepan, and bring to a boil over medium-high heat. Add cream, and cook, whisking often, 6 minutes or until slightly thick. Remove from heat, and whisk in butter until melted.

how to:
grill shrimp

1. Thread shrimp onto skewers. Don't overcrowd them so they'll cook evenly.

2. Brush shrimp with olive oil. Place on grill over medium-high heat.

3. Grill shrimp 4 to 6 minutes, or until shrimp turn pink, basting with glaze.

Greek Snapper on the Grill

Hands-on Time: 25 min.
Total Time: 40 min.
Makes: 12 servings

- ¼ cup olive oil
- 1 Tbsp. Greek seasoning
- 12 (8-oz.) snapper or grouper fillets
- 24 (¼-inch-thick) lemon slices
- Dot's Tartar Sauce
- Garnish: fresh oregano

1. Combine oil and Greek seasoning. Brush fish fillets with oil mixture. Top each fillet with 2 lemon slices.
2. Place a large piece of lightly greased heavy-duty aluminum foil over grill cooking grate. Arrange fish on foil.
3. Grill fillets, covered with grill lid, over medium-high heat (350° to 400°) 15 minutes or until fish flakes with a fork. For extra flavor, grill lemon slices. Serve with Dot's Tartar Sauce and garnish, if desired.

Dot's Tartar Sauce

Hands-on Time: 10 min.
Total Time: 10 min.
Makes: 1½ cups

- 1 cup mayonnaise
- 2 Tbsp. dill pickle relish
- 2 Tbsp. drained capers
- 2 Tbsp. chopped fresh chives
- 1 Tbsp. chopped fresh tarragon
- 1 Tbsp. Dijon mustard
- 2 tsp. fresh lemon juice
- ¼ tsp. black pepper

1. Stir together all ingredients until blended. Cover and chill until ready to serve.

Note: For testing purposes only, we used Wickles Relish.

how to:
grill fish

1. Brush fish fillets with oil and seasoning mixture.

2. Place a large piece of lightly greased heavy-duty foil on grill grate. Arrange fish on foil; top each fillet with 2 lemon slices. Grill fish over medium-high heat 15 minutes or until fish flakes with a fork.

3. If you'd prefer, a grill basket works well as a substitute for foil. It holds the lemon slices in place and makes fillets easy to turn.

Sweet-and-Savory Burgers

If the weather is cold, or you don't feel like firing up the grill, a grill pan works just as well.

Hands-on Time: 25 min.
Total Time: 4 hr., 25 min.
Makes: 8 servings

- ¼ cup soy sauce
- 2 Tbsp. light corn syrup
- 1 Tbsp. fresh lemon juice
- ½ tsp. ground ginger
- ¼ tsp. garlic powder
- 2 green onions, thinly sliced
- 2 lb. ground beef
- ¼ cup chili sauce
- ¼ cup hot red pepper jelly
- 8 hamburger buns, toasted
- Toppings: grilled sweet onion and pineapple slices

1. Stir together first 6 ingredients. Reserve 3 Tbsp. mixture; cover and chill. Pour remaining soy sauce mixture into a shallow pan or baking dish.
2. Shape beef into 8 (½-inch-thick) patties; place in a single layer in soy sauce mixture in pan, turning to coat. Cover and chill 4 hours.
3. Preheat grill to 350° to 400° (medium-high) heat. Remove patties from marinade, discarding marinade. Grill patties, covered with grill lid, 5 minutes on each side or until beef is no longer pink in center, basting occasionally with reserved 3 Tbsp. soy sauce mixture.
4. Stir together chili sauce and jelly. Serve burgers on buns with chili sauce mixture and desired toppings.

kitchen secret:

Press your thumb into centers of patties before grilling for burgers that cook up flat rather than domed across the top.

how to:
grill burgers on a grill pan

1. Coat grill pan with cooking spray. Heat pan over medium-high heat until hot.

2. Add burgers to pan. Grill 5 minutes on each side or until a meat thermometer registers 160° and meat is no longer pink.

Fiesta Brisket

Hands-on Time: 40 min.
Total Time: 8 hr., 35 min.
Makes: 8 servings

Don't shy away from this slow-cooked, robust brisket because of the long ingredients list—you'll love it.

      4 guajillo chiles
      4 cups boiling water
    ½ cup cider vinegar
    ½ cup low-sodium chicken broth
      8 garlic cloves
      1 medium onion, chopped
      3 fresh thyme sprigs
      2 tsp. dried Mexican oregano leaves*
  1½ tsp. ground cumin
    ½ tsp. ground cloves
    ½ tsp. ground allspice
      3 tsp. salt, divided
      2 tsp. ground black pepper
      1 (4- to 5-lb.) beef brisket flat
      8 cups hickory wood chips
      2 large limes, cut into wedges
    Garnish: fresh cilantro sprig

1. Cook chiles in a skillet over high heat 5 minutes or until fragrant, turning often. Remove stems and seeds from chiles. Place chiles in a large bowl; add 4 cups boiling water, and let stand 20 minutes. Drain.
2. Process chiles, vinegar, next 8 ingredients, and ³⁄₄ tsp. salt in a blender or food processor until smooth, stopping to scrape down sides as needed.
3. Sprinkle ground black pepper and remaining 2 ¹⁄₄ tsp. salt over brisket. Place brisket in an extra-large zip-top plastic freezer bag or a large shallow dish. Pour chile mixture over brisket; rub brisket with chile mixture. Seal or cover, and chill 2 to 24 hours.
4. Soak wood chips in water 30 minutes. Prepare gas grill by removing cooking grate from one side of grill. Close grill lid, and light side of grill without cooking grate, leaving other side unlit. Preheat grill to 250° to 300° (low) heat.
5. Spread 4 cups soaked and drained wood chips on a large sheet of heavy-duty aluminum foil. Cover with

another sheet of heavy-duty foil, and fold edges to seal. Poke several holes in top of pouch with a fork. Place pouch directly on lit side of grill. Cover with cooking grate.
6. Remove brisket from marinade, discarding marinade. Place brisket, fat side up, in a 12- x 10-inch disposable foil roasting pan. Place pan on unlit side of grill; cover with grill lid.
7. Grill brisket, maintaining internal temperature of grill between 225° and 250°, for 1¹⁄₂ hours. Carefully tear open foil pouch with tongs, and add remaining 4 cups soaked and drained wood chips to pouch.
8. Cover with grill lid, and grill, maintaining internal temperature of grill between 225° and 250°, until a meat thermometer inserted into thickest portion of brisket registers 165° (about 1¹⁄₂ hours).
9. Remove brisket from grill. Place brisket on a large sheet of heavy-duty foil, and pour ¹⁄₂ cup pan drippings over brisket; wrap with foil, sealing edges.
10. Return brisket to unlit side of grill, and grill, covered with grill lid, until meat thermometer registers 195° (about 2 hours). Remove from grill, and let stand 10 minutes. Cut brisket across the grain into thin slices. Squeeze juice from limes over brisket before serving. Garnish, if desired.

Note: Guajillo chiles and Mexican oregano may be found on the spice aisle of specialty grocery stores or in Mexican markets.

*Dried oregano may be substituted for Mexican oregano.

Oven-Roasted Fiesta Brisket: Prepare recipe as directed through Step 3. Preheat oven to 350°. Remove brisket from marinade, discarding marinade. Wrap brisket with heavy-duty aluminum foil, and place in a jelly-roll pan. Bake 3 hours or until a meat thermometer inserted into thickest portion registers 195° and brisket is very tender. Remove from oven, and let stand 10 minutes. Cut brisket across the grain into thin slices.

how to:
smoke brisket

1. Trim excess fat from brisket.

2. Pour marinade into an extra-large zip-top plastic freezer bag. Place seasoned brisket in bag, turning to coat with marinade. Seal and chill 2 to 24 hours.

3. Prepare grill for smoking. Place 4 cups soaked wood chips in heavy-duty foil; fold edges and seal. Poke holes in pouch and place directly on lit side of grill. Remove brisket from marinade; discard marinade. Place brisket, fat side up, in a disposable foil roasting pan. Place pan on unlit side of grill; cover with grill lid. Grill brisket 1½ hours, maintaining grill between 225° and 250°. Carefully add remaining 4 cups wood chips to foil pouch. Continue grilling brisket about 1½ more hours, or until a meat thermometer inserted into thickest portion registers 165°. Remove from grill and place on a large sheet of heavy-duty foil. Pour ½ cup pan drippings over brisket; wrap with foil, sealing edges. Return to unlit side of grill, and grill, covered, 2 hours or until a meat thermometer registers 195°.

4. Remove brisket from grill; let stand 10 minutes. Cut across the grain into thin slices.

how to:
prepare charcoal briquettes using a chimney

1. Place a few pieces of balled newspaper in the bottom of chimney. Pour desired amount of briquettes over paper. (The longer the recipe takes to cook, the more you will need.)

2. Light paper through the holes in the bottom of the chimney.

3. Heat briquettes until they are uniformly ashy gray in color and the flames have died down.

Grilling over Direct Heat vs. Indirect Heat

Direct Heat

This grilling method involves cooking the food directly over the heat source. It is ideal for items that can be fully cooked in 30 minutes or less.

Using a charcoal grill: Spread hot coals in a single even layer over charcoal grate. Preheat at least 10 minutes. To adjust the temperature before grilling the food, open the vents to give more air to the fire (increase the heat), or close the vents to decrease the heat.

Using a gas grill: Light all burners according to manufacturer's instructions. Turn burners to high, and preheat 10 minutes. Adjust burners to temperature recommended in recipe when ready to cook.

Indirect Heat

This grilling method has the heat source off to the side and allows the heat to circulate around the food slowly for even cooking. It's best for large cuts of meat and foods that require a cooking time of 30 minutes or longer.

Using a charcoal grill:

There are several ways to set up indirect grilling using a charcoal grill. In each setup you'll want to grill the food directly over the drip pan:

a. Place the drip pan on one side of the charcoal grate. Arrange hot coals on the other side. This setup is great for recipes that involve both direct and indirect grilling.
b. Place the drip pan in the center of the charcoal grate. Arrange hot coals on both sides. This setup is great if you want one side of the direct heat to have a higher or lower temperature than the other.
c. Place the drip pan in the center of the charcoal grate. Arrange hot coals completely surrounding the drip pan. This setup is great when grilling large items like whole chickens.

Using a gas grill:

Light all burners according to manufacturer's instructions. Turn burners to high, and preheat 10 minutes. Adjust outside burners to temperature requirements in recipe. Place food on grate, and turn off burners directly beneath the food.

Smoked Salmon

Hands-on Time: 25 min.
Total Time: 5 hr., 35 min.
Makes: 6 servings

Disposable turkey roasting pans from the supermarket are great for brining the fish. Try mackerel, bluefish, amberjack, or even mullet. Split fish will have the same smoking time, but lower the smoking time for fillets.

¾ to 1 cup kosher salt
1 cup firmly packed brown sugar
1 Tbsp. onion powder
5 bay leaves, crushed
1 (5-lb.) side of salmon
Pepper
Hickory wood chips
Garnish: fresh dill
Crackers (optional)
Hot sauce (optional)
Lemon wedges (optional)

1. Combine 1 gal. water, salt, and next 3 ingredients in a large bowl, stirring until salt dissolves. Add salmon; cover and chill 45 minutes to 2 hours or to desired degree of saltiness. (Cut off a small piece of fish, and fry it to determine degree of saltiness by tasting. Longer soak times yield saltier fish.)
2. Rinse fish, discarding brine mixture; pat fish dry with paper towels. Place fish on wire rack in roasting pan; cover with paper towels, and chill 2 to 3 hours or until dry. Rub pepper on both sides of fish.
3. Soak wood chips in water at least 30 minutes.
4. Prepare charcoal fire in smoker; let burn 15 to 20 minutes.
5. Drain chips, and place on coals. Place water pan in smoker; add water to depth of fill line.
6. Place fish, skin side down, on upper or lower food rack; cover with smoker lid.
7. Cook 2 hours or just until fish flakes with a fork. Garnish, if desired. Serve with crackers, hot sauce, and lemon wedges, if desired.

how to:
smoke fish

 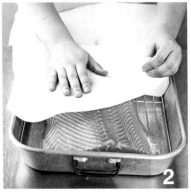 

1. Place fish in brine mixture. Cover and chill 45 minutes to 2 hours.

2. Place rinsed and dried fish on a wire rack in roasting pan; cover with paper towels. Chill 2 to 3 hours or until dry.

3. Place prepared wood chips on coals in smoker. Place water pan (to regulate temperature) in smoker; add water to depth of fill line. Place fish, skin side down, on upper or lower food racks. Cook, covered, 2 hours or until fish flakes with a fork.

Smoked Corn

Hands-on Time: 20 min.
Total Time: 1 hr., 30 min.
Makes: 8 servings

> Hickory wood chips
> ½   cup butter, softened
> 2   Tbsp. chopped fresh thyme
> 8   ears fresh corn with husks

1. Soak wood chips in water at least 30 minutes. Prepare charcoal fire in smoker; let burn 15 to 20 minutes.

2. Stir together butter and thyme. Remove heavy outer husks from corn; pull back inner husks. Remove and discard silks. Rub corn with butter mixture. Pull husks back over corn.

3. Drain chips, and place on coals. Place water pan in smoker; add water to depth of fill line. Place corn on upper food rack; cover with smoker lid. Cook 30 to 40 minutes. Remove from smoker, and let stand 10 minutes. Pull husks back, and serve.

how to:
smoke corn

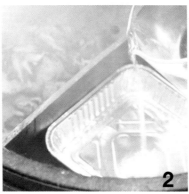

1. Prepare charcoal fire; let burn 15 to 20 minutes. Drain soaked chips and place on coals.

2. Place water pan in smoker; add water to depth of fill line.

3. Place prepared corn on upper food rack; cover with smoker lid. Cook 30 to 40 minutes or until tender. Remove from smoker and let stand 10 minutes.

ROAST

Roasting is an **indirect cooking** method involving dry heat in an oven or over an open flame.The low and slow cooking of meats, vegetables, and fruit creates **caramelization** on the surface of the food to equal an added boost in flavor. Roasting is also a great method for making **large, inexpensive** cuts of meat tender and juicy.

Marian's Easy Roast Chicken

Hands-on Time: 10 min.
Total Time: 1 hr., 50 min.
Makes: 8 servings

- 4 tsp. kosher salt
- 2 tsp. freshly ground pepper
- 2 (4- to 5-lb.) whole chickens
- 1 Tbsp. olive oil

Garnish: fresh parsley

1. Preheat oven to 375°. Stir together salt and pepper.

2. If applicable, remove necks and giblets from chickens, and reserve for another use. Pat chickens dry. Sprinkle $^1/_2$ tsp. salt mixture inside cavity of each chicken. Rub $1^1/_2$ tsp. olive oil into skin of each chicken. Sprinkle with remaining salt mixture; rub into skin. Place chickens, breast sides up, facing in opposite directions (for even browning), on a lightly greased wire rack in a lightly greased roasting pan.

3. Bake at 375° for $1^1/_2$ hours or until a meat thermometer inserted into thigh registers 165°. Let stand 10 minutes before slicing. Garnish, if desired.

how to:
roast chicken

1. Combine salt and pepper. Sprinkle chicken cavity with salt mixture.

2. Rub oil over skin. Sprinkle with salt mixture.

3. Place chickens, breast sides up, on a lightly greased wire rack in a lightly greased roasting pan.

4. Bake at 375° for $1^1/_2$ hours or until a meat thermometer inserted into thigh registers 165°. Let stand 10 minutes before slicing. (Letting the chicken stand allows the juices to absorb into the meat. Cutting it too quickly causes the juices to escape and leave the chicken dry.)

Roasted Lamb

Hands-on Time: 20 min.
Total Time: 2 hr., 35 min.
Makes: 8 servings

- 1 (5-lb.) boneless leg of lamb
- 2 lemons, halved and divided
- ¼ cup chopped fresh oregano
- 2½ tsp. salt
- 2 tsp. pepper
- Kitchen string
- 1 garlic bulb, unpeeled
- ¼ cup olive oil
- 1 cup low-sodium chicken broth
- Garnish: fresh parsley leaves

1. Preheat oven to 350°. Unroll lamb, if necessary. Rub 1 lemon half on all sides of lamb, squeezing juice from lemon. Stir together oregano, salt, and pepper; rub on lamb. Roll up lamb, and tie with kitchen string.

2. Place lamb on a lightly greased rack in a roasting pan. Separate unpeeled garlic cloves, and place around roast. Drizzle olive oil over lamb and garlic cloves.

3. Squeeze juice from remaining 1½ lemons into a bowl. Stir together juice and chicken broth; pour into roasting pan.

4. Bake at 350° for 2 hours to 2 hours and 15 minutes or until a meat thermometer inserted into thickest portion registers 140° (medium) or to desired degree of doneness. Remove lamb from pan; cover with aluminum foil, and let stand 10 minutes before slicing. Garnish, if desired.

Roasted Boston Butt: Substitute 1 (5-lb.) bone-in pork shoulder roast (Boston butt) for lamb. Rub lemon and oregano mixture over roast as directed. (Do not tie up roast.) Proceed as directed, increasing bake time to 3 to 3½ hours or until fork-tender. Shred pork into large pieces using two forks, if desired.

kitchen secret:

Separating garlic cloves from the bulb is easy. Place the whole garlic bulb on a cutting board. Apply pressure with your hand while moving the garlic in a steady circular motion. The individual cloves will come apart easily.
Want to remove the papery skin from the garlic clove? Place one clove on a cutting board. Place the broad flat side of a chef's knife over the garlic. Gently smash the flat side of the knife with the palm of your hand. Remove the knife, and peel back the skin of the garlic.

how to:
roast lamb

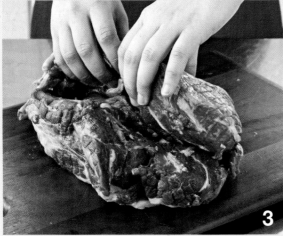

1. Rub a lemon half on skin side of lamb.

2. Turn lamb over and rub lemon on inside of lamb.

3. Roll up lamb, and tie with kitchen string.

4. Place seasoned lamb on a lightly greased rack in a roasting pan. Sprinkle unpeeled garlic cloves around lamb. Drizzle olive oil over lamb and garlic.

5. Squeeze juice from remaining $1^{1}/_{2}$ lemons into a bowl. Stir together juice and broth; pour into roasting pan. (The moisture from the juice mixture will infuse the lamb while it cooks to give it added flavor and juiciness.) Bake at 350° for 2 hours or until a meat thermometer inserted into thickest portion registers 140° or to desired degree of doneness. Remove lamb from pan; cover with aluminum foil. Let stand 10 minutes before slicing.

how to:
make gravy

Don't toss the pan drippings when roasting meats—they make the perfect gravy!

1. For 2 cups of liquid, melt enough butter with pan drippings to equal $1/4$ cup. Whisk in $1/4$ cup flour. Cook, whisking constantly, 3 to 5 minutes.

2. Slowly whisk 1 cup broth into roux in pan.

3. Cook over medium heat, stirring constantly, 5 minutes or until gravy is thickened. Season to taste with salt and pepper.

Roasted Fall Vegetables

Hands-on Time: 20 min.
Total Time: 50 min.
Makes: 8 servings

Candy cane beets are also known as Chioggia beets. We love this variety because they don't stain like traditional red beets.

  8   baby yellow and red beets
  8   baby candy cane beets
 10   small carrots with greenery
  3   Tbsp. olive oil, divided
  1   tsp. kosher salt, divided
  ½   tsp. pepper, divided

1. Preheat oven to 425°. Cut tops from beets, leaving ½-inch stems. Peel beets, and cut in half. Cut tops from carrots, leaving ½ inch of greenery on each.
2. Toss yellow beets and carrots with 2 Tbsp. olive oil in a large bowl; place in a single layer on one side of an aluminum foil-lined 15- x 10-inch jelly-roll pan. Sprinkle vegetables in pan with ½ tsp. salt and ¼ tsp. pepper.
3. Toss candy cane beets and red beets with remaining 1 Tbsp. olive oil; arrange beets in a single layer on remaining side of jelly-roll pan. Sprinkle with remaining ½ tsp. salt and ¼ tsp. pepper.
4. Bake at 425° for 15 minutes; stir once, and bake 15 more minutes or until tender.

how to:
roast root vegetables

1. Cut the tops from the beets, leaving ½-inch stems.

2. Cut tops from carrots, leaving ½ inch of greenery. Toss yellow beets with carrots and olive oil in a large bowl. Toss peeled red beets and candy cane beets with remaining olive oil.

3. Place carrots and yellow beets in a single layer on one side of a foil-lined jelly-roll pan. Arrange remaining beets on remaining side of pan. Sprinkle vegetables with salt and pepper. Bake at 425° for 15 minutes. Stir and bake 15 more minutes or until tender.

Roasted Winter Squash

Hands-on Time: 15 min.
Total Time: 1 hr., 25 min.
Makes: 6 to 8 servings

- 1 (2- to 3-lb.) butternut squash
- 1 (2- to 3-lb.) spaghetti squash
- 1 (1- to 2-lb.) acorn squash
- ¼ cup butter
- 2 Tbsp. honey
- 1 tsp. salt
- ¼ tsp. pepper

1. Preheat oven to 400°. Cut butternut squash, spaghetti squash, and acorn squash in half lengthwise, and remove seeds. Place squash, cut sides up, on an aluminum foil-lined baking sheet. Microwave butter and honey at HIGH 1 minute or until melted; stir until blended. Brush cut sides of squash with butter mixture. Sprinkle with salt and pepper. Bake, uncovered, 1 hour or until tender; let stand 10 minutes. Cut into large pieces and serve.

Roasted Acorn Squash: Omit butternut and spaghetti squash. Cut acorn squash in half; remove and discard seeds. Cut squash into ¹/₂-inch slices. Proceed with recipe as directed, decreasing bake time to 45 minutes or until tender. Garnish with sage sprigs, if desired.

how to:
roast winter squash

1. Cut squash in half lengthwise.

2. Remove seeds.

3. Place squash, cut sides up, on an aluminum foil-lined baking sheet. Brush cut sides of squash with honey-butter mixture. Sprinkle with salt and pepper.

4. Bake squash, uncovered, at 400° for 1 hour or until tender. Let stand 10 minutes.

Roasted Grape Chutney

Hands-on Time: 10 min.
Total Time: 1 hr.
Makes: 1⅓ cups

This sweet chutney is great served with chicken or pork.

- 1 cup seedless red grapes, halved
- 1 cup seedless green grapes, halved
- 1 Tbsp. olive oil
- 1 Tbsp. red wine vinegar
- 1 tsp. dried thyme
- ½ tsp. kosher salt
- ¼ tsp. pepper

1. Preheat oven to 425°. Combine all ingredients on an aluminum foil-lined baking sheet. Bake 20 minutes or until grapes begin to shrivel. Remove from oven, and let cool 30 minutes. Store in refrigerator up to 3 days.

how to:
roast grapes

1. Halve grapes lengthwise. Line a baking sheet with aluminum foil (to prevent sticking).

2. Combine grapes, olive oil, vinegar, thyme, salt, and pepper on prepared baking sheet.

3. Bake at 425° for 20 minutes or until grapes begin to shrivel. Remove from oven and let cool 30 minutes.

Sauté in French literally means **"to jump,"** and this cooking method involves heating foods in a small amount of oil or fat in a shallow pan over relatively **high heat.** These foods are cooked quickly and stirred frequently to create a savory **brown crust** while preserving a tender, moist center. So whether you're stir-frying some vegetables to serve over rice or sautéeing some shrimp, this method **is ideal for** weeknight meals when schedules are busy.

Shrimp and Grits

Hands-on Time: 41 min.
Total Time: 41 min.
Makes: 4 to 6 servings

 2 bacon slices
 1 lb. unpeeled, medium-size raw shrimp
 ¼ tsp. pepper
 ⅛ tsp. salt
 ¼ cup all-purpose flour
 1 cup sliced fresh mushrooms
 2 tsp. canola oil
 ½ cup chopped green onions
 2 garlic cloves, minced
 1 cup low-sodium fat-free chicken broth
 2 Tbsp. fresh lemon juice
 ¼ tsp. hot sauce
  Cheese Grits

1. Cook bacon in a large nonstick skillet over medium heat 10 minutes or until crisp; remove bacon, and drain on paper towels, reserving 1 tsp. drippings in skillet. Crumble bacon.
2. Peel shrimp; devein, if desired. Sprinkle shrimp with pepper and salt; dredge in flour.
3. Sauté mushrooms in hot drippings with oil in skillet 5 minutes or until tender. Add green onions; sauté 2 minutes. Add shrimp and garlic, and sauté

2 minutes or until shrimp are lightly browned. Stir in chicken broth, lemon juice, and hot sauce, and cook 2 more minutes, stirring to loosen particles from bottom of skillet. Spoon shrimp mixture over hot Cheese Grits; sprinkle with crumbled bacon.

Cheese Grits

Hands-on Time: 30 min.
Total Time: 30 min.
Makes: 4 to 6 servings

 1 (14-oz.) can low-sodium fat-free chicken broth
 1 cup fat-free milk
 ½ tsp. salt
 1 cup uncooked quick-cooking grits
 ¾ cup (3 oz.) shredded 2% reduced-fat sharp Cheddar cheese
 ¼ cup freshly grated Parmesan cheese
 ½ tsp. hot sauce
 ¼ tsp. ground white pepper

1. Bring first 3 ingredients and 1⅓ cups water to a boil in a medium saucepan over medium-high heat; gradually whisk in grits. Reduce heat to low; simmer, stirring occasionally, 10 minutes or until thickened. Stir in Cheddar cheese and next 3 ingredients.

how to:
sauté shrimp for shrimp and grits

1. Sauté mushrooms in hot bacon drippings and oil in skillet 5 minutes or until tender. Add green onions, and sauté 2 minutes.

2. Add seasoned and dredged shrimp and garlic to skillet.

3. Sauté shrimp and garlic 2 minutes or until shrimp are lightly browned.

4. Stir in chicken broth, lemon juice, and hot sauce. Cook 2 more minutes, stirring to loosen particles from bottom of skillet (also known as deglazing).

Tacos al Pastor

Hands-on Time: 25 min.
Total Time: 4 hr., 25 min.
Makes: 6 tacos

- 1 lb. pork tenderloin, cut into ½-inch cubes
- 1 (8-oz.) can pineapple tidbits in juice, drained
- 1 medium onion, chopped
- ¼ cup chopped fresh cilantro
- 1 Tbsp. Mexican-style chili powder
- 1 tsp. ground cumin
- 1 tsp. dried oregano
- 1 tsp. pepper
- 1 tsp. chopped garlic
- ¾ tsp. salt
- 1 Tbsp. canola oil
- 6 (8-inch) soft taco-size corn or flour tortillas, warmed

Toppings: chopped radishes, fresh cilantro leaves, crumbled queso fresco, chopped onions, chopped jalapeño

1. Combine pork and next 9 ingredients in a large zip-top plastic freezer bag. Seal and chill 4 to 24 hours.

2. Cook pork mixture in hot oil in a large nonstick skillet over medium-high heat, stirring often, 10 minutes or until pork is done. Serve mixture with warm tortillas and desired toppings.

Spicy Chicken-Pineapple Tacos: Substitute 1 lb. skinned and boned chicken thighs, chopped, for pork tenderloin. Proceed with recipe as directed.

fix it!

Problem: The tortillas have dried out.

Solution: Wrap sets of 2 tortillas in damp paper towels. Microwave at HIGH 10 to 20 seconds or until warm. The moisture from the towels will soften the tortillas.

how to:
make tacos al pastor

1. Heat 1 Tbsp. canola oil in a large nonstick skillet over medium-high heat.

2. Add marinated pork mixture to hot oil.

3. Cook pork mixture, stirring often, 10 minutes or until pork is done. Serve with warm tortillas and desired toppings.

Okra-and-Corn Maque Choux

Hands-on Time: 28 min.
Total Time: 28 min.
Makes: 8 servings

- ¼ lb. spicy smoked sausage, diced
- ½ cup chopped sweet onion
- ½ cup chopped green bell pepper
- 2 garlic cloves, minced
- 3 cups fresh corn kernels
- 1 cup sliced fresh okra
- 1 cup peeled, seeded, and diced tomato (½ lb.)

Salt and freshly ground pepper to taste

1. Sauté sausage in a large skillet over medium-high heat 3 minutes or until browned. Add onion, bell pepper, and garlic; sauté 5 minutes or until tender Add corn, okra, and tomato; cook, stirring often, 10 minutes. Season with salt and pepper to taste.

Note: We tested with Conecuh Original Spicy and Hot Smoked Sausage.

Southern foodlore

Maque choux is a traditional dish of southern Louisiana similar to succotash. It is believed that the name of this dish is a Cajun French translation of the Native American name.

how to:
sauté vegetables for maque choux

1. Sauté sausage in a large skillet over medium-high heat 3 minutes or until browned.

2. Add onion, bell pepper, and garlic to sausage in skillet. Sauté 5 minutes or until vegetables are tender.

3. Add corn, okra, and tomato to mixture in skillet. Cook, stirring often, 10 minutes. Season with salt and pepper to taste.

Zucchini-Potato Soup

Hands-on Time: 31 min.
Total Time: 56 min.
Makes: 7 cups

Inspired by the classic potato-and-leek vichyssoise (vihsh-ee-SWAHZ), we added zucchini and gave this recipe our Southern twist with the addition of crisp, crumbled bacon.

- 1 medium leek
- 4 bacon slices
- ½ cup chopped celery
- 1 garlic clove, minced
- 4 cups low-sodium fat-free chicken broth
- 1 lb. zucchini, sliced (about 3 small squash)
- ½ lb. small new potatoes, quartered
- 1 cup half-and-half
- ⅓ cup chopped fresh parsley
- ¼ tsp. kosher salt
- ¼ tsp. pepper

1. Remove root, tough outer leaves, and tops from leek, leaving 2 inches of dark leaves. Thinly slice leek; rinse well, and drain.

2. Cook bacon in a large Dutch oven over medium-high heat 8 to 10 minutes or until crisp; remove bacon, and drain on paper towels, reserving 2 Tbsp. drippings in Dutch oven. Crumble bacon.

3. Sauté leek, celery, and garlic in hot drippings 3 to 4 minutes or until tender. Add chicken broth, zucchini, and potatoes, and simmer 20 to 25 minutes. Stir in half-and-half, parsley, salt, and pepper. Remove from heat, and cool 5 minutes.

4. Process potato mixture, in batches, in a blender or food processor until smooth, stopping to scrape down sides as needed. Sprinkle with crumbled bacon and serve immediately, or, if desired, cover and chill 4 to 6 hours.

how to:
make zucchini-potato soup

1. Sauté leek, celery, and garlic in hot bacon drippings in a large Dutch oven 3 to 4 minutes or until tender.

2. Add broth, zucchini, and potatoes to pan. Simmer 20 to 25 minutes.

3. Stir in remaining ingredients except bacon. Remove pan from heat, and let cool 5 minutes.

4. Process potato mixture, in batches, in a blender or food processor until smooth, stopping to scrape down sides as needed. (Be sure to remove the center of the lid to let steam escape while pureeing.)

kitchen secret:

Be very careful when pureeing hot soup in a blender. Sometimes, the pressure from the heat can cause an overflow, so always remove the center vent of the lid, and cover it with a kitchen towel.

Cabbage Stir-Fry

Hands-on Time: 20 min.
Total Time: 20 min.
Makes: 4 to 6 servings

The beautiful color and fresh flavor of this dish will entice the whole family.

- 2 Tbsp. vegetable oil
- ½ red cabbage, thinly sliced
- 1 green bell pepper, thinly sliced
- 1 small onion, thinly sliced
- ¾ cup chopped fresh cilantro
- 1 Tbsp. lime juice
- 1 tsp. salt
- ½ tsp. pepper

1. Heat oil in a large skillet or wok at high heat 3 to 4 minutes. Add cabbage, bell pepper, and onion, and stir-fry 7 to 10 minutes or until crisp-tender or to desired degree of doneness. Stir in cilantro and remaining ingredients.

Spicy Cabbage Stir-Fry: Stir in 3 Tbsp. jalapeño jelly with cabbage, bell pepper, and onion. Proceed as directed.

how to:
stir-fry cabbage

1. Heat 2 Tbsp. vegetable oil in a large wok or skillet 3 to 4 minutes.

2. Add cabbage, bell pepper, and onion. Stir-fry 7 to 10 minutes or until crisp-tender.

3. Stir in cilantro, lime juice, salt, and pepper.

Peanut-Broccoli Stir-Fry

Hands-on Time: 40 min.
Total Time: 1 hr., 35 min.
Makes: 6 servings

 1 (16-oz.) package firm tofu
 2 cups uncooked brown rice
 ½ tsp. salt
 1½ cups vegetable broth
 1 Tbsp. light brown sugar
 2 Tbsp. fresh lime juice
 2 Tbsp. sweet chili sauce
 2 Tbsp. creamy peanut butter
 1 Tbsp. lite soy sauce
 1 tsp. grated fresh ginger
 ¾ tsp. cornstarch
 1 Tbsp. peanut or vegetable oil
 1 tsp. dark sesame oil
 2 cups fresh broccoli florets
 1 cup carrot sticks
 2 Tbsp. chopped peanuts
Garnish: lime wedges

1. Place tofu between 2 flat plates. Weight the top with a heavy can. (Sides of tofu should be bulging slightly but not cracking.) Let stand 45 minutes; discard liquid. Cut tofu into ½-inch cubes.

2. Prepare rice according to package directions, adding ½ tsp. salt.

3. Meanwhile, combine vegetable broth and next 7 ingredients in a medium bowl, stirring well. Add tofu, and toss to coat. Let stand 10 minutes. Remove tofu from marinade, reserving marinade.

4. Heat oils in a nonstick skillet or wok over high heat 1 minute. Add tofu; stir-fry 4 to 5 minutes or until browned. Add broccoli and carrot sticks; stir-fry 2 minutes. Add reserved marinade, and bring to a boil. Cook, stirring constantly, 2 minutes or until thickened. Serve over hot cooked rice. Sprinkle with chopped peanuts. Garnish, if desired.

how to:
make peanut-broccoli stir-fry

1. Place tofu between 2 flat plates. Place a heavy can on plate and let stand 45 minutes to remove excess moisture; discard liquid. Cut tofu into 1/2-inch cubes.

2. Combine tofu and marinade in a medium bowl. Let stand 10 minutes. Remove tofu from marinade, reserving marinade.

3. Heat peanut and sesame oils in a wok or skillet over high heat 1 minute. Add tofu, and stir-fry 4 to 5 minutes or until browned.

4. Add broccoli and carrots to wok; stir-fry 2 minutes. Add reserved marinade, and bring to a boil. Cook, stirring constantly, 2 minutes or until thickened.

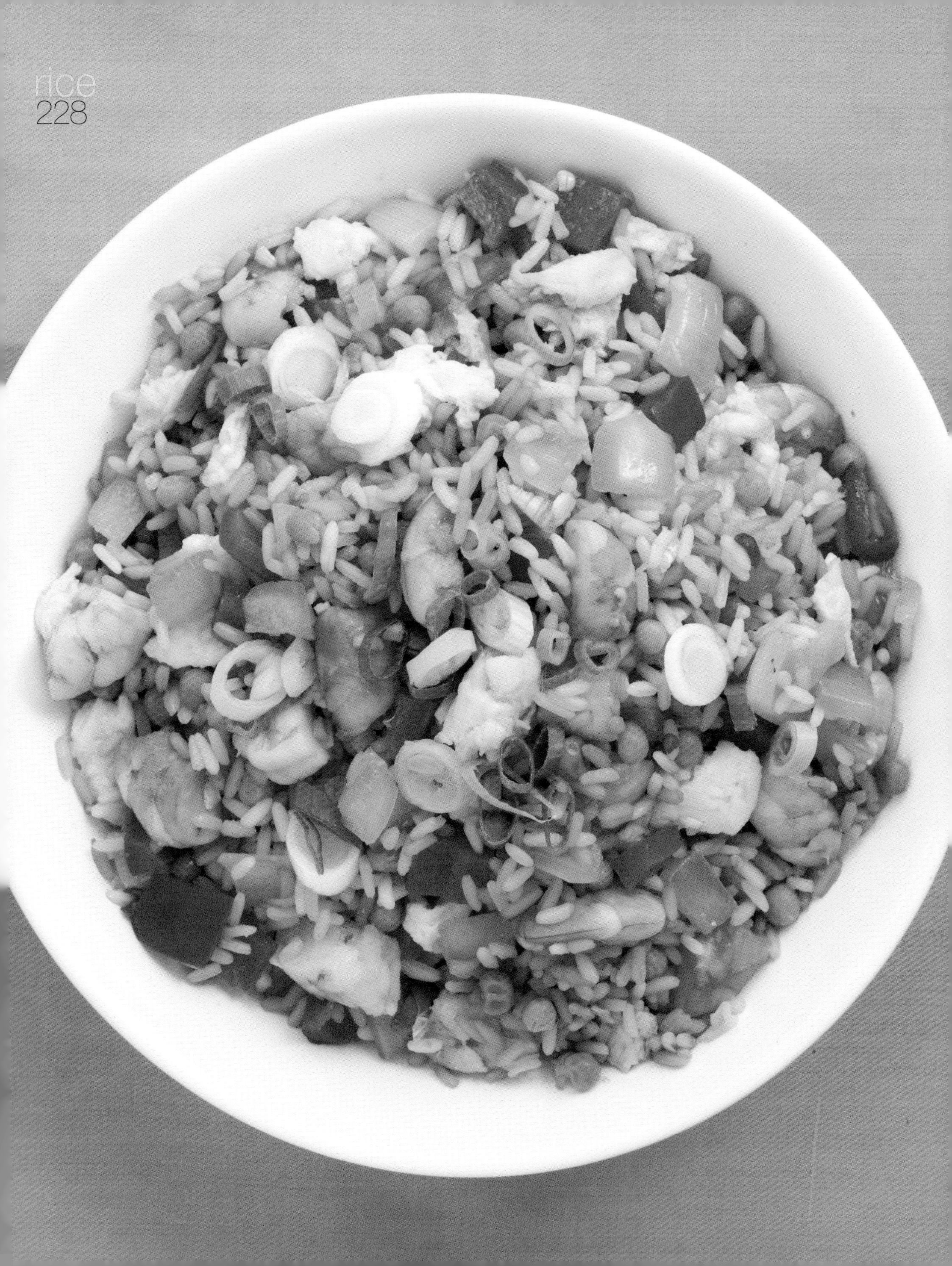

Combination Fried Rice

Hands-on Time: 26 min.
Total Time: 26 min.
Makes: 4 servings

Use a mix of whatever meat you have on hand. Spicy chili-garlic sauce adds a kick, and, once opened, keeps indefinitely in the refrigerator.

    3 Tbsp. vegetable oil, divided
    2 large eggs, lightly beaten
    ½ cup diced onion
    ½ cup diced bell pepper
    1 cup chopped cooked meat, poultry,
       or shrimp
    ½ cup frozen English peas
    3 cups cooked rice
    ¼ cup soy sauce
    1 tsp. Asian chili-garlic sauce
    Garnish: sliced green onions

1. Heat 1 Tbsp. oil in a wok or skillet over medium-high heat 1 to 2 minutes; add eggs, and gently stir 1 minute or until softly scrambled. Remove eggs from skillet; chop.

2. Heat remaining 2 Tbsp. oil in skillet; add onion and bell pepper, and stir-fry 3 minutes. Add chopped cooked meat and peas; stir-fry 2 minutes. Add rice, eggs, soy sauce, and chili-garlic sauce; stir-fry 5 minutes or until thoroughly heated. Garnish, if desired.

how to:
make combination fried rice

1. Cook eggs in oil in a wok or large nonstick skillet 1 minute or until softly scrambled. Remove eggs from skillet, and chop.

2. Heat remaining oil in wok; add onion and bell pepper. Stir-fry 3 minutes. Add peas and chopped cooked meat; stir-fry 2 minutes.

3. Add cooked rice, chili-garlic sauce, eggs, and soy sauce. Cook 5 minutes or until thoroughly heated.

Steaming is one of the most healthy cooking methods and involves using the steam from a boiling liquid to cook the food. The food is kept separate from the boiling liquid, but because it has direct contact with the steam, the result is a tender and moist texture. Steaming can be achieved with the use of a steamer basket, a water bath, a parchment pouch, or by cooking in a flavored hot liquid.

Steamed Mussels With Herbs

Hands-on Time: 23 min.
Total Time: 23 min.
Makes: 4 servings

Serve with crusty bread to dip into the flavorful broth.

- 2 lb. fresh mussels
- 4 garlic cloves, minced
- 2 shallots, minced
- 2 Tbsp. olive oil
- 2 cups dry white wine
- 2 Tbsp. Dijon mustard
- 1 (14.5-oz.) can vegetable broth
- ¼ tsp. salt
- ¼ cup chopped fresh basil
- ¼ cup chopped fresh cilantro

1. Scrub mussels thoroughly with a scrub brush, removing beards. Discard any opened shells.
2. Sauté garlic and shallots in hot oil in a Dutch oven over medium heat 1 to 2 minutes. Stir in wine and mustard; cook 2 to 3 minutes. Add broth and salt, and bring to a boil. Add mussels. Cook, covered, stirring occasionally, 5 minutes or until all mussels have opened. Remove from heat. Stir in basil and cilantro.

how to:
steam mussels

1. Scrub mussels with a scrub brush and remove beards. (Pinch the beard with your thumb and index finger and gently pull.) If some shells are opened, tap them gently to see if they close. If they don't, discard them.

2. Sauté garlic and shallots in hot olive oil in a Dutch oven over medium heat 1 to 2 minutes. Stir in wine and mustard; cook 2 to 3 minutes. Add broth and salt; bring to a boil. Add mussels to mixture.

3. Cook mussels, covered, stirring occasionally, 5 minutes or until all mussels are opened.

Lemon-Dill Tilapia

Hands-on Time: 15 min.
Total Time: 35 min.
Makes: 4 servings

Aluminum foil can be substituted for parchment paper.

- 4 (5-oz.) fresh tilapia fillets
- 1 tsp. salt
- ½ tsp. pepper
- 2 lemons, sliced
- ¼ cup shredded carrots
- 2 Tbsp. fresh dill
- 2 Tbsp. fresh parsley
- 2 Tbsp. butter

1. Preheat oven to 375°. Sprinkle fillets with salt and pepper.
2. Cut parchment paper into 4 (13- x 9-inch) rectangles. Place 3 lemon slices crosswise in center of 1 parchment rectangle. Top with 1 fillet. Repeat with remaining lemon slices, fillets, and parchment paper rectangles. Sprinkle fillets evenly with carrot, dill, and parsley. Top each fillet with ½ Tbsp. butter. Fold 1 side of parchment paper over fillets; tuck excess parchment under fillets, pressing folds to form a crease.
3. Bake at 375° for 20 to 25 minutes or until fish flakes with a fork. Serve immediately.

how to:
steam fish in parchment

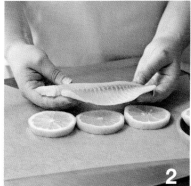

1. Cut parchment paper into 4 (13- x 9-inch) rectangles.

2. Place 3 lemon slices lengthwise in center of each parchment rectangle. Top lemon with fish.

3. Sprinkle fillets evenly with carrot, dill, and parsley. Top each fillet with butter. Fold 1 side of parchment paper over fillets; tuck excess parchment under fillets, pressing folds to form a crease. Bake at 375° for 20 to 25 minutes or until fish flakes with a fork.

Sugar Snap-Snow Pea Salad

Hands-on Time: 10 min.
Total Time: 17 min.
Makes: 4 servings

- 1½ cups trimmed fresh sugar snap peas (about 5 oz.)
- 1½ cups trimmed fresh snow peas (about 6 oz.)
- 1 Tbsp. soy sauce
- 1 Tbsp. pomegranate or cranberry juice
- 1 Tbsp. white vinegar
- 1 Tbsp. canola oil
- 1 tsp. sugar
- 2 tsp. minced fresh ginger
- 1 Tbsp. black or regular sesame seeds
- 1 cup frozen baby English peas, thawed

1. Arrange sugar snap peas and snow peas in a steamer basket over boiling water. Cover and steam 1 to 2 minutes or until crisp-tender. Plunge peas into ice water to stop the cooking process; drain.
2. Whisk together soy sauce and next 5 ingredients in a large bowl.
3. Heat sesame seeds in a small nonstick skillet over medium-low heat, stirring often, 4 to 5 minutes or until toasted and fragrant. Add hot sesame seeds to soy sauce mixture, stirring until blended. Add sugar snap peas, snow peas, and thawed English peas, tossing gently to coat. Serve immediately.

how to:
steam sugar snap and snow peas

1. Arrange peas in a steamer basket over boiling water.

2. Cover and steam 1 to 2 minutes or until crisp-tender.

3. Plunge peas into ice water to stop the cooking process; drain.

Caramel Custard

Hands-on Time: 10 min.
Total Time: 4 hr., 15 min.
Makes: 10 servings

The hot water bath helps insulate the custard from the direct heat of the oven and provides a more gentle environment for even baking.

- ½ cup sugar
- 2 egg yolks
- 1 large egg
- 1 (14-oz.) can fat-free sweetened condensed milk
- 1 (12-oz.) can fat-free evaporated milk
- 3 oz. ⅓-less-fat cream cheese, softened
- 1 Tbsp. vanilla extract

1. Cook sugar in an 8-inch round cake pan (with 2-inch sides) over medium heat, shaking pan occasionally, 5 minutes or until sugar melts and turns light golden brown. Remove pan from heat, and let stand 5 minutes. (Sugar will harden.)

2. Preheat oven to 350°. Process egg yolks and next 5 ingredients in a blender until smooth. Pour mixture over caramelized sugar in pan. Cover mixture with aluminum foil.

3. Place cake pan in a broiler pan. Add hot water (150°) to pan to a depth of ⅔ inch.

4. Bake at 350° for 1 hour or until a knife inserted in center of custard comes out clean. Remove cake pan from water bath; cool completely on a wire rack. Cover and chill at least 3 hours.

5. Run a knife around edge of pan to loosen; invert onto a serving plate.

Banana-Caramel Custard: Prepare custard recipe as directed, adding 1 medium-size ripe banana to egg yolk mixture in blender.

kitchen secret:

The 8-oz. blocks of ⅓-less-fat cream cheese have marks on the packaging noting 1-oz. measurements. By using these marks, it is easy to measure the 3 oz. of cream cheese that you need for this recipe.

how to:
steam custard

1. Cook sugar in a cake pan over medium heat, shaking pan occasionally, 5 minutes or until sugar melts and turns light golden brown.

2. Pour prepared custard mixture over caramelized sugar in pan. Cover with aluminum foil. Place cake pan in a broiler pan. Add hot water to pan to a depth of ²/₃ inch.

3. Bake at 350° for 1 hour or until a knife inserted in center of custard comes out clean.

4. Run a knife around the edge of pan (of cooled and chilled custard) to loosen; carefully invert custard onto a serving plate.

the RECIPES

Applying your cooking skills to make these delicious dishes

APPETIZERS & BEVERAGES

From refreshing cocktails to delicious nibbles, these party starters will satisfy any crowd.

Lemonade Iced Tea

Hands-on Time: 15 min.
Total Time: 25 min.
Makes: 8 cups

Also known as an Arnold Palmer, this refreshing beverage serves a crowd, so it's perfect for summer get-togethers.

- 2 family-size tea bags
- 1 (1-oz.) package fresh mint leaves (about 1 cup loosely packed)
- ½ cup sugar
- 4 cups cold water
- 1 (6-oz.) can frozen lemonade concentrate, thawed

Garnish: fresh citrus slices

1. Bring 3 cups water to a boil in a 2-qt. saucepan. Remove from heat, add tea bags, and stir in fresh mint. Cover and steep 10 minutes.
2. Remove and discard tea bags and mint. Stir in sugar until dissolved.
3. Pour tea into a 3-qt. container, and stir in 4 cups cold water and lemonade concentrate. Serve over ice. Garnish, if desired.

Bourbon-Lemonade Iced Tea: Prepare recipe as directed, and stir in 1 cup bourbon.

Spiced Dark Rum-Lemonade Iced Tea: Prepare recipe as directed, and stir in 1 cup spiced dark rum.

Lemonade Iced Tea

Rich 'n' Thick Hot Chocolate

Hands-on Time: 14 min.
Total Time: 18 min., including whipped cream
Makes: 8 servings

This is a luxurious, unexpected offering for dessert. Take it over the top with a dollop of Marshmallow Whipped Cream.

> 4 cups milk, divided
> 2 tsp. cornstarch
> 2 (3.5-oz.) dark chocolate bars (at least 70% cacao), chopped
> ⅓ cup honey
> 1 tsp. vanilla extract
> Pinch of salt
> Marshmallow Whipped Cream (optional)

1. Whisk together ½ cup milk and cornstarch until smooth.
2. Cook remaining 3½ cups milk in a nonaluminum saucepan over medium heat until bubbles appear around edge of saucepan (about 4 minutes; do not boil). Whisk in chocolate, honey, vanilla, and salt until blended and smooth. Whisk in cornstarch mixture.
3. Bring milk mixture to a boil, whisking frequently (about 4 minutes). Remove from heat. Let cool slightly. (Mixture will thicken as it cools.) Serve immediately with Marshmallow Whipped Cream, if desired.

fix it!

Problem: The mixture became lumpy after you added cornstarch to it.

Solution: Strain the hot liquid and let it cool. Avoid adding cornstarch to hot liquids to prevent lumps from forming. Always combine it with a cool liquid and then heat.

Mexican Rich 'n' Thick Hot Chocolate: Prepare recipe as directed through Step 2, whisking in 1¼ tsp. ground cinnamon and 1 tsp. ancho chili powder with chocolate. Proceed with recipe as directed.

Orange-Almond Rich 'n' Thick Hot Chocolate: Prepare recipe as directed through Step 2, whisking in 3 Tbsp. orange juice and 2 Tbsp. almond liqueur with chocolate. Proceed with recipe as directed.

Marshmallow Whipped Cream

Hands-on Time: 10 min.
Total Time: 10 min.
Makes: about 1½ cups

Maximum make-ahead time is 2 hours. After that, the marshmallows start to dissolve.

> ½ cup whipping cream
> 1 Tbsp. powdered sugar
> ½ cup miniature marshmallows

1. Beat whipping cream at medium-high speed with an electric mixer until foamy; gradually add powdered sugar, beating until soft peaks form. Fold in marshmallows. Serve immediately, or cover and chill up to 2 hours.

Rich 'n' Thick Hot Chocolate

Banana-Pecan Smoothies

Hands-on Time: 8 min.
Total Time: 8 min.
Makes: about 3 cups

- 1½ cups low-fat vanilla yogurt
- 2 large ripe bananas, sliced and frozen
- 1 cup ice
- ½ cup finely chopped toasted pecans
- ½ cup milk
- 1 Tbsp. honey
- ½ tsp. ground cinnamon

1. Process yogurt, bananas, ice, pecans, milk, honey, and cinnamon in a blender until smooth. Pour into glasses, and serve immediately.

Homemade Orange Soda

Hands-on Time: 3 min.
Total Time: 3 min.
Makes: about 2½ qt.

Stir this refreshing beverage occasionally to keep the ingredients thoroughly mixed.

- 1 (12-oz.) can frozen, pulp-free orange juice concentrate, thawed and undiluted
- 2 (2-liter) bottles lemon-lime soft drink, chilled
- 1 to 2 oranges, thinly sliced

1. Stir together orange juice concentrate and lemon-lime soft drink when ready to serve. Serve over ice in individual glasses with an orange slice.

Maple Coffee

Hands-on Time: 5 min.
Total Time: 5 min.
Makes: 6 cups

- 2 cups half-and-half
- ¾ cup maple syrup
- 3 cups strong brewed coffee
- Half-and-half, frothed (optional)

1. Cook 2 cups half-and-half and maple syrup in a saucepan over medium heat until thoroughly heated. (Do not boil.) Stir in brewed coffee. Top with frothed half-and-half, if desired.

kitchen secret:
If you don't have an espresso machine with a frother, beat the half-and-half with a handheld mixer until frothy.

Banana-Pecan Smoothies

Carolina Peach Sangria

Hands-on Time: 10 min.
Total Time: 8 hr., 10 min.
Makes: about 9 cups

Be sure to use rosé, not white Zinfandel, in this cool drink.

- 1 (750-milliliter) bottle rosé wine
- ¾ cup vodka*
- ½ cup peach nectar
- 2 Tbsp. sugar
- 6 Tbsp. thawed, frozen lemonade concentrate
- 1 lb. ripe peaches, peeled and sliced
- 1 (6-oz.) package fresh raspberries**
- 2 cups club soda, chilled

1. Combine first 5 ingredients in a pitcher; stir until sugar is dissolved. Stir in peaches and raspberries. Cover and chill 8 hours.
2. Stir in chilled club soda just before serving.

*Peach-flavored vodka may be substituted. Omit peach nectar.
**1 cup frozen raspberries may be substituted.

Raspberry Beer Cocktail

Hands-on Time: 5 min.
Total Time: 5 min.
Makes: 6 servings

- ¾ cup frozen raspberries*
- 3½ (12-oz.) bottles beer, chilled
- 1 (12-oz.) can frozen raspberry lemonade concentrate, thawed
- ½ cup vodka
- Garnishes: lemon and lime slices

1. Stir together first 4 ingredients. Serve over ice. Garnish, if desired.

*Fresh raspberries may be substituted.

Raspberry Beer Cocktail

kitchen secret:

To make ahead, combine lemonade concentrate and vodka in a large container. Chill up to 3 days. Stir in raspberries and beer just before serving. Garnish, if desired.

Puff Pastry Cheese Tray

Hands-on Time: 10 min.
Total Time: 1 hr., 9 min.
Makes: 1 tray

Top this edible cheese board with a selection of your favorite cheeses.

- 1 large egg
- 1 (17.3-oz.) package frozen puff pastry sheets, thawed
- 1 tsp. seasoning blend
Fresh herb sprigs (optional)

1. Preheat oven to 400°. Whisk together egg and 2 tsp. water. Unfold 1 thawed puff pastry sheet on an ungreased baking sheet; brush with egg mixture. Cut 4 (¹/₂-inch-wide) strips from one side of pastry, cutting parallel to seam of pastry. Place strips along outer edges of pastry, overlapping and trimming ends of strips as needed.
2. Prick bottom of pastry generously with a fork. Sprinkle bottom of pastry with 1 tsp. of your favorite seasoning blend. If desired, gently press fresh herb sprigs onto bottom of pastry. Bake at 400° for 6 minutes. Prick bottom of pastry generously with fork again (to prevent center from rising). Bake 6 more minutes or until lightly brown. Let cool on pan 2 minutes; transfer to a wire rack, and let cool 45 minutes or until completely cool.

Puff Pastry Cheese Tray

Gorgonzola Truffles

Marinated Mozzarella

Hands-on Time: 20 min.
Total Time: 8 hr., 20 min.
Makes: about 4 cups

- 3 (8-oz.) blocks mozzarella cheese
- 1 (8.5-oz.) jar sun-dried tomatoes, drained and halved
- ½ cup olive oil
- 3 Tbsp. finely chopped fresh flat-leaf parsley
- 1 tsp. garlic powder
- 1 tsp. onion powder
- ½ tsp. dried oregano
- ½ tsp. Italian seasoning
- ¼ tsp. salt
- ¼ tsp. freshly ground pepper
- Garnish: fresh rosemary stems

1. Cut blocks of cheese into 1-inch cubes. Arrange cheese cubes and tomato halves in an 8-inch square baking dish.
2. Whisk together ¹/₂ cup olive oil, chopped parsley, and next 6 ingredients; pour evenly over cheese cubes. Cover and chill at least 8 hours or up to 24 hours. Transfer mixture to a serving plate. Spear tomato halves and cheese cubes with short rosemary stems, if desired. Drizzle with marinade, if desired.

Gorgonzola Truffles

Hands-on Time: 20 min.
Total Time: 1 hr., 20 min.
Makes: 6 appetizer servings

- 4 oz. cream cheese, softened
- 1 (4-oz.) container crumbled Gorgonzola cheese
- 2 tsp. finely chopped onion
- ½ tsp. Worcestershire sauce
- ¼ tsp. freshly ground pepper
- ½ cup cooked and crumbled bacon
- Apple slices, pear slices, and grapes

1. Beat first 5 ingredients at medium speed with an electric mixer until well combined. Cover tightly, and chill at least 1 hour or until firm. (Mixture can chill up to 3 days.)
2. Roll cheese mixture into ³/₄-inch-round balls. Roll each ball in bacon. Serve immediately, or cover and chill until ready to serve. If chilled, let stand 30 minutes before serving. Serve with apple and pear slices and grapes.

Blue Cheese Ranch Dip

Hands-on Time: 5 min.
Total Time: 5 min.
Makes: 2¹/₂ cups

- 1 (16-oz.) container sour cream
- 1 (1-oz.) envelope Ranch dip mix
- 1 (4-oz.) package blue cheese crumbles
- 2 Tbsp. chopped fresh chives
- Carrot and celery sticks, potato chips, and hot wings

1. Stir together first 4 ingredients. Serve with carrot and celery sticks, potato chips, and hot wings.

Warm Turnip Green Dip

Hands-on Time: 35 min.
Total Time: 40 min.
Makes: 4 cups

To make the dish spicier, offer guests several brands of hot sauce on the side.

5	bacon slices, chopped
½	medium-size sweet onion, chopped
2	garlic cloves, chopped
¼	cup dry white wine
1	(16-oz.) package frozen chopped turnip greens, thawed
12	oz. cream cheese, cut into pieces
1	(8-oz.) container sour cream
½	tsp. dried crushed red pepper
¼	tsp. salt
¾	cup freshly grated Parmesan cheese

Garnish: dried crushed red pepper
Assorted crackers, flatbread, and wafers

1. Preheat broiler with oven rack 6 inches from heat. Cook bacon in a Dutch oven over medium-high heat 5 to 6 minutes or until crisp; remove bacon, and drain on paper towels, reserving 1 Tbsp. drippings in Dutch oven.

2. Sauté onion and garlic in hot drippings 3 to 4 minutes. Add wine, and cook 1 to 2 minutes, stirring to loosen particles from bottom of Dutch oven. Stir in turnip greens, next 4 ingredients, and ½ cup Parmesan cheese. Cook, stirring often, 6 to 8 minutes or until cream cheese is melted and mixture is thoroughly heated. Transfer to a lightly greased 1½-qt. baking dish. (Make certain that you use a broiler-safe baking dish.) Sprinkle with remaining ¼ cup Parmesan cheese.

3. Broil 4 to 5 minutes or until cheese is lightly browned. Sprinkle with bacon. Garnish, if desired. Serve with assorted crackers, flatbread, and wafers.

Warm Spinach-Artichoke Dip: Substitute 2 (10-oz.) packages frozen spinach, thawed and drained, and 1 (14-oz.) can quartered artichoke hearts, drained and coarsely chopped, for turnip greens. Proceed with recipe as directed.

kitchen secret:

To make ahead, prepare recipe as directed through Step 2. Cover and chill 8 hours. Bake, covered with aluminum foil, at 350° for 30 minutes. Uncover and bake 30 more minutes. Sprinkle with bacon. Serve with assorted crackers and chips.

Warm Turnip Green Dip

Roasted Garlic-Edamame Spread

Hands-on Time: 15 min.
Total Time: 50 min.
Makes: about 2¹⁄₂ cups

This is delicious on toasted crostini and topped with fresh basil. It also works well as a sandwich spread and can be made up to three days ahead.

- 1 garlic bulb
- 1 Tbsp. olive oil
- 2 cups fully cooked, shelled edamame (green soybeans)*
- ½ cup ricotta cheese
- ¼ cup chopped fresh basil
- 2 Tbsp. lemon juice
- ¼ cup olive oil
- 1 tsp. kosher salt
- ½ tsp. freshly ground pepper
- Assorted fresh vegetables

1. Preheat oven to 425°. Cut off pointed end of garlic; place garlic on a piece of aluminum foil, and drizzle with 1 Tbsp. olive oil. Fold foil to seal. Bake 30 minutes; let cool 5 minutes. Squeeze pulp from garlic cloves into a bowl.

2. Process edamame in a food processor 30 seconds or until smooth, stopping to scrape down sides. Add roasted garlic, ricotta, basil, and lemon juice; pulse 2 to 3 times or until blended.

3. With processor running, pour ¹⁄₄ cup oil through food chute in a slow, steady stream, processing until smooth. Stir in salt and pepper. Serve with assorted fresh vegetables.

*2 cups uncooked, frozen, shelled edamame (green soybeans) may be substituted. Prepare edamame according to package directions. Plunge into ice water to stop the cooking process; drain. Proceed with recipe as directed.

Note: We tested with Marjon Shelled Fully Cooked Edamame.

Roasted Garlic-Lima Bean Spread: Substitute 2 cups frozen lima beans for edamame. Prepare lima beans according to package directions. Proceed with recipe as directed.

Roasted Garlic-Edamame Spread

Tex-Mex Shrimp Cocktail

Hands-on Time: 15 min.
Total Time: 4 hr., 15 min.
Makes: 4 to 6 servings

Serve this festive favorite in individual glasses, if you'd like.

- ¼ cup hot red jalapeño pepper jelly
- 1 Tbsp. lime zest
- ¼ cup fresh lime juice
- 1 lb. peeled, large cooked shrimp (31/40 count)
- 1 cup diced mango
- ½ cup diced red bell pepper
- ¼ cup chopped fresh cilantro
- 1 small avocado, diced

Garnishes: lime slices, fresh cilantro sprigs
Tortilla chips

1. Whisk together first 3 ingredients. Pour into a large zip-top plastic freezer bag; add shrimp and next 3 ingredients, turning to coat. Seal and chill 4 hours, turning occasionally. Add avocado just before serving.
2. Divide mixture into 4 to 6 servings. Garnish, if desired. Serve with tortilla chips.

Baked Fig Crostini

Baked Fig Crostini

Hands-on Time: 12 min.
Total Time: 19 min.
Makes: 12 servings

If figs are out of season, sliced pears or apples are a great substitute.

- 4 oz. chopped cooked bacon or country ham
- 4 oz. crumbled goat cheese, softened
- 1 Tbsp. finely chopped toasted pecans
- 1 tsp. chopped fresh thyme
- 12 fresh figs
- 1 Tbsp. honey

Toasted baguette slices

1. Preheat oven to 350°. Stir together bacon or country ham, softened goat cheese, finely chopped toasted pecans, and chopped fresh thyme. Cut figs in half. Press back of a small spoon into centers of fig halves, making a small indentation in each. Spoon bacon mixture into indentations. Bake on a baking sheet 7 minutes. Drizzle with honey. Serve immediately with toasted baguette slices.

Tex-Mex Shrimp Cocktail

Warm Olive Sauté

Hands-on Time: 10 min.
Total Time: 16 min.
Makes: 12 servings

1	lemon
1	tsp. minced garlic
¾	tsp. fennel seeds
½	tsp. dried crushed red pepper
⅓	cup extra virgin olive oil
1½	cups mixed olives
8	pickled okra, cut in half lengthwise
1	fennel bulb, cored and sliced
½	cup roasted, lightly salted almonds

1. Peel lemon into strips, being careful to avoid the white pith. Reserve remaining lemon for another use. Sauté lemon peel, minced garlic, fennel seeds, and dried crushed red pepper in hot extra virgin olive oil in a large skillet over medium heat 1 minute. Add olives, pickled okra, sliced fennel, and almonds. Cook, stirring occasionally, 5 to 7 minutes or until fennel is crisp-tender.

kitchen secret:

Use a swivel-head vegetable peeler to remove the zest of the lemon with ease.

Warm Olive Sauté

Red Pepper Jelly-Brie Bites

Hands-on Time: 10 min.
Total Time: 15 min.
Makes: 30 tartlets

Use frozen mini phyllo pastry shells as the base for this colorful appetizer.

- 2 (1.9-oz.) packages frozen mini phyllo pastry shells, thawed
- 3 oz. Brie round, rind removed
- Red pepper jelly
- 3 Tbsp. chopped roasted salted almonds

1. Preheat oven to 350°. Place mini phyllo pastry shells on a baking sheet. Cut Brie into 30 very small pieces. Spoon rounded ¼ tsp. red pepper jelly into each shell; top with cheese. Sprinkle with almonds. Bake tartlets 5 to 6 minutes or until cheese is melted.

Ham-Stuffed Biscuits

Hands-on Time: 1 hr.
Total Time: 2 hr., 17 min., including butter
Makes: 5 dozen

- 1 (¼-oz.) envelope active dry yeast
- ½ cup warm water (100° to 110°)
- 2 cups buttermilk
- 5½ cups all-purpose flour
- ¼ cup sugar
- 1½ Tbsp. baking powder
- 1½ tsp. salt
- ½ tsp. baking soda
- ¾ cup shortening
- Mustard Butter
- 2 lb. thinly sliced cooked ham

1. Combine yeast and warm water in a 4-cup liquid measuring cup; let stand 5 minutes. Stir in buttermilk.

Red Pepper Jelly-Brie Bites

2. Combine flour and next 4 ingredients in a large bowl; cut in shortening with a pastry blender or fork until mixture resembles coarse meal. Add buttermilk mixture, stirring with a fork just until dry ingredients are moistened.

3. Turn dough out onto a well-floured surface, and knead 4 to 5 times.

4. Roll dough to ½-inch thickness; cut with a 2-inch round cutter, and place on lightly greased baking sheets. Cover and let rise in a warm place (85°), free from drafts, 1 hour.

5. Preheat oven to 425°. Bake 10 to 12 minutes or until golden. Split each biscuit, and spread evenly with Mustard Butter. Stuff biscuits with ham.

Mustard Butter

Hands-on Time: 5 min.
Total Time: 5 min.
Makes: about 1 cup

  1 cup butter, softened
  2 Tbsp. minced sweet onion
  2 Tbsp. spicy brown mustard

1. Stir together all ingredients until blended.

Curried Shrimp Tarts

Hands-on Time: 15 min.
Total Time: 15 min.
Makes: 4 to 6 servings

  15 frozen mini phyllo pastry shells
   1 cup chopped cooked shrimp
   ½ (8-oz.) package cream cheese, softened
   3 Tbsp. chopped green onions
   1 Tbsp. fresh lime juice
   ¾ tsp. curry powder
   ¼ tsp. ground red pepper
  2½ Tbsp. jarred mango chutney
  Toppings: chopped fresh chives, toasted sweetened flaked coconut

Curried Shrimp Tarts

1. Bake pastry shells according to package directions.

2. Stir together first 6 ingredients. Spoon mixture into pastry shells. Spoon ½ tsp. mango chutney over each tart; sprinkle with desired toppings.

Mini Crab Cakes with Garlic-Chive Sauce

Hands-on Time: 10 min.
Total Time: 26 min.
Makes: 8 servings

This crowd-pleaser can also serve 4 as a main dish.

- 1 (8-oz.) package fresh lump crabmeat, drained
- 3 whole grain white bread slices
- ⅓ cup reduced-fat mayonnaise
- 3 green onions, thinly sliced
- 1 tsp. Old Bay seasoning
- 1 tsp. Worcestershire sauce
- 2 large eggs, lightly beaten

Salt to taste
Garlic-Chive Sauce
Garnish: lemon slices

1. Pick crabmeat, removing any bits of shell. Pulse bread slices in a blender or food processor 5 times or until finely crumbled. (Yield should be about 1½ cups.)
2. Stir together mayonnaise and next 4 ingredients in a large bowl. Gently stir in breadcrumbs and crabmeat. Shape mixture into 16 (2-inch) cakes (about 2 Tbsp. each).
3. Cook cakes, in batches, on a hot, large griddle or nonstick skillet coated with cooking spray over medium-low heat 4 minutes on each side or until golden brown. Season with salt to taste. (Keep cakes warm in a 200° oven for up to 30 minutes.) Serve with Garlic-Chive Sauce. Garnish, if desired.

kitchen secret:

You may also use jumbo lump crabmeat to avoid having to pick through the meat to find shells.

Mini Crab Cakes with Garlic-Chive Sauce

Garlic-Chive Sauce

Hands-on Time: 10 min.
Total Time: 40 min.
Makes: 1 cup

- ¾ cup reduced-fat sour cream*
- 1 garlic clove, minced
- 1 Tbsp. chopped fresh chives
- ¾ tsp. lemon zest
- 1½ Tbsp. fresh lemon juice
- ¼ tsp. salt
- ⅛ tsp. pepper

1. Stir together all ingredients in a small bowl. Cover and chill 30 minutes before serving.

*Reduced-fat mayonnaise may be substituted.

Stuffed Mushrooms with Pecans

Hands-on Time: 28 min.
Total Time: 53 min.
Makes: 8 appetizer servings

Use mushrooms of equal size for even cooking.

2	medium leeks
1	(16-oz.) package fresh mushrooms (about 24 medium-size mushrooms)
1	tsp. salt, divided
2	shallots, minced
2	garlic cloves, minced
2	Tbsp. olive oil
½	cup grated Parmesan cheese
¼	cup fine, dry breadcrumbs
¼	cup pecans, chopped
2	Tbsp. chopped fresh basil

Garnish: fresh basil sprigs

1. Preheat oven to 350°. Remove and discard root ends and dark green tops of leeks. Thinly slice leeks, and rinse thoroughly under cold running water to remove grit and sand.

2. Wipe mushrooms with a damp paper towel. Remove and discard stems. Place mushrooms, upside down, on a wire rack in an aluminum foil-lined jelly-roll pan. Sprinkle with ½ tsp. salt; invert mushrooms.

3. Bake at 350° for 15 minutes.

4. Sauté leeks, shallots, and garlic in hot oil in a large skillet over medium heat 3 to 5 minutes or until tender. Transfer mixture to a large bowl. Stir in ¼ cup Parmesan cheese, next 3 ingredients, and remaining ½ tsp. salt until well combined. Spoon 1 heaping teaspoonful leek mixture into each mushroom cap. Sprinkle with remaining ¼ cup Parmesan cheese. Bake at 350° for 10 minutes or until golden. Garnish, if desired.

fake it!

Out of dry breadcrumbs? You can still achieve a crisp texture by substituting finely crushed crackers instead.

Stuffed Mushrooms with Pecans

Dixie Caviar Cups

Dixie Caviar Cups

Hands-on Time: 15 min.
Total Time: 24 hr., 15 min.
Makes: 15 appetizer servings

- 1 (15.8-oz.) can black-eyed peas, drained and rinsed
- 1 cup frozen whole kernel corn
- 1 medium-size plum tomato, seeded and finely chopped
- ½ medium-size green bell pepper, finely chopped
- ½ small sweet onion, finely chopped
- 2 green onions, sliced
- 1 jalapeño pepper, seeded and minced
- 1 garlic clove, minced
- ½ cup Italian dressing
- 2 Tbsp. chopped fresh cilantro
- 30 Belgian endive leaves (about 3 bunches)
- ½ cup sour cream

1. Combine first 9 ingredients in a large zip-top plastic freezer bag. Seal bag, and chill 24 hours; drain.
2. Spoon mixture into a bowl; stir in cilantro. Spoon about 1 rounded Tbsp. mixture into each endive leaf. Dollop with sour cream.

kitchen secret:

If you'd like, substitute 2¼ tsp. finely chopped pickled jalapeño peppers for the fresh jalapeño.

Macaroni-and-Pimiento Cheese Bites

Hands-on Time: 52 min.
Total Time: 8 hr., 52 min.
Makes: 5$^1/_2$ dozen

- 1 (8-oz.) package elbow macaroni
- 3 Tbsp. butter
- ¼ cup all-purpose flour
- 2 cups milk
- 1 tsp. salt
- ¼ tsp. ground red pepper
- ⅛ tsp. garlic powder
- 1 (8-oz.) block sharp Cheddar cheese, shredded
- 1 (4-oz.) jar diced pimiento, drained
- ¾ cup fine, dry breadcrumbs
- ¾ cup freshly grated Parmesan cheese
- 2 large eggs, lightly beaten
- ½ cup milk
- Vegetable oil

1. Prepare pasta according to package directions.
2. Meanwhile, melt butter in a large skillet over medium heat. Gradually whisk in flour until smooth; cook, whisking constantly, 1 minute. Gradually whisk in 2 cups milk and next 3 ingredients. Cook mixture, whisking constantly, 3 to 5 minutes or until thickened. Stir in Cheddar cheese and pimiento until melted and smooth. Remove from heat, and stir in pasta.
3. Line a 13- x 9-inch pan with plastic wrap, allowing several inches to extend over edges of pan. Pour mixture into prepared pan. Cool slightly; cover and chill 8 hours. Remove macaroni mixture from pan, and cut into 1-inch squares.
4. Stir together breadcrumbs and Parmesan cheese in a shallow dish or pie plate. Whisk together eggs and $^1/_2$ cup milk in another shallow dish or pie plate; dip macaroni bites in egg mixture, and dredge in breadcrumb mixture.
5. Pour oil to a depth of 1 inch into a large skillet; heat to 350°. Fry bites, in batches, 2 minutes on each side or until golden.

Golden Baked Macaroni and Pimiento Cheese:
Prepare recipe as directed through Step 2. Pour macaroni mixture into a lightly greased 13- x 9-inch baking dish; do not chill. Omit eggs and $^1/_2$ cup milk. Stir together breadcrumbs and Parmesan cheese; sprinkle over mixture. Omit oil. Bake at 350° for 15 to 20 minutes or until golden and bubbly.

Macaroni-and-Pimiento Cheese Bites

Sweet Potato Squares with Lemon-Garlic Mayonnaise

Hands-on Time: 38 min.
Total Time: 58 min., including mayonnaise
Makes: 8 appetizer servings

Serve Sweet Potato Squares warm or at room temperature. Prepare the Lemon-Garlic Mayonnaise first if you choose to serve the Sweet Potato Squares warm.

2	lb. sweet potatoes, peeled and cut into 32 (1-inch) cubes
2	Tbsp. olive oil
½	tsp. pepper
¼	tsp. salt
½	lb. spicy smoked sausage, cut into 32 (½-inch) pieces
32	wooden picks
	Lemon-Garlic Mayonnaise
	Garnish: fresh thyme sprigs

1. Preheat oven to 450°. Place sweet potato cubes on a lightly greased 15- x 10-inch jelly-roll pan. Drizzle potatoes with 2 Tbsp. oil, and sprinkle with pepper and salt. Toss to coat.
2. Bake at 450° for 15 to 20 minutes, turning cubes twice.

3. Cook sausage in a large nonstick skillet over medium-high heat 3 to 4 minutes on each side or until browned. Drain on paper towels.
4. Place 1 sausage slice on top of 1 sweet potato cube; secure with a wooden pick. Repeat with remaining sausage slices and potato cubes. Serve with Lemon-Garlic Mayonnaise. Garnish, if desired.

Lemon-Garlic Mayonnaise

Hands-on Time: 10 min.
Total Time: 10 min.
Makes: about 1¼ cups

1	cup mayonnaise
2	Tbsp. chopped fresh flat-leaf parsley
2	tsp. minced garlic
1	tsp. lemon zest
2	Tbsp. fresh lemon juice
½	tsp. pepper
¼	tsp. salt

1. Stir together all ingredients. Store in an airtight container in the refrigerator up to 7 days.

Southern foodlore

In the South, "sweet potatoes" and "yams" are often used synonymously. It is believed that Louisiana sweet potato growers began calling their potatoes "yams" in order to distinguish them from what they believed were far inferior "Yankee" sweet potatoes. Yams are in fact a different species than sweet potatoes, but "canned yams" sold in the U.S., are actually a variety of sweet potato that is grown in the South.

Sweet Potato Squares with Lemon-Garlic Mayonnaise

BREAKFAST & BRUNCH

Everyone knows that breakfast is the most important meal of the day so rise and shine to these hearty favorites.

Cinnamon-Pecan Rolls

Hands-on Time: 20 min.
Total Time: 1 hr., 20 min.
Makes: 12 rolls

- 1 cup chopped pecans
- 1 (16-oz.) package hot roll mix
- ½ cup butter, softened
- 1 cup firmly packed light brown sugar
- 2 tsp. ground cinnamon
- 1 cup powdered sugar
- 2 Tbsp. milk
- 1 tsp. vanilla extract

1. Preheat oven to 350°. Bake pecans in a single layer in a shallow pan 5 to 7 minutes or until toasted and fragrant, stirring halfway through.

2. Prepare hot roll dough according to package directions; let dough stand 5 minutes. Roll dough into a 15- x 10-inch rectangle; spread with softened butter. Stir together brown sugar and cinnamon; sprinkle over butter. Sprinkle pecans over brown sugar mixture. Roll up tightly, starting at one long side; cut into 12 slices. Place rolls, cut sides down, in a lightly greased 12-inch cast-iron skillet or 13- x 9-inch pan. Cover loosely with plastic wrap and a cloth towel; let rise in a warm place (85°), free from drafts, 30 minutes or until doubled in bulk.

Cinnamon-Pecan Rolls

3. Preheat oven to 375°. Uncover rolls, and bake for 20 to 25 minutes or until center rolls are golden brown and done. Let cool in pan on a wire rack 10 minutes. Stir together powdered sugar, milk, and vanilla; drizzle over rolls.

Buttermilk-Pear Pancakes

Hands-on Time: 26 min.
Total Time: 46 min., including topping
Makes: about 14 pancakes

- 2 cups reduced-fat, all-purpose baking mix
- 2 cups nonfat buttermilk
- 1 large egg
- Fresh Pear-Cinnamon Topping

1. Whisk together baking mix, buttermilk, and egg in a bowl. Pour ¼ cup batter for each pancake onto a hot, lightly greased griddle or large nonstick skillet. Cook pancakes 3 to 4 minutes or until tops are covered with bubbles and edges look dry and cooked; turn and cook other side. Spoon on Fresh Pear-Cinnamon Topping, and serve immediately.

Fresh Pear-Cinnamon Topping

Hands-on Time: 20 min.
Total Time: 20 min.
Makes: about 1¼ cups

- 4 pears, peeled, cored, and sliced
- 1 Tbsp. fresh lemon juice
- 1 Tbsp. honey
- ¼ tsp. ground cinnamon
- ½ Tbsp. butter

1. Toss pears with lemon juice, honey, and cinnamon in a medium bowl. Melt butter in a nonstick skillet over medium-high heat; sauté mixture, stirring occasionally, 8 to 10 minutes or until slightly thickened.

Pancakes with Buttered Honey Syrup

Hands-on Time: 34 min.
Total Time: 39 min., including syrup
Makes: about 16 (4-inch) pancakes

1¾ cups all-purpose flour
 2 tsp. sugar
1½ tsp. baking powder
 1 tsp. baking soda
 1 tsp. salt
 2 cups buttermilk
 2 large eggs
 ¼ cup melted butter
 Garnishes: apricot preserves, fresh blueberries
 Buttered Honey Syrup

1. Combine flour and next 4 ingredients in a large bowl. Whisk together buttermilk and eggs. Gradually stir buttermilk mixture into flour mixture. Gently stir in butter. (Batter will be lumpy.)

2. Pour about ¼ cup batter for each pancake onto a hot buttered griddle or large nonstick skillet. Cook pancakes 3 to 4 minutes or until tops are covered with bubbles and edges look dry and cooked. Turn and cook 3 to 4 minutes or until golden brown. Place pancakes in a single layer on a baking sheet, and keep warm in a 200° oven up to 30 minutes. Garnish, if desired, and serve with Buttered Honey Syrup.

Buttered Honey Syrup

Hands-on Time: 5 min.
Total Time: 5 min.
Makes: about ¾ cup

 ⅓ cup butter
 ½ cup honey

1. Melt butter in a small saucepan over medium-low heat. Stir in honey, and cook 1 minute or until warm.

Note: Buttered Honey Syrup cannot be made ahead. The heated honey will crystallize when cooled and will not melt if reheated.

Pancakes with Buttered Honey Syrup

Lemon-Poppy Seed Belgian Waffles with Blackberry Maple Syrup

Hands-on Time: 25 min.
Total Time: 30 min., including syrup
Makes: 4 servings

 2 cups all-purpose baking mix
 1 to 2 Tbsp. poppy seeds
 1 Tbsp. lemon zest
1¼ cups cold club soda
 1 large egg, lightly beaten
 ¼ cup melted butter
 Blackberry Maple Syrup
 Crème fraîche (optional)

1. Stir together baking mix, poppy seeds, and lemon zest. Whisk together club soda, egg, and butter in a small bowl; gently whisk egg mixture into poppy seed mixture. (Mixture will be lumpy.) Let stand 3 minutes.

2. Cook batter in a preheated, oiled Belgian-style waffle iron until golden (about ³/₄ to 1 cup batter each). Serve with Blackberry Maple Syrup and, if desired, crème fraîche.

kitchen secret:

If you don't have a Belgian-style waffle iron, use ½ cup batter for each waffle in a traditional waffle iron.

Blackberry Maple Syrup

Hands-on Time: 5 min.
Total Time: 5 min.
Makes: 2 cups

- ½ cup maple syrup
- 1 (12-oz.) package frozen blackberries, thawed
- 1 tsp. lemon zest
- 2 tsp. lemon juice

1. Combine all ingredients in a medium bowl.

Lemon-Poppy Seed Pancakes: Prepare batter as directed. Pour about ¼ cup batter for each pancake onto a hot, lightly greased griddle or large nonstick skillet. Cook pancakes 3 to 4 minutes or until tops are covered with bubbles and edges look dry and cooked; turn and cook other side.

Guiltless French Toast

Hands-on Time: 16 min.
Total Time: 16 min.
Makes: 4 servings

A little dab of butter, maple syrup, and fresh fruit are the finishing touches to Guiltless French Toast.

- 8 egg whites
- ¼ cup fresh orange juice
- 1 Tbsp. vanilla extract
- 1 tsp. ground cinnamon
- 4 whole grain bakery bread slices
- 1 Tbsp. butter
- ¼ cup maple syrup
- Fresh blueberries and kiwifruit slices

1. Whisk together first 4 ingredients in a shallow dish. Dip bread slices in egg mixture, coating both sides evenly.

2. Melt butter on a griddle or in a large nonstick skillet over medium heat. Place bread slices on hot griddle, and pour remaining egg mixture over bread slices. Cook 3 to 4 minutes on each side or until golden. Drizzle with maple syrup, and top with fruit.

Guiltless French Toast

One-Dish Blackberry French Toast

Hands-on Time: 21 min.
Total Time: 8 hr., 51 min.
Makes: 8 to 10 servings

Make-ahead baked French toast makes getting breakfast on the table easy.

- 1 cup blackberry jam
- 1 (12-oz.) French bread loaf, cut into 1½-inch cubes
- 1 (8-oz.) package ⅓-less-fat cream cheese, cut into 1-inch cubes
- 4 large eggs
- 2 cups half-and-half
- 1 tsp. ground cinnamon
- 1 tsp. vanilla extract
- ½ cup firmly packed light brown sugar

Toppings: maple syrup, whipped cream

1. Cook jam in a saucepan over medium heat 1 to 2 minutes or until melted and smooth, stirring once.
2. Place half of bread cubes in bottom of a lightly greased 13- x 9-inch baking dish. Top with cream cheese cubes, and drizzle with melted jam. Top with remaining bread cubes.
3. Whisk together eggs and next 3 ingredients. Pour over bread mixture. Sprinkle with brown sugar. Cover tightly, and chill 8 to 24 hours.
4. Preheat oven to 325°. Bake, covered, 20 minutes. Uncover and bake 10 to 15 minutes or until bread is golden brown and mixture is set. Serve with desired toppings.

One-Dish Blackberry French Toast

Streusel Coffee Cake

Hands-on Time: 20 min.
Total Time: 1 hr., 25 min., including topping
Makes: 8 to 10 servings

To make one day ahead, just bake, cool completely, and wrap in aluminum foil.

- ½ cup butter, softened
- 1 (8-oz.) package cream cheese, softened
- 1¼ cups sugar
- 2 large eggs
- 2 cups all-purpose flour
- 2 tsp. baking powder
- ½ tsp. baking soda
- ½ tsp. salt
- ½ cup milk
- 1 tsp. vanilla extract
- ½ tsp. almond extract
  Crumb Topping

1. Preheat oven to 350°. Beat butter and cream cheese at medium speed with an electric mixer until creamy. Gradually add sugar, beating at medium speed until light and fluffy. Add eggs, one at a time, beating just until yellow disappears.
2. Sift together flour and next 3 ingredients; add to butter mixture alternately with milk, beginning and ending with flour mixture. Beat at low speed just until blended after each addition. Stir in vanilla and almond extracts. Pour batter into a greased 13- x 9-inch pan; sprinkle with Crumb Topping.
3. Bake at 350° for 35 to 40 minutes or until a wooden pick inserted in center comes out clean. Let cool 20 minutes before serving.

Streusel Coffee Cake

Crumb Topping

Hands-on Time: 10 min.
Total Time: 10 min.
Makes: about 1½ cups

- ½ cup all-purpose flour
- ½ cup sugar
- ½ cup coarsely chopped pecans
- ¼ cup butter, softened

1. Stir together flour, sugar, and pecans in a bowl. Cut in butter with a pastry blender or fork until mixture resembles small peas.

Cranberry-Orange Tea Bread Muffins

Cranberry-Orange Tea Bread Muffins

Hands-on Time: 25 min.
Total Time: 1 hr., including glaze
Makes: 2 dozen

½	cup chopped pecans
2	cups all-purpose flour
1½	tsp. baking powder
1	tsp. salt
½	(12-oz.) package fresh cranberries (about 2 cups)
1	cup sugar
¼	cup butter, softened
1	large egg, lightly beaten
¾	cup orange juice
24	aluminum foil miniature baking cups

Orange-Cream Cheese Glaze
Garnish: Candied Kumquat Slices

1. Preheat oven to 350°. Bake pecans in a single layer in a shallow pan 8 to 10 minutes or until toasted and fragrant, stirring occasionally.
2. Whisk together flour, baking powder, and salt.
3. Combine cranberries and sugar in a food processor; pulse 3 to 4 times or just until chopped.
4. Beat butter at medium speed with an electric mixer until creamy. Add egg, beating until well blended. Gradually add flour mixture alternately with orange juice, beginning and ending with flour mixture. Beat at low speed until blended after each addition. Stir in cranberry mixture and pecans. Place baking cups in 1 (24-cup) miniature muffin pan. Coat cups with cooking spray. Spoon batter into cups, filling full.
5. Bake at 350° for 25 minutes or until a wooden pick inserted in center comes out clean. Remove from pans to a wire rack; spoon Orange-Cream Cheese Glaze over warm muffins. Garnish with Candied Kumquat Slices, if desired.

Orange-Cream Cheese Glaze

Hands-on Time: 10 min.
Total Time: 10 min.
Makes: about 1 cup

- 1 (3-oz.) package cream cheese, softened
- 1 Tbsp. orange juice
- ¼ tsp. vanilla extract
- 1½ cups sifted powdered sugar

1. Beat cream cheese at medium speed with an electric mixer until creamy. Add orange juice and vanilla; beat until smooth. Gradually add powdered sugar, beating until smooth.

Candied Kumquat Slices

Hands-on Time: 15 min.
Total Time: 24 hr., 25 min.
Makes: about 3½ dozen

You can strain the syrup left after making kumquat slices to flavor iced tea or lemonade.

- 8 kumquats
- ¾ cup sugar, divided

1. Cut kumquats into ⅛-inch-thick slices. Stir together ½ cup sugar and ½ cup water in a small heavy saucepan. Bring to a boil over medium heat.
2. Reduce heat to medium-low, and stir in kumquat slices; simmer 10 minutes. Remove from heat; remove kumquat slices, one at a time, shaking off excess sugar-water mixture. Place kumquats in a bowl with remaining ¼ cup sugar; toss to coat. Transfer kumquats to wax paper. Cover loosely with plastic wrap, and let stand 24 hours.

Praline Pull-Apart Bread

Hands-on Time: 15 min.
Total Time: 9 hr., 25 min.
Makes: 12 servings

Don't skip the quick step of whipping the cream before stirring in the brown sugar—that's the secret to the smooth texture of the caramel-flavored sauce.

- 1 cup granulated sugar
- 4 tsp. ground cinnamon, divided
- 1 (2-lb.) package frozen bread roll dough
- ½ cup melted butter
- 1 cup chopped pecans
- ¾ cup whipping cream
- ¾ cup firmly packed light brown sugar

1. Stir together granulated sugar and 3 tsp. cinnamon. Coat each roll in butter; dredge rolls in sugar mixture. Arrange in a lightly greased 10-inch tube pan; sprinkle with pecans. Cover and chill 8 to 18 hours.
2. Preheat oven to 325°. Beat whipping cream at high speed with an electric mixer until soft peaks form; stir in brown sugar and remaining 1 tsp. cinnamon. Pour mixture over dough.
3. Place pan on an aluminum foil-lined baking sheet.
4. Bake at 325° for 1 hour or until golden brown. Cool on a wire rack 10 minutes; invert onto a serving plate, and drizzle with any remaining glaze in pan.

> ### kitchen secret:
>
> Use a tube pan rather than a Bundt pan for the Praline Pull-Apart Bread. (Tube pans have straight, high sides; Bundt pans are shallower and fluted.) Both may measure 10 inches in diameter, but each holds a different amount of batter.

Peach-Oat Muffins

Hands-on Time: 15 min.
Total Time: 35 min.
Makes: about 2 dozen

These muffins are loaded with many components of a well-rounded breakfast: fiber and whole grains from oats and bran cereal, good fats from pecans and canola oil, dairy from nonfat buttermilk, and fruit from dried peaches.

- ¼ cup chopped pecans
- 1¾ cups uncooked regular oats
- 1 cup sugar
- ½ cup canola oil
- 2 large eggs
- 1¼ cups all-purpose flour
- 1 tsp. baking soda
- ½ tsp. salt
- 1 cup peach nectar
- 1 cup nonfat buttermilk
- 5 cups wheat bran cereal
- ⅓ cup chopped dried peaches

Paper baking cups

1. Preheat oven to 375°. Heat pecans in a small nonstick skillet over medium-low heat, stirring often, 2 to 4 minutes or until toasted.

2. Process oats in a food processor or blender, about 45 seconds or until finely ground.

3. Beat sugar and oil at medium speed with an electric mixer 1 minute. Add eggs, one at a time, beating until blended after each addition. (Mixture will be light yellow.)

4. Combine ground oats, flour, baking soda, and salt in a small bowl. Stir together peach nectar and buttermilk in a small bowl. Add oat mixture to sugar mixture alternately with peach mixture, beginning and ending with oat mixture. Stir until blended after each addition. Gently stir in bran cereal, dried peaches, and toasted pecans. Place paper baking cups in 2 (12-cup) muffin pans, and coat with cooking spray. Spoon batter into cups, filling three-fourths full.

5. Bake at 375° for 20 minutes or until golden brown.

Note: Muffins may be frozen for up to 1 month. Heat in toaster oven, or microwave at HIGH 30 seconds.

Peach-Oat Muffins

Buttermilk Breakfast Cake

Buttermilk Breakfast Cake

Hands-on Time: 20 min.
Total Time: 1 hr., 40 min., including glaze
Makes: 10 to 12 servings

Buttermilk replaces sour cream in our twist on this not-too-sweet Bundt cake.

    1 (18.25-oz.) package white cake mix
    1 cup buttermilk
   ½ cup melted butter
    5 large eggs
    3 Tbsp. light brown sugar
    2 tsp. ground cinnamon
Shortening
    1 Tbsp. granulated sugar
Buttermilk-Vanilla Glaze

1. Preheat oven to 350°. Beat first 3 ingredients at medium speed with an electric mixer 1½ minutes or until thoroughly blended; add eggs, one at a time, beating well after each addition.
2. Stir together brown sugar and cinnamon in a small bowl.

3. Grease a 12-cup Bundt pan with shortening; sprinkle with 1 Tbsp. granulated sugar.
4. Spoon one-third of batter into prepared pan; sprinkle brown sugar mixture evenly over batter. Top with remaining batter.
5. Bake at 350° for 45 minutes or until a long wooden pick inserted in center of cake comes out clean. Cool cake in pan on a wire rack 15 minutes; remove from pan to wire rack, and cool 20 minutes. Drizzle Buttermilk-Vanilla Glaze over slightly warm cake.

Buttermilk-Vanilla Glaze

Hands-on Time: 5 min.
Total Time: 5 min.
Makes: about ⅓ cup

    1 cup powdered sugar
    1 Tbsp. melted butter
    1 tsp. vanilla extract
    1 to 2 Tbsp. buttermilk

1. Combine first 3 ingredients and 1 Tbsp. buttermilk until smooth, adding additional 1 Tbsp. buttermilk, if necessary, for desired consistency.

Sausage-and-Cheese Frittata

Hands-on Time: 25 min.
Total Time: 48 min.
Makes: 6 servings

For an easy side, toss together fresh spinach leaves, sliced red onions, and toasted almonds with your favorite bottled vinaigrette.

- 1 (12-oz.) package reduced-fat ground pork sausage
- 8 large eggs
- ⅓ cup milk
- ½ tsp. pepper
- ¼ tsp. salt
- 1 Tbsp. butter
- 1 cup (4 oz.) shredded 2% reduced-fat Cheddar cheese

1. Preheat oven to 350°. Brown sausage in a 10-inch ovenproof nonstick skillet over medium-high heat 10 minutes or until meat crumbles and is no longer pink; drain and transfer to a bowl. Wipe skillet clean.
2. Whisk together eggs and next 3 ingredients until well blended.
3. Melt butter in skillet over medium heat; remove from heat, and pour half of egg mixture into skillet. Sprinkle with cooked sausage and cheese. Top with remaining egg mixture.
4. Bake at 350° for 23 to 25 minutes or until set.

Angela's Vegetable Frittata

Hands-on Time: 36 min.
Total Time: 46 min.
Makes: 6 to 8 servings

- 2 large leeks
- 2 Tbsp. olive oil
- 1 cup diced, cooked potato
- 1 lb. summer squash, sliced
- 2 Tbsp. chopped fresh parsley
- ½ tsp. chopped fresh thyme
- ½ tsp. freshly ground pepper
- ¾ tsp. salt, divided
- 8 large eggs
- ½ cup milk
- ¾ cup (3 oz.) shredded Parmesan cheese

1. Preheat oven to 450°. Remove and discard root ends and dark green tops of leeks. Cut leeks in half lengthwise, and rinse thoroughly under cold running water to remove grit and sand. Thinly slice leeks.
2. Sauté leeks in 1 Tbsp. hot oil in a 10-inch ovenproof skillet over medium-high heat 4 to 5 minutes or until tender. Remove from skillet. Sauté potato in remaining 1 Tbsp. oil in skillet 3 to 4 minutes or until golden. Add squash, and sauté 10 minutes. Stir in leeks, parsley, thyme, pepper, and ½ tsp. salt until blended.
3. Process eggs, milk, ½ cup Parmesan cheese, ¼ cup water, and remaining ¼ tsp. salt in a blender until blended; pour over leek mixture in skillet. Cook over medium heat, without stirring, 2 minutes or until edges of frittata are set. (Edges should appear firm when pan is gently shaken; the top layer should appear wet.) Sprinkle with remaining ¼ cup cheese.
4. Bake at 450° for 10 to 12 minutes or until center is set.

Sausage-and-Cheese Frittata

Spinach-and-Cheese Omelet

Hands-on Time: 14 min.
Total Time: 14 min.
Makes: 1 serving

    2   large eggs
    1   Tbsp. butter
    1   cup coarsely chopped spinach
  ⅓   cup chopped tomatoes
  ⅛   tsp. salt
  ⅓   cup (1½ oz.) shredded Swiss cheese
  ⅛   tsp. pepper

1. Process eggs and 2 Tbsp. water in a blender until blended. Melt butter in an 8-inch nonstick skillet over medium heat; add spinach and tomatoes, and sauté 1 minute or until spinach is wilted. Add salt and egg mixture to skillet.

2. As egg mixture starts to cook, gently lift edges of omelet with a spatula, and tilt pan so that uncooked egg mixture flows underneath, cooking until almost set (about 1 minute). Cover skillet, and cook 1 minute.

3. Sprinkle omelet with cheese and pepper. Fold omelet in half, allowing cheese to melt. Slide cooked omelet onto a serving plate, and season with salt to taste. Serve with buttered toast and fresh fruit.

Spinach-and-Cheese Omelet

Tomato-Leek Pie

Hands-on Time: 15 min.
Total Time: 1 hr., 33 min.
Makes: 6 servings

½ (14.1-oz.) package refrigerated piecrusts
2 medium-size red tomatoes
2 medium-size yellow tomatoes
1 green tomato
½ tsp. kosher salt
1 medium leek
2 Tbsp. butter
¼ tsp. pepper
½ cup grated Parmesan cheese
½ cup reduced-fat mayonnaise
1 large egg, lightly beaten
Garnish: fresh flat-leaf parsley sprigs

1. Preheat oven to 450°. Fit piecrust into a 9-inch pie plate according to package directions; fold edges under, and crimp.
2. Bake at 450° for 8 to 10 minutes or until golden brown. Remove from oven, and let cool 5 minutes. Reduce oven temperature to 375°.
3. Cut tomatoes into ¼-inch slices. Place on a paper towel-lined wire rack. Sprinkle tomatoes with kosher salt. Let stand 20 minutes. Pat dry with paper towels.
4. Remove and discard root end and dark green top of leek. Cut in half lengthwise, and rinse thoroughly under cold running water to remove grit and sand. Thinly slice leek.
5. Melt butter in a large skillet over medium heat; add leek, and sauté 3 to 5 minutes or until tender.
6. Layer leek on bottom of prepared crust. Top with tomato slices, and sprinkle with pepper. Stir together cheese, mayonnaise, and egg in a medium bowl until blended. Spread cheese mixture over top of tomatoes.
7. Bake at 375° for 30 minutes or until thoroughly heated. Let stand 10 minutes. Garnish, if desired.

fix it!

Problem: Your tomato pie is watery.

Solution: Salting the tomatoes before baking them removes any excess liquid and prevents them from watering out.

Tomato-Leek Pie

Breakfast Pizza Cups

Hands-on Time: 30 min.
Total Time: 50 min.
Makes: 12 servings

To make this recipe more heart healthy, we decreased the saturated fat and cholesterol by using egg substitute, lean ground turkey sausage, reduced-fat Cheddar cheese, and fat-free milk.

- ½ lb. lean ground turkey sausage
- 2 (13.8-oz.) cans refrigerated pizza crust dough
- ½ cup frozen hash browns, thawed
- ½ cup (2 oz.) shredded 2% reduced-fat sharp Cheddar cheese
- 1¼ cups egg substitute
- ½ cup fat-free milk
- ⅛ tsp. pepper
- 2 Tbsp. grated Parmesan cheese
- 1½ cups pizza sauce

1. Cook sausage in a large skillet over medium-high heat 10 minutes or until sausage crumbles and is no longer pink. Drain well on paper towels; set aside.
2. Roll or pat 1 can pizza dough into a 15- x 10-inch rectangle on a lightly floured surface; cut into 6 (5-inch) squares. Press squares into a lightly greased (12-cup) muffin pan, skipping every other muffin cup. Repeat procedure with remaining can of pizza dough.
3. Spoon sausage evenly into crusts; sprinkle evenly with hash browns and Cheddar cheese.
4. Stir together egg substitute and next 2 ingredients; pour evenly into pizza cups, and sprinkle with grated Parmesan cheese.
5. Bake at 375° for 18 to 20 minutes or until golden. Serve with pizza sauce.

Cheddar Cheese Grits Casserole

Hands-on Time: 15 min.
Total Time: 55 min.
Makes: 6 servings

- 4 cups milk
- 1 cup uncooked quick-cooking grits
- ¼ cup butter
- 1 large egg, lightly beaten
- 2 cups (8 oz.) shredded sharp Cheddar cheese
- 1 tsp. salt
- ½ tsp. pepper
- ¼ cup grated Parmesan cheese

1. Preheat oven to 350°. Bring milk just to a boil in a large saucepan over medium-high heat; gradually whisk in grits and butter. Reduce heat, and simmer, whisking constantly, 5 to 7 minutes or until grits are done. Remove from heat.
2. Stir in egg and next 3 ingredients. Pour into a lightly greased 11- x 7-inch baking dish. Sprinkle with grated Parmesan cheese.
3. Bake, covered, at 350° for 35 to 40 minutes or until mixture is set. Serve immediately.

Cheddar Cheese Grits Casserole

Sunny Skillet Breakfast

Hands-on Time: 21 min.
Total Time: 40 min.
Makes: 6 servings

Soaking the shredded potatoes in cold water keeps them from turning gray before cooking. It also rinses off some of the starch. Drain and pat them dry so that they won't stick to the cast-iron skillet.

3   (8-oz.) baking potatoes, peeled and
     shredded (about 3 cups firmly packed)*
1   Tbsp. butter
2   Tbsp. vegetable oil
1   small red bell pepper, diced
1   medium onion, diced
1   garlic clove, pressed
¾   tsp. salt, divided
6   large eggs
¼   tsp. pepper

1. Preheat oven to 350°. Place shredded potatoes in a large bowl; add cold water to cover. Let stand 5 minutes; drain and pat dry.
2. Melt butter with oil in a 10-inch cast-iron skillet over medium heat. Add bell pepper and onion, and sauté 3 to 5 minutes or until tender. Add garlic; sauté 1 minute. Stir in shredded potatoes and ½ tsp. salt; cook, stirring often, 10 minutes or until potatoes are golden and tender.
3. Remove from heat. Make 6 indentations in potato mixture, using back of a spoon. Break 1 egg into each indentation. Sprinkle eggs with pepper and remaining ¼ tsp salt.
4. Bake at 350° for 12 to 14 minutes or until eggs are set. Serve immediately.

*3 cups firmly packed thawed frozen shredded potatoes may be substituted, omitting Step 1.

Veggie Confetti Frittata: Prepare recipe as directed through Step 2, sautéing ½ (8-oz.) package sliced fresh mushrooms with bell peppers and onion. Remove from heat, and stir in ¼ cup sliced ripe black olives, drained, and ¼ cup thinly sliced sun-dried tomatoes in oil, drained. Whisk together eggs, pepper, and remaining ¼ tsp. salt; whisk in ½ cup (2 oz.) shredded Swiss cheese. Pour egg mixture over potato mixture in skillet. Bake at 350° for 9 to 10 minutes or until set. Cut into wedges, and serve immediately.

Sunny Skillet Breakfast

Brie-and-Veggie Breakfast Strata

Hands-on Time: 42 min.
Total Time: 9 hr., 32 min.
Makes: 8 to 10 servings

Two cups (8 oz.) shredded Swiss cheese may be substituted for the Brie, if you'd like.

- 1 large sweet onion, halved and thinly sliced
- 1 large red bell pepper, diced
- 1 large Yukon gold potato, peeled and diced
- 2 Tbsp. olive oil
- 1 (8-oz.) Brie round
- 1 (12-oz.) package sourdough bread loaf, cubed
- 1 cup (4 oz.) shredded Parmesan cheese
- 8 large eggs
- 3 cups milk
- 2 Tbsp. Dijon mustard
- 1 tsp. seasoned salt
- 1 tsp. pepper

1. Preheat oven to 350°. Sauté first 3 ingredients in hot oil 10 to 12 minutes or just until vegetables are tender and onion slices begin to turn golden.
2. Trim and discard rind from Brie. Cut cheese into $^{1}/_{2}$-inch cubes.
3. Layer a lightly greased 13- x 9-inch baking dish with half each of bread cubes, onion mixture, Brie cubes, and Parmesan cheese.
4. Whisk together eggs and next 4 ingredients; pour half of egg mixture evenly over cheeses. Repeat layers once. Cover and chill at least 8 hours or up to 24 hours.
5. Bake at 350° for 45 to 50 minutes or until lightly browned on top and set in center.

Brie-and-Veggie Breakfast Strata

kitchen secrets:

- Refrigerate eggs in their original carton at a temperature below 40°.
- Use raw eggs within 4 weeks and leftover yolks and whites within 4 days.
- Never leave eggs at room temperature for more than an hour.
- ¼ cup egg substitute = 1 large egg

BREADS

From yeast rolls to quick breads, these fresh-from-the-oven baked goods will be a welcome addition to any meal.

Easy Garlic Rolls

Hands-on Time: 12 min.
Total Time: 20 min.
Makes: 4 to 6 servings

Who says you can't have fresh-tasting bread in 20 minutes flat? Wow the whole family with "Mom's secret recipe" tonight.

    4 artisan rolls
    ½ cup butter
    2 garlic cloves, minced
    ¼ to ½ tsp. dried Italian seasoning

1. Preheat oven to 400°. Cut rolls in half horizontally. Melt butter in a small saucepan over medium-low heat. Add minced garlic and dried Italian seasoning, and cook, stirring constantly, 1 to 2 minutes or until fragrant. Brush butter mixture on cut sides of bread. Place bread, cut sides up, on a lightly greased baking sheet.
2. Bake at 400° for 7 to 8 minutes or until lightly toasted.

Double Whammy Yeast Rolls

Hands-on Time: 30 min.
Total Time: 2 hr., 53 min.
Makes: 1 dozen

The double whammy comes from using beer and potato flakes in the recipe.

    ⅔ cup sugar, divided
    1 cup milk
    ⅓ cup butter
    ¼ cup instant potato flakes
    1¼ tsp. salt
    2 (¼-oz.) envelopes active dry yeast
    ¼ cup beer, at room temperature
    1 large egg, lightly beaten
    4½ cups bread flour, divided
    Butter (optional)

1. Remove and reserve 1 Tbsp. sugar. Cook milk, next 3 ingredients, and remaining sugar in a medium saucepan over medium-low heat, stirring constantly, until butter melts. Cool to 110°.
2. Stir together yeast, beer, and reserved 1 Tbsp. sugar in a 2-cup liquid measuring cup; let stand 5 minutes.
3. Combine milk mixture and yeast mixture in a large bowl; stir in egg. Gradually stir in 4 cups flour to form a dough. (Dough will be very stiff.)

Easy Garlic Rolls

Double Whammy Yeast Rolls

4. Turn dough out onto a lightly floured surface, and knead, adding additional flour (up to ½ cup) as needed, until smooth and elastic (about 6 to 8 minutes). Place in a bowl coated with cooking spray, turning to coat top of dough. Cover and let rise in a warm place (85°), free from drafts, 1 hour or until doubled in bulk.
5. Coat 1 (12-cup) muffin pan with cooking spray. Punch dough down; shape dough into 36 (1-inch) balls. Place 3 dough balls in each muffin cup. (Handle the dough as little as possible to prevent over-kneading.) Cover and let rise in a warm place, free from drafts, 1 hour.
6. Preheat oven to 350°. Bake 15 to 18 minutes or until golden. Place a small pat of butter on top of each roll after baking 5 minutes, or brush with melted butter after baking, if desired.

Pimiento Cheese Rolls

Hands-on Time: 15 min.
Total Time: 1 hr., 25 min., including Cheese
Makes: 1 dozen

  1 (26.4-oz.) package frozen biscuits
All-purpose flour
  2 cups Pimiento Cheese

1. Arrange frozen biscuits, with sides touching, in 3 rows of 4 biscuits on a lightly floured surface. Let stand 30 to 45 minutes or until biscuits are thawed but cool to the touch.
2. Preheat oven to 375°. Sprinkle thawed biscuits lightly with flour. Press biscuit edges together, and pat to form a 10- x 12-inch rectangle of dough; spread evenly with Pimiento Cheese.
3. Roll up, starting at one long side; cut into 12 (about 1-inch-thick) slices. Place 1 slice into each cup of 1 lightly greased 12-cup muffin pan.
4. Bake at 375° for 20 to 25 minutes or until golden brown. Cool slightly, and remove from pan.

Pimiento Cheese

Hands-on Time: 10 min.
Total Time: 10 min.
Makes: 2 cups

  2 cups (8 oz.) shredded sharp Cheddar cheese
  ¾ cup mayonnaise
  1 (2-oz.) jar diced pimiento, drained
  1 tsp. minced onion
  ¼ tsp. ground red pepper

1. Stir together all ingredients until blended.

Ham-and-Swiss Rolls: Omit Pimiento Cheese. Stir together ¼ cup each of softened butter, spicy brown mustard, and finely chopped sweet onion. Spread butter mixture evenly over a 12- x 10-inch rectangle of thawed dough; sprinkle evenly with 1 cup each of shredded Swiss cheese and chopped cooked ham. Proceed with recipe as directed.

Easy Three-Seed Pan Rolls

Hands-on Time: 10 min.
Total Time: 4 hr., 25 min.
Makes: 9 rolls

The initial cost for these rolls is money well spent. You can make 3 scrumptious batches from the ingredients.

- 4 tsp. fennel seeds
- 4 tsp. poppy seeds
- 4 tsp. sesame seeds
- 9 frozen bread dough rolls
- 1 egg white, beaten
- Melted butter

1. Combine first 3 ingredients in a small bowl. Dip dough rolls, one at a time, in egg white; roll in seed mixture. Arrange rolls, 1 inch apart, in a lightly greased 8-inch pan. Cover with lightly greased plastic wrap, and let rise in a warm place (85°), free from drafts, 3 to 4 hours or until doubled in bulk.
2. Preheat oven to 350°. Uncover rolls, and bake at 350° for 15 minutes or until golden. Brush with melted butter.

Three-Seed French Bread: Substitute 1 (11-oz.) can refrigerated French bread dough for frozen bread dough rolls. Combine seeds in a shallow dish. Brush dough loaf with egg white. Roll top and sides of dough loaf in seeds. Place, seam side down, on a baking sheet. Cut and bake dough loaf according to package directions.

Easy Three-Seed Pan Rolls

Hurry-Up Homemade Crescent Rolls

Hands-on Time: 25 min.
Total Time: 1 hr., 40 min.
Makes: 1 dozen

Who knew crescent rolls could be so easy to make? This recipe only requires five ingredients and offers several variations for dressing up.

- 1 (¼-oz.) envelope active dry yeast
- ¾ cup warm water (100° to 110°)
- 3 to 3½ cups all-purpose baking mix
- 2 Tbsp. sugar
- All-purpose flour

1. Stir together yeast and warm water in a 1-cup measuring cup; let stand 5 minutes. Combine 3 cups baking mix and sugar in a large bowl; gradually stir in yeast mixture.

2. Turn dough out onto a floured surface, and knead, adding additional baking mix (up to ½ cup) as needed, until dough is smooth and elastic (about 10 minutes).

3. Roll dough into a 12-inch circle; cut circle into 12 wedges. Roll up wedges, starting at wide end, to form a crescent shape; place, point sides down, on a lightly greased baking sheet. Cover and let rise in a warm place (85°), free from drafts, 1 hour or until doubled in bulk.

4. Preheat oven to 425°. Bake 10 to 12 minutes or until golden.

Note: Rolls may be frozen up to 2 months. Bake at 425° for 5 minutes; cool completely (about 30 minutes). Wrap in aluminum foil, and freeze in an airtight container. Thaw at room temperature on a lightly greased baking sheet; bake at 425° for 7 to 8 minutes or until golden.

Three-Seed Crescent Rolls: Brush unbaked rolls with lightly beaten egg white, and sprinkle with sesame seeds, poppy seeds, and fennel seeds.

Italian Crescent Rolls: Brush unbaked rolls with melted butter; sprinkle with Parmesan cheese, kosher salt, coarsely ground pepper, and dried Italian seasoning.

Hurry-Up Homemade Crescent Rolls

kitchen secret:

To make rolls in a heavy-duty electric stand mixer, prepare as directed in Step 1. Beat dough at medium speed, using dough hook attachment, about 5 minutes, beating in ½ cup additional baking mix, if needed, until dough leaves the sides of the bowl and pulls together, becoming soft and smooth. Proceed with recipe as directed in Step 3.

Easy Asiago-Olive Rolls

Hands-on Time: 10 min.
Total Time: 25 min.
Makes: 8 to 10 servings

Asiago [ah-SYAH-goh] has a sweeter flavor than Parmesan and Romano.

- 1 (13.8-oz.) can refrigerated classic pizza crust dough
- ¼ cup refrigerated olive tapenade
- ½ cup grated Asiago cheese
- 1 tsp. chopped fresh rosemary
- 1 Tbsp. melted butter

1. Preheat oven to 450°. Unroll pizza crust dough. Spread olive tapenade over dough, leaving a ¼-inch border. Sprinkle with cheese and rosemary. Gently roll up dough, starting at one long side. Cut into 10 (1¼-inch-thick) slices. Place slices in a lightly greased 9-inch round cake pan. Brush top of dough with melted butter.
2. Bake at 450° for 15 to 20 minutes or until golden. Serve immediately.

Fresh Herb Spoon Rolls

Easy Asiago-Olive Rolls

Fresh Herb Spoon Rolls

Hands-on Time: 20 min.
Total Time: 45 min.
Makes: 2 dozen

- 1 (¼-oz.) envelope active dry yeast
- 2 cups warm water (100° to 110°)
- 4 cups self-rising flour
- ¾ cup melted butter
- ¾ cup chopped fresh chives
- ½ cup chopped fresh parsley
- ¼ cup sugar
- 1 large egg, lightly beaten

1. Preheat oven to 400°. Combine yeast and 2 cups warm water in a large bowl; let stand 5 minutes. Stir in flour and remaining ingredients. Spoon batter into 2 lightly greased 12-cup muffin pans, filling three-fourths full.
2. Bake at 400° for 20 to 22 minutes or until golden brown.

Easy Orange Rolls

Hands-on Time: 15 min.
Total Time: 45 min.
Makes: 11 rolls

Your family will definitely want to rise, shine, and dine when they smell these baking in the oven.

- ½ (8-oz.) package cream cheese, softened
- ¼ cup firmly packed light brown sugar
- 1½ tsp. orange zest
- 1 (11-oz.) can refrigerated French bread dough
- 2 Tbsp. granulated sugar
- 1 Tbsp. melted butter
- ½ cup powdered sugar
- 1 Tbsp. orange juice

1. Preheat oven to 375°. Beat cream cheese, light brown sugar, and orange zest at medium speed with an electric mixer until smooth. Unroll French bread dough onto a lightly floured surface. Spread cream cheese mixture over dough, leaving a $^1/_4$-inch border. Sprinkle with granulated sugar. Gently roll up dough, starting at one long side. Cut into 11 ($1^1/_4$-inch) slices. Place slices in a lightly greased 8-inch round cake pan. Brush top of dough with melted butter.
2. Bake at 375° for 25 to 30 minutes or until golden. Stir together powdered sugar and orange juice in a small bowl until smooth. Drizzle over hot rolls. Serve immediately.

Easy Orange Rolls

Best-Ever Scones

Hands-on Time: 15 min.
Total Time: 33 min.
Makes: 8 servings

This is the only scone recipe you will ever need! Start with the basic dough and add your favorite combinations.

  2 cups all-purpose flour
 ⅓ cup sugar
  1 Tbsp. baking powder
 ½ tsp. salt
 ½ cup cold butter, cut into ½-inch cubes
  1 cup whipping cream, divided
Wax paper

1. Preheat oven to 450°. Stir together first 4 ingredients in a large bowl. Cut butter into flour mixture with a pastry blender until crumbly and mixture resembles small peas. Freeze 5 minutes. Add ¾ cup plus 2 Tbsp. cream, stirring just until dry ingredients are moistened.
2. Turn dough out onto wax paper; gently press or pat dough into a 7-inch round. (Mixture will be crumbly.) Cut round into 8 wedges. Place wedges 2 inches apart on a lightly greased baking sheet. Brush tops with remaining 2 Tbsp. cream just until moistened.
3. Bake at 450° for 13 to 15 minutes or until golden.

Sweet Variations

Chocolate-Cherry Scones: Stir in ¼ cup coarsely chopped dried cherries and 2 oz. coarsely chopped semisweet chocolate with the cream.
Apricot-Ginger Scones: Stir in ½ cup finely chopped dried apricots and 2 Tbsp. finely chopped crystallized ginger with the cream. Drizzle with Vanilla Glaze (recipe at right) after baking.
Cranberry-Pistachio Scones: Stir in ¼ cup sweetened dried cranberries and ¼ cup coarsely chopped roasted salted pistachios with the cream.
Brown Sugar-Pecan Scones: Substitute brown sugar for granulated sugar. Stir in ½ cup chopped toasted pecans with the cream.

Savory Variations

Bacon, Cheddar, and Chive Scones: Omit sugar. Stir in ¾ cup (3 oz.) shredded sharp Cheddar cheese, ¼ cup finely chopped cooked bacon, 2 Tbsp. chopped fresh chives, and ½ tsp. freshly ground pepper with the cream.
Ham-and-Swiss Scones: Omit sugar. Stir in ¾ cup (3 oz.) shredded Swiss cheese and ¾ cup finely chopped baked ham with the cream. Serve warm with Mustard Butter: Stir together ½ cup softened butter, 1 Tbsp. spicy brown mustard, and 1 Tbsp. minced sweet onion.
Pimiento Cheese Scones: Omit sugar. Stir in ¾ cup (3 oz.) shredded sharp Cheddar cheese and 3 Tbsp. finely chopped pimiento with the cream.
Rosemary, Pear, and Asiago Scones: Omit sugar. Stir in ¾ cup finely chopped fresh pear, ½ cup grated Asiago cheese, and 1 tsp. chopped fresh rosemary with the cream.

Festive Touches

• Add a Vanilla Glaze: Whisk together 1 cup powdered sugar, 1 Tbsp. milk, and ½ tsp. vanilla extract until smooth, adding up to 2 tsp. additional milk for desired consistency. Drizzle over tops of scones.
• Make Bite-Size Scones: Pat dough into 2 (4-inch) rounds. Cut rounds into 8 wedges. Bake as directed for 12 to 13 minutes.
• Sprinkle scones with sparkling sugar before baking.

fix it!

Problem: Your scones are tough and dry.

Solution: Handle the dough as little as possible—the less you work it, the more tender the scones will be. Also be sure to cut ice-cold butter into the flour mixture, leaving crumbly pieces the size of small peas. If the butter is softened or cut in too finely, the texture of the scones will be dense and coarse.

Biscuit Beignets

Hands-on Time: 5 min.
Total Time: 17 min.
Makes: 4 to 6 servings

Tip your hat to the Crescent City by preparing these New Orleans-style treats.

 1 (12-oz.) can refrigerated buttermilk biscuits
Vegetable oil
Powdered sugar

Biscuit Beignets

1. Separate biscuits into individual rounds, and cut into quarters. Pour oil to a depth of 2 inches into a Dutch oven, and heat over medium heat to 350°. Fry biscuit quarters, in batches, 1 to 1$\frac{1}{2}$ minutes on each side or until golden. Drain on paper towels, and dust generously with powdered sugar. Serve immediately.

Frenchie Flats

Hands-on Time: 15 min.
Total Time: 40 min.
Makes: 10 to 12 servings

 1 (14-oz.) package soft flatbreads
 3 Tbsp. olive oil
Creole seasoning

1. Preheat oven to 350°. Cut flatbreads into 1-inch strips. Place on a baking sheet. Brush with olive oil; sprinkle with desired amount of Creole seasoning.
2. Bake at 350° for 15 minutes or until toasted; cool 10 minutes.

Garlic-Herb Bread

Hands-on Time: 10 min.
Total Time: 25 min.
Makes 8 servings

This quick and easy bread is also great with a little grated Parmesan cheese sprinkled on top.

 3 garlic cloves, minced
 2 Tbsp. extra virgin olive oil
 2 Tbsp. melted butter
 1 Tbsp. chopped fresh chives
 ½ tsp. dried crushed red pepper
 1 (16-oz.) French bread loaf

1. Preheat oven to 350°. Combine first 5 ingredients in a small bowl.
2. Cut bread in half lengthwise. Brush cut sides with garlic mixture; place on a baking sheet.
3. Bake at 350° for 13 to 15 minutes or until golden brown. Cut each bread half into 8 slices.

Sour Cream Cornbread

Hands-on Time: 10 min.
Total Time: 37 min.
Makes: 8 servings

- 1½ cups self-rising white cornmeal mix
- ½ cup all-purpose flour
- 1 (14.75-oz.) can low-sodium cream-style corn
- 1 (8-oz.) container light sour cream
- 3 large eggs, lightly beaten
- 2 Tbsp. chopped fresh cilantro
- ½ cup (2 oz.) 2% reduced-fat shredded Cheddar cheese (optional)

1. Preheat oven to 450°. Heat a 10-inch cast-iron skillet in oven 5 minutes.

2. Stir together cornmeal mix and flour in a large bowl; add corn and next 3 ingredients, stirring just until blended. Pour batter into hot lightly greased skillet. Top with cheese, if desired.

3. Bake at 450° for 22 to 24 minutes or until golden brown and cornbread pulls away from sides of skillet.

Farmhouse Eggs Benedict: Prepare Sour Cream Cornbread, omitting cheese topping. Prepare 1 (0.9-oz.) envelope hollandaise sauce mix according to package directions, using 1 cup 2% reduced-fat milk and 2 Tbsp. lemon juice and omitting butter. Cut 4 cornbread wedges in half lengthwise, and toast under the broiler. Top 2 toasted cornbread halves with 1 low-sodium ham slice, 1 poached egg, and 1 Tbsp. hollandaise sauce. Repeat with remaining cornbread.

Pam's Country Crust Bread

Hands-on Time: 25 min.
Total Time: 3 hr., 50 min.
Makes: 2 loaves

     2   (¼-oz.) envelopes active dry yeast
     2   cups warm water (100° to 115°)
     ½   cup sugar
     2   large eggs
     ¼   cup vegetable oil
     1   Tbsp. salt
     1   Tbsp. lemon juice
     6   to 6½ cups bread flour
     1   Tbsp. vegetable oil
    1½   Tbsp. melted butter

1. Combine yeast, 2 cups warm water, and 2 tsp. sugar in bowl of a heavy-duty electric stand mixer; let stand 5 minutes. Stir in eggs, next 3 ingredients, 3 cups flour, and remaining sugar. Beat dough at medium speed, using paddle attachment, until smooth. Gradually beat in remaining 3 to 3½ cups flour until a soft dough forms.
2. Turn dough out onto a well-floured surface, and knead until smooth and elastic (about 8 to 10 minutes), sprinkling surface with flour as needed. Place dough in a lightly greased large bowl, turning to grease top. Cover and let rise in a warm place (85°), free from drafts, about 1 hour or until doubled in bulk.
3. Punch dough down; turn out onto a lightly floured surface. Divide dough in half.
4. Roll each dough half into an 18- x 9-inch rectangle. Starting at one short end, tightly roll up each rectangle, jelly-roll fashion, pressing to seal edges as you roll. Pinch ends of dough to seal, and tuck ends under dough. Place each dough roll, seam side down, in a lightly greased 9- x 5-inch loaf pan. Brush tops with oil. Cover and let rise in a warm place (85°), free from drafts, 1 hour or until doubled in bulk.
5. Preheat oven to 375°. Bake 25 to 30 minutes or until loaves are deep golden brown and sound hollow when tapped. Remove from pans to a wire rack, and brush loaves with melted butter. Let cool completely (about 1 hour).

Pam's Country Crust Bread

Country Crust Wheat Bread: Substitute 3 cups wheat flour for 3 cups bread flour.

Country Crust Cheese Bread: Sprinkle 1 cup (4 oz.) freshly shredded sharp Cheddar cheese onto each dough rectangle before rolling up.

kitchen secret:

Create the perfect "warm place, free from drafts" to allow the dough to rise. Fill a metal pan with 1 inch of boiling water and place on the bottom rack of your oven. Place the dough, covered in a lightly greased bowl, on the top rack to rise.

Southern Soda Bread

Hands-on Time: 15 min.
Total Time: 2 hr., 45 min.
Makes: 2 loaves

- 4½ cups all-purpose flour
- ⅔ cup sugar
- 4½ tsp. baking powder
- 1½ tsp. baking soda
- 1½ tsp. salt
- 3 cups buttermilk
- 3 large eggs, lightly beaten
- 4½ Tbsp. melted butter

1. Preheat oven to 350°. Combine first 5 ingredients in a large bowl. Make a well in center of mixture. Add buttermilk, eggs, and butter, whisking just until thoroughly blended. (Batter should be almost smooth.) Pour batter into 2 lightly greased 8½- x 4½-inch loaf pans.

2. Bake at 350° for 45 minutes. Rotate pans in oven; shield with aluminum foil. Bake 30 to 35 minutes or until a long wooden pick inserted in center comes out clean. Cool in pans on a wire rack 10 minutes. Carefully run a knife along edges of bread to loosen from pans. Remove from pans to wire rack, and cool completely (about 1 hour).

Southern Soda Bread

Cranberry-Orange Bread

Hands-on Time: 15 min.
Total Time: 1 hr., 12 min.
Makes: 12 servings

This sweet bread also makes a perfect gift during the holidays.

- 1 cup nutlike cereal nuggets
- 1 cup uncooked regular oats
- ½ cup whole wheat flour
- ⅓ cup sugar
- ½ tsp. baking soda
- ½ tsp. salt
- ½ cup nonfat buttermilk
- ¼ cup vegetable oil
- 2 large eggs
- 1 tsp. grated orange zest
- ½ cup low-sugar orange marmalade
- ½ cup sweetened dried cranberries

1. Preheat oven to 375°. Combine first 6 ingredients in a large bowl; make a well in center of mixture.
2. Whisk together buttermilk, oil, and eggs; add to dry mixture, stirring just until moistened. Gently fold in grated orange zest, marmalade, and cranberries. Spoon into a lightly greased 8½- x 4½-inch loaf pan.
3. Bake at 375° for 28 to 32 minutes or until a wooden pick inserted in center comes out clean. Cool in pan on wire rack 5 minutes. Remove from pan to wire rack; let cool 20 minutes or until completely cool.

Cranberry-Orange Muffins: Prepare recipe as directed through Step 2, spooning batter into one lightly greased 12-cup muffin pan, filling two-thirds full. Bake at 375° for 16 to 18 minutes or until golden brown. Cool in pan on wire rack 5 minutes; remove from pan to wire rack, and cool 10 minutes or until completely cool.

Praline-Apple Bread

Hands-on Time: 25 min.
Total Time: 2 hr., 41 min.
Makes: 1 loaf

Sour cream is the secret to the rich, moist texture of this bread. There's no butter or oil in the batter—only in the glaze.

1½	cups chopped pecans, divided
1	(8-oz.) container sour cream
1	cup granulated sugar
2	large eggs
1	Tbsp. vanilla extract
2	cups all-purpose flour
2	tsp. baking powder
½	tsp. baking soda
½	tsp. salt
1½	cups finely chopped, peeled Granny Smith apple (about ¾ lb.)
½	cup butter
½	cup firmly packed light brown sugar

1. Preheat oven to 350°. Bake ½ cup pecans in a single layer in a shallow pan 6 to 8 minutes or until toasted and fragrant, stirring after 4 minutes.
2. Beat sour cream and next 3 ingredients at low speed with an electric mixer 2 minutes or until blended.
3. Stir together flour and next 3 ingredients. Add to sour cream mixture, beating just until blended. Stir in apple and ½ cup toasted pecans. Spoon batter into a greased and floured 9- x 5-inch loaf pan. Sprinkle with remaining 1 cup chopped pecans; lightly press pecans into batter.
4. Bake at 350° for 1 hour to 1 hour and 5 minutes or until a wooden pick inserted into center comes out clean, shielding with aluminum foil after 50 minutes to prevent excessive browning. Cool in pan on a wire rack 10 minutes; remove from pan to wire rack.
5. Bring butter and brown sugar to a boil in a 1-qt. heavy saucepan over medium heat, stirring constantly; boil 1 minute. Remove from heat, and spoon over top of bread; let cool completely (about 1 hour).

Note: To freeze, cool bread completely; wrap in plastic wrap and then in aluminum foil. Freeze up to 3 months. Thaw at room temperature.

Praline-Apple Bread

Cornbread Focaccia

Hands-on Time: 20 min.
Total Time: 1 hr., 50 min.
Makes: 8 servings

We love this fun, pizza-like flatbread.

- 1 (¼-oz.) envelope rapid-rise yeast
- 1 cup warm water (100° to 110°)
- 1 Tbsp. sugar
- 2 cups all-purpose flour
- ½ cup plain yellow cornmeal
- 1 Tbsp. chopped fresh rosemary
- 1 tsp. salt
- 3 Tbsp. olive oil, divided
- 1 Tbsp. balsamic vinegar
- 1 (14.5-oz.) can fire-roasted diced tomatoes, drained
- ⅓ cup (1½ oz.) shredded Parmesan cheese
- ½ tsp. kosher salt
- ¼ tsp. freshly ground pepper

1. Combine rapid-rise yeast, 1 cup warm water, and sugar in a small bowl, and let stand 5 minutes or until mixture bubbles.
2. Stir together 2 cups flour and next 3 ingredients in a large bowl; stir in yeast mixture and 2 Tbsp. oil until well blended. (Dough will be sticky.) Turn dough out onto a well-floured surface, and knead until smooth and elastic (about 3 to 5 minutes). Place in a well-greased bowl, turning to grease top. Cover with plastic wrap, and let stand 15 minutes.
3. Sprinkle cornmeal onto a baking sheet. Place dough on baking sheet, and roll into a 12-inch square, sprinkling with flour as needed to prevent sticking (about 1 Tbsp.). Cover with plastic wrap, and let rise in a warm place (85°), free from drafts, 45 minutes.

4. Preheat oven to 400°. Brush dough with balsamic vinegar. Gently press end of a wooden spoon into top of dough, forming indentations. Top with tomatoes and cheese. Sprinkle with salt and pepper. Drizzle with remaining 1 Tbsp. oil.
5. Bake at 400° for 20 minutes or until golden and cheese is melted. Cool 5 minutes, and cut into squares.

Cornbread Focaccia

Caramelized Onion Flatbread

Hands-on Time: 25 min.
Total Time: 45 min.
Makes: 8 servings

- 1 large sweet onion, sliced
- 3 Tbsp. olive oil, divided
- 1 lb. bakery pizza dough
- 1¼ tsp. kosher salt
- 1 tsp. chopped fresh rosemary

1. Preheat oven to 425°. Sauté onion in 1 Tbsp. hot oil over medium-high heat 15 minutes or until golden brown.

2. Press dough into a 15- x 10-inch jelly-roll pan, pressing to about ¼-inch thickness. Press handle of a wooden spoon into dough to make indentations at 1-inch intervals; drizzle with remaining 2 Tbsp. oil, and sprinkle with salt, rosemary, and caramelized onions.

3. Bake at 425° on lowest oven rack 20 minutes or until lightly browned.

bake it!

Substitute 1 (13.8-oz.) can refrigerated pizza crust dough for bakery pizza dough. Reduce salt to ¾ tsp. Reduce bake time to 10 minutes or until lightly browned.

Caramelized Onion Flatbread

SANDWICHES & SOUPS

Whether the weather is hot or cold, this classic combination is ideal for an easy lunch or light dinner.

Arkansas Tomato Sandwiches

Hands-on Time: 20 min.
Total Time: 55 min., including griddle cakes
Makes: 8 servings

This sandwich is summertime between two pieces of bread with juicy heirloom tomatoes, a fresh herb mayonnaise, and a slice of sweet onion.

  1 cup mayonnaise
  1 cup loosely packed fresh cilantro leaves
  1 tsp. lime zest
  1 Tbsp. fresh lime juice
  1 garlic clove
Summer Griddle Cakes
Heirloom tomatoes, sliced
Salt and freshly ground pepper to taste
Salad greens
Red onion, thinly sliced

1. Process first 5 ingredients in a blender until smooth. Spread mayonnaise mixture over warm Summer Griddle Cakes. Sprinkle tomato slices with salt and freshly ground pepper to taste, and sandwich tomato slices with salad greens and thinly sliced red onion between griddle cakes.

Summer Griddle Cakes

Hands-on Time: 35 min.
Total Time: 35 min.
Makes: 17 (3½-inch) cakes

Stir finely chopped fresh cilantro into softened butter, and serve alongside a bread basket of these treats.

  4 bacon slices
  1 cup finely chopped okra
1½ cups self-rising white cornmeal mix
 ½ cup all-purpose flour
  1 Tbsp. sugar
1⅔ cups buttermilk
  3 Tbsp. melted butter
  2 large eggs, lightly beaten

1. Cook bacon in a large skillet over medium-high heat 8 to 10 minutes or until crisp; remove bacon, and drain on paper towels, reserving drippings in skillet. Finely chop bacon.
2. Sauté okra in hot drippings 3 minutes or until crisp-tender.
3. Whisk together cornmeal mix, flour, and sugar. Combine buttermilk, butter, and eggs in a separate bowl. Add to dry ingredients, and stir just until moistened. Stir in okra and bacon.
4. Pour about ¼ cup batter for each griddle cake onto a hot, lightly greased griddle or large nonstick skillet. Cook cakes 2 to 3 minutes or until tops are covered with bubbles and edges look dry and cooked; turn and cook other side 1 to 2 minutes or until done.

Arkansas Tomato Sandwiches

Goat Cheese and Strawberry Grilled Cheese

Goat Cheese and Strawberry Grilled Cheese

Hands-on Time: 20 min.
Total Time: 20 min.
Makes: 3 servings

- 1 (4-oz.) goat cheese log, softened
- 6 whole grain bread slices
- 4½ tsp. red pepper jelly
- ¾ cup sliced fresh strawberries
- 6 large fresh basil leaves
- 1½ cups fresh watercress or arugula
- Salt and pepper to taste

1. Spread goat cheese on one side of 3 bread slices. Spread pepper jelly on one side of remaining bread slices; layer with strawberries, basil leaves, and watercress. Sprinkle with salt and pepper to taste. Top with remaining bread, goat cheese sides down.
2. Cook sandwiches in a large, lightly greased nonstick skillet over medium heat 2 to 3 minutes on each side or until golden brown.

Grilled Pimiento Cheese Sandwiches
Basil-Tomato Soup (page 298)

Grilled Pimiento Cheese Sandwiches

Hands-on Time: 19 min.
Total Time: 19 min.
Makes: 11 servings

- 1 cup mayonnaise
- 1 (4-oz.) jar diced pimiento, drained
- 1 tsp. Worcestershire sauce
- 1 tsp. finely grated onion
- 2 (8-oz.) blocks sharp Cheddar cheese, shredded

White bread slices
Mayonnaise

1. Stir together 1 cup mayonnaise, diced pimiento, Worcestershire sauce, and onion. Stir in shredded sharp Cheddar cheese. (Store in an airtight container in refrigerator up to 1 week, if desired.) Spread ¼ cup pimiento cheese mixture on one side of a white bread slice; top with another bread slice. Lightly spread both sides of sandwich with mayonnaise. Repeat with remaining pimiento cheese mixture for desired number of sandwiches.

2. Cook, in batches, on a hot griddle or large nonstick skillet over medium heat 4 to 5 minutes on each side or until golden brown and cheese melts.

Mini Bacon, Tomato, and Basil Sandwiches

Hands-on Time: 30 min.
Total Time: 30 min.
Makes: 12 appetizer servings

These sandwiches can be assembled up to two hours ahead. Simply cover with a damp paper towel to keep the bread from drying out.

9	slices ready-to-serve bacon, halved
½	cup (2 oz.) shredded Parmesan cheese
⅓	cup mayonnaise
1	garlic clove, minced
9	slices extra-thin white bread slices
3	plum tomatoes, sliced
12	fresh basil leaves

1. Cook bacon according to package directions until crisp; set aside.

2. Stir together cheese, mayonnaise, and garlic. Spread mayonnaise mixture evenly onto one side of each bread slice. Layer 3 bread slices, mayonnaise sides up, with 3 bacon slices each. Top bacon evenly with 3 bread slices, tomato slices, and basil. Top each with remaining bread slices, mayonnaise sides down. Cut each sandwich into quarters.

Mini Bacon, Tomato, and Basil Sandwiches

Easy Mini Muffulettas

Hands-on Time: 15 min.
Total Time: 31 min.
Makes: 12 servings

     1   (32-oz.) jar Italian olive salad
    12   small deli rolls, cut in half
    12   thin Swiss cheese slices
    12   thin deli ham slices
    12   thin provolone cheese slices
    12   Genoa salami slices

1. Preheat oven to 350°. Spread 1 Tbsp. olive salad evenly over each cut side of roll bottoms. Top each with 1 Swiss cheese slice, 1 ham slice, 1 Tbsp. olive salad, 1 provolone cheese slice, 1 salami slice, and 1 Tbsp. olive salad. Cover with roll tops, and wrap sandwiches together in a large piece of aluminum foil. Place on a baking sheet.
2. Bake at 350° for 14 to 16 minutes or until cheeses are melted.

Note: We tested with Boscoli Italian Olive Salad.

Easy Mini Muffulettas

Hot Brown Panini

Hands-on Time: 23 min.
Total Time: 23 min., including cheese sauce
Makes: 8 servings

This richly delicious sandwich was inspired by a recipe for a Kentucky classic.

- 2 Tbsp. melted butter
- 16 (½-inch-thick) Italian bread slices
- 1 cup (4 oz.) shredded Swiss cheese, divided
- 3 cups chopped cooked chicken or turkey
- 4 plum tomatoes, sliced
- 3 cups warm White Cheese Sauce, divided
- 13 cooked bacon slices, crumbled

1. Brush melted butter on one side of 16 bread slices. Place bread slices, butter sides down, on wax paper.
2. Sprinkle 1 Tbsp. Swiss cheese on top of each of 8 bread slices; top evenly with chicken, tomato slices, and 1 cup warm White Cheese Sauce. Sprinkle with bacon and remaining Swiss cheese, and top with remaining bread slices, butter sides up.
3. Cook sandwiches, in batches, in a preheated panini press 2 to 3 minutes or until golden brown. Serve with remaining 2 cups warm White Cheese Sauce for dipping.

fake it!

Don't have a panini press? No need to worry! A cast-iron or heavy skillet is a great substitute. Place the sandwich in a lightly greased skillet and top with a piece of aluminum foil and another skillet or flat-bottomed pan. Place a few heavy cans into the pan and you've created a pressed sandwich.

White Cheese Sauce

Hands-on Time: 20 min.
Total Time: 20 min.
Makes: 3 cups

- ¼ cup butter
- ¼ cup all-purpose flour
- 3½ cups milk
- 1 cup (4 oz.) shredded Swiss cheese
- 1 cup grated Parmesan cheese
- ½ tsp. salt
- ¼ tsp. ground red pepper

1. Melt butter in a heavy saucepan over low heat; whisk in flour until smooth. Cook 1 minute, whisking constantly. Gradually whisk in milk; cook over medium heat, whisking constantly, until mixture is thickened and bubbly. Whisk in Swiss and Parmesan cheeses, salt, and red pepper, whisking until cheeses are melted and sauce is smooth.

Hot Brown Panini

Pressed Cuban Sandwiches

Hands-on Time: 22 min.
Total Time: 1 hr., 52 min., including pork loin
Makes: 4 servings

We made these sandwiches in a skillet, but feel free to use a hot panini press instead. You'll still get the same tasty results.

- 1 (12-oz.) Cuban bread loaf, cut in half crosswise
- 6 to 8 Tbsp. yellow mustard
- ⅓ lb. thinly sliced Baked Pork Loin Roast (about 8 to 10 slices)
- ⅓ lb. thinly sliced baked ham
- ⅓ lb. thinly sliced provolone cheese
- ¼ to ⅓ cup dill pickle chips
- 2 Tbsp. butter, softened

1. Cut bread halves lengthwise, cutting to but not through opposite side. Spread mustard on cut sides of bread. Layer with Baked Pork Loin Roast and next 3 ingredients. Close sandwiches, and spread outsides with butter.

2. Place 1 sandwich in a hot, large skillet over medium heat. Place a heavy skillet on top of sandwich. Cook 2 to 3 minutes on each side or until cheese is melted and sandwich is flat. Repeat with remaining sandwich. Cut each sandwich in half, and serve immediately.

Baked Pork Loin Roast

Hands-on Time: 10 min.
Total Time: 1 hr., 40 min.
Makes: 8 to 10 servings

This simple pork loin recipe is great alone, and leftovers make great sandwiches. Add lettuce, tomato, and serve on ciabatta rolls with mayonnaise or honey mustard.

- 1 (3- to 4-lb.) boneless pork loin
- 1 Tbsp. olive oil
- 2 tsp. salt
- 2 tsp. pepper

Pressed Cuban Sandwiches

1. Preheat oven to 350°. Trim boneless pork loin roast. Rinse and pat dry. Rub roast with olive oil. Sprinkle with salt and pepper; place in an aluminum foil-lined 13- x 9-inch pan.

2. Bake at 350° for 1½ to 2 hours or until a meat thermometer inserted into thickest portion registers 150°. Let stand 15 minutes before slicing.

Baked Pork Butt Roast: Substitute 1 (4- to 5-lb.) boneless pork shoulder roast (Boston butt) for boneless pork loin roast. Prepare recipe as directed in Step 1. Bake at 350° for 4 to 4½ hours or until a meat thermometer inserted into thickest portion registers 180°. Let stand 15 minutes before slicing.

Easy Barbecue Sliders

Hands-on Time: 10 min.
Total Time: 10 min.
Makes: 18 appetizer servings

This easy sandwich is perfect for serving at a party. Pick up your favorite pulled pork from a local barbecue joint and top with your favorite slaw.

  2 (12-oz.) packages French rolls, split
1½ lb. shredded barbecued pork
     Barbecue sauce
     Coleslaw

1. Bake rolls according to package directions. Serve pork on rolls with barbecue sauce and coleslaw.

Fried Fish Sandwiches

Hands-on Time: 28 min.
Total Time: 28 min.
Makes: 4 servings

This superb sandwich is inspired by the Black Grouper Sandwich served at Dockside Dave's in St. Pete Beach, Florida.

  2 lb. grouper, mahi-mahi, cod, or halibut fillets
  2 tsp. Greek seasoning, divided
1½ tsp. salt, divided
  1 tsp. freshly ground pepper, divided
2¼ cups all-purpose flour
 ¼ cup plain yellow cornmeal
  2 tsp. baking powder
  2 cups cold beer
  1 large egg, lightly beaten
     Vegetable oil
  4 sesame seed hamburger buns
     Tartar sauce or mayonnaise
  4 green leaf lettuce leaves
  4 tomato slices

1. Cut fish into 3-inch strips. Sprinkle evenly with 1 tsp. Greek seasoning, 1 tsp. salt, and ½ tsp. pepper.
2. Combine flour, cornmeal, baking powder, remaining 1 tsp. Greek seasoning, ½ tsp. salt, and ½ tsp. pepper; stir well. Add 2 cups cold beer and egg, stirring until thoroughly blended and smooth.
3. Pour oil to a depth of 2 to 3 inches into a Dutch oven; heat to 375°.
4. Dip fish strips into batter, coating both sides well; shake off excess. Fry fish, in batches, 2 minutes on each side or until golden. (Do not crowd pan.) Drain on paper towels.
5. Spread top half of each bun evenly with tartar sauce. Place 1 lettuce leaf and 1 tomato slice on bottom half of each bun; top each with 2 fried fish strips and top half of bun.

Fried Fish Sandwiches

Roasted Red Pepper Soup with Pesto Croutons

Hands-on Time: 45 min.
Total Time: 55 min.
Makes: 6 servings

If you'd like to serve the soup cold, stir in an extra ¼ teaspoon salt.

- ¼ cup refrigerated pesto, at room temperature
- 6 sourdough bread slices
- 1 Tbsp. butter
- 1 Tbsp. olive oil
- 1 garlic clove, minced
- 1 shallot, finely chopped
- 1 Tbsp. tomato paste
- 4 cups low-sodium chicken broth
- 1 (15-oz.) jar roasted red bell peppers, drained and rinsed
- ¼ cup half-and-half
- 1 Tbsp. chopped fresh parsley

Salt and pepper to taste
Garnishes: fresh flat-leaf parsley sprigs, shaved Parmesan cheese

1. Preheat oven to 350°. Spread pesto on one side of each bread slice. Cut each bread slice into ½- to 1-inch cubes. Place bread cubes in a single layer on a lightly greased aluminum foil-lined jelly-roll pan.

2. Bake at 350° for 16 to 20 minutes or until golden, turning once after 10 minutes. Remove from oven, and let cool.

3. Melt butter with oil in a large Dutch oven over medium-high heat. Add garlic and shallot, and cook, stirring constantly, 2 minutes or until vegetables are tender. Add tomato paste, and cook, stirring constantly, 1 minute. Stir in chicken broth and bell peppers; bring to a boil. Reduce heat to medium, and simmer, stirring occasionally, 5 minutes. Remove from heat; let cool 10 minutes.

4. Process red pepper mixture, in batches, in a blender or food processor 8 to 10 seconds or until smooth, stopping to scrape down sides. Return red pepper mixture to Dutch oven; stir in half-and-half and parsley, and cook over medium heat 5 minutes or until thoroughly heated. Season with salt and pepper to taste.

5. Ladle soup into 6 bowls; top with croutons. Garnish, if desired.

Roasted Red Pepper Soup with Pesto Croutons

Pumpkin-Acorn Squash Soup

Hands-on Time: 45 min.
Total Time: 1 hr., 55 min.
Makes: 6 to 8 servings

1	medium pie pumpkin (about 3½ lb.)
1	medium acorn squash (about 2 lb.)
4	Tbsp. butter, divided
2	Tbsp. honey, divided
½	tsp. salt, divided
1	medium-size sweet onion, chopped
4	tsp. chopped fresh thyme
4½	cups chicken broth
¼	cup half-and-half
1	tsp. cider vinegar
⅛	tsp. ground ginger
⅛	tsp. ground nutmeg
	Freshly ground pepper to taste
	Garnish: fresh thyme sprigs, roasted pumpkin seeds

1. Preheat oven to 400°. Cut pumpkin and squash in half lengthwise, cutting through stem and bottom ends. Reserve seeds for another use. Place pumpkin and squash halves, cut sides up, in an aluminum foil-lined shallow pan.

2. Microwave 2 Tbsp. butter in a microwave-safe bowl at HIGH 25 seconds or until melted; stir in 1 Tbsp. honey and ¼ tsp. salt. Brush cut sides of pumpkin and squash with butter mixture.

3. Bake pumpkin and acorn squash at 400° for 45 minutes or until tender. Let cool completely (about 15 minutes). Scoop out pulp, discarding shells.

4. Melt remaining 2 Tbsp. butter in a Dutch oven over medium heat. Add onion, and sauté 5 minutes or until tender. Add thyme; sauté 1 minute.

5. Stir in broth and pumpkin and squash pulp. Increase heat to medium-high; bring to a boil. Reduce heat to low, and simmer 10 minutes. Remove from heat, and let cool 10 minutes.

6. Process soup, in batches, in a blender or food processor until smooth. Return soup to Dutch oven. Stir in half-and-half, next 4 ingredients, and remaining 1 Tbsp. honey and ¼ tsp. salt. Cook, over low heat, stirring often, 3 minutes or until thoroughly heated. Garnish, if desired. Serve immediately.

fake it!

Substitute 1 (15-oz.) can of pumpkin for the fresh pie pumpkin and 2 (12-oz.) packages of frozen cooked pureed squash, thawed, for the fresh acorn squash. Decrease butter to 2 Tbsp. Omit Steps 1, 2, and 3. Proceed with Steps 4 through 6, simmering 6 minutes in Step 5 and stirring in 2 Tbsp. honey and ½ tsp. salt with half-and-half in Step 6.

Pumpkin-Acorn Squash Soup

Baby Carrot Soup

Hands-on Time: 35 min.
Total Time: 45 min.
Makes: 4 servings

Smoky adobo sauce gives this creamy soup a subtle touch of heat.

- 1 (7-oz.) can chipotle peppers in adobo sauce
- 1 small sweet onion, chopped
- 1 Tbsp. olive oil
- 1 (32-oz.) container low-sodium fat-free chicken broth
- 1 (16-oz.) package baby carrots
- ⅓ cup half-and-half
- 1 tsp. salt
- Toppings: chopped fresh chives, chopped dried chile peppers, reduced-fat sour cream

1. Remove 2 tsp. adobo sauce from can; reserve peppers and remaining sauce for another use.
2. Sauté onion in hot oil in a Dutch oven over medium heat 3 minutes or until tender. Stir in broth, carrots, and 2 tsp. adobo sauce; cover, increase heat to medium-high, and bring to a boil. Reduce heat to medium, and simmer, partially covered, 15 to 20 minutes or until carrots are tender. Remove from heat, and let cool 10 minutes.

3. Process carrot mixture in a blender or food processor 1 minute or until smooth, stopping to scrape down sides as needed. Return carrot mixture to Dutch oven. Stir in half-and-half and salt. Cook over low heat 2 to 4 minutes or until thoroughly heated. Serve with desired toppings.

Basil-Tomato Soup

Hands-on Time: 40 min.
Total Time: 1 hr., 10 min.
Makes: 8 to 10 servings

Enjoy ripe tomatoes all year long with this hearty classic. The addition of a fried okra garnish gives it a special Southern twist. (pictured on page 290)

- 2 medium onions, chopped
- 4 Tbsp. olive oil, divided
- 3 (35-oz.) cans Italian-style whole peeled tomatoes with basil
- 1 (32-oz.) box chicken broth
- 1 cup loosely packed fresh basil leaves
- 3 garlic cloves
- 1 tsp. lemon zest
- 1 Tbsp. lemon juice
- 1 tsp. salt
- 1 tsp. sugar
- ½ tsp. pepper
- 1 (16-oz.) package frozen breaded cut okra

1. Sauté onions in 2 Tbsp. hot oil in a large Dutch oven over medium-high heat 9 to 10 minutes or until tender. Add tomatoes and chicken broth. Bring mixture to a boil, reduce heat to medium-low, and simmer, stirring occasionally, 20 minutes. Process mixture with a handheld blender until smooth.
2. Process basil, next 4 ingredients, ¼ cup water, and remaining 2 Tbsp. oil in a food processor until smooth, stopping to scrape down sides as needed. Stir basil mixture, sugar, and pepper into soup. Cook 10 minutes or until thoroughly heated.
3. Meanwhile, cook okra according to package directions. Serve with soup.

Baby Carrot Soup

Loaded Potato Soup

Loaded Potato Soup

Hands-on Time: 17 min.
Total Time: 33 min.
Makes: 4 servings

This hearty soup uses leftover ham, mashed potatoes, sweet peas, and dinner rolls.

    2 Tbsp. butter
    1 cup diced smoked ham
    4 sliced green onions
    1 garlic clove, minced
    2 cups mashed potatoes
    1 (14-oz.) can low-sodium fat-free chicken
       broth
    1 cup milk
    ⅓ cup sweet peas
    2 tsp. chopped fresh thyme
  Salt and pepper
    2 cups torn dinner rolls
    1 cup (4 oz.) shredded Cheddar cheese
  Garnish: chopped parsley

1. Preheat broiler. Melt butter in a 3-qt. saucepan; add diced ham, sliced green onions, and minced garlic. Sauté until golden. Stir in mashed potatoes, chicken broth, milk, peas, and chopped fresh thyme. Bring to a boil; reduce heat. Simmer 8 minutes or until thickened. Season with salt and pepper.
2. Spoon into 4 broiler-safe bowls. Top with torn dinner rolls; sprinkle with shredded Cheddar cheese. Place bowls on a baking sheet. Broil 3 minutes or until golden brown. Garnish, if desired.

Turnip Greens Stew

Hands-on Time: 11 min.
Total Time: 41 min.
Makes: 6 to 8 servings

Frozen seasoning blend is a mixture of diced onion, red and green bell peppers, and celery.

    2 cups chopped cooked ham
    1 Tbsp. vegetable oil
    3 cups chicken broth
    2 (16-oz.) packages frozen chopped turnip
       greens
    1 (16-oz.) package frozen seasoning blend
    1 tsp. sugar
    1 tsp. seasoned pepper

1. Sauté ham in hot oil in a Dutch oven over medium-high heat 5 minutes or until lightly browned. Add chicken broth and remaining ingredients; bring greens mixture to a boil. Cover, reduce heat to low, and simmer, stirring occasionally, 25 minutes.

Note: We tested with McKenzie's Seasoning Blend.

Collard Greens Stew: Substitute 1 (16-oz.) package frozen chopped collard greens and 1 (16-oz.) can black-eyed peas, drained, for 2 packages turnip greens. Prepare recipe as directed, cooking collard greens 15 minutes; add black-eyed peas, and cook 10 more minutes.

Southern Tortellini Minestrone

Hands-on Time: 20 min.
Total Time: 42 min.
Makes: 8 to 10 servings

Use your favorite frozen greens in this soup or substitute a bag of thoroughly washed fresh spinach.

- 1 medium onion, chopped
- 1 Tbsp. olive oil
- 3 garlic cloves, chopped
- 2 (32-oz.) containers chicken broth
- ¾ cup dry white wine
- 2 (14.5-oz.) cans Italian-seasoned diced tomatoes
- 1 (16-oz.) package frozen green beans
- 1 (16-oz.) package chopped frozen collard greens
- 3 Tbsp. chopped fresh parsley
- 1 Tbsp. chopped fresh rosemary
- ½ tsp. dried crushed red pepper
- 1 (16-oz.) package frozen cheese tortellini

1. Sauté onion in hot oil in a large Dutch oven over medium heat 8 minutes or until onion is tender. Add garlic, and cook 1 minute. Stir in chicken broth, white wine, and tomatoes; bring to a boil over medium-high heat. Add green beans, collard greens, and next 3 ingredients. Reduce heat to medium, and simmer, stirring occasionally, 15 minutes. Add pasta, and cook 10 to 12 minutes or until pasta is done.

Southern Tortellini Minestrone

Easy Chicken and Dumplings

Hands-on Time: 30 min.
Total Time: 40 min.
Makes: 4 to 6 servings

Deli-roasted chicken, cream of chicken soup, and canned biscuits make a quick-and-tasty version of this favorite. One roasted chicken yields 3 cups of meat.

- 1 (32-oz.) container low-sodium fat-free chicken broth
- 3 cups shredded cooked chicken (about 1½ lb.)
- 1 (10¾-oz.) can reduced-fat cream of chicken soup
- ¼ tsp. poultry seasoning
- 1 (10.2-oz.) can refrigerated jumbo buttermilk biscuits
- 2 carrots, diced
- 3 celery ribs, diced

1. Bring first 4 ingredients to a boil in a Dutch oven over medium-high heat. Cover, reduce heat to low, and simmer, stirring occasionally, 5 minutes. Increase heat to medium-high; return to a low boil.
2. Place biscuits on a lightly floured surface. Roll or pat each biscuit to ⅛-inch thickness; cut into ½-inch-wide strips.
3. Drop strips, one at a time, into boiling broth mixture. Add carrots and celery. Cover, reduce heat to low, and simmer 15 to 20 minutes, stirring occasionally to prevent dumplings from sticking.

Easy Chicken and Dumplings

She-Crab Soup

Hands-on Time: 10 min.
Total Time: 1 hr., 20 min.
Makes: 4 servings

Traditionally, this soup is made with female crab and crab roe. It hails from the Low Country and is especially delicious doused with sherry just before serving.

- 1 qt. whipping cream
- ⅛ tsp. salt
- ⅛ tsp. pepper
- 2 fish bouillon cubes
- 2 cups boiling water
- ¼ cup unsalted butter
- ⅓ cup all-purpose flour
- 1 lb. fresh crabmeat
- 2 Tbsp. lemon juice
- ¼ tsp. ground nutmeg
  Garnish: chopped parsley
- ⅓ cup sherry (optional)

1. Combine first 3 ingredients in a heavy saucepan; bring to a boil over medium heat. Reduce heat, and simmer 1 hour. Set aside.
2. Stir together fish bouillon cubes and 2 cups boiling water until bouillon dissolves.
3. Melt butter in a large, heavy saucepan over low heat; add flour, stirring until smooth. Cook 1 minute, stirring constantly. Gradually add hot fish broth; cook over medium heat until thickened. Stir in cream mixture, and cook until thoroughly heated. Add crabmeat, lemon juice, and nutmeg. Ladle into individual serving bowls. Garnish, if desired. Add a spoonful of sherry to each serving, if desired.

Note: We tested with Knorr Fish Bouillon. It is important to use good-quality sherry, not cooking sherry, for this soup.

Matzo Ball Soup

Hands-on Time: 30 min.
Total Time: 4 hr., including matzo balls
Makes: 8 to 10 servings

- 1 (1-oz.) package fresh dill
- 1 bunch fresh parsley
- Kitchen string
- 3 skin-on, bone-in chicken breasts (about 3 lb.)
- 4 medium carrots, thinly sliced
- 3 parsnips, thinly sliced
- 3 celery ribs
- 1 medium onion, quartered
- Matzo Balls
- 1½ to 2 Tbsp. fresh lemon juice
- 2½ tsp. kosher salt
- ½ tsp. ground white pepper
- Garnish: fresh dill sprigs

1. Tie half of dill and half of parsley in a bunch with kitchen string. Chop remaining dill and parsley to equal 2 tsp. each.

2. Bring chicken, next 4 ingredients, dill-parsley bunch, and 3½ qt. water to a boil in a large Dutch oven over medium-high heat; skim any foam with a slotted spoon. Cover, reduce heat to medium-low and simmer, 2½ to 3 hours or until chicken is tender and falls off the bone.

3. Remove soup from heat. Skim fat from surface of broth. Remove chicken and celery. Pour broth through a fine wire-mesh strainer into a large bowl. Return broth, carrots, and parsnips to Dutch oven, discarding onion and herb bunch. Let chicken, celery, and broth mixture cool 30 minutes.

4. Squeeze juice from cooled celery ribs into broth. Discard celery ribs. Skin and bone chicken; shred chicken. Add Matzo Balls, shredded chicken, lemon juice, kosher salt, and ground white pepper to broth. Bring to a boil over medium-high heat. Reduce heat to medium-low; simmer 8 minutes. Stir in reserved dill and parsley; cook 2 minutes. Garnish, if desired.

Matzo Balls

Hands-on Time: 17 min.
Total Time: 1 hr., 27 min.
Makes: 18

- 2 Tbsp. vegetable oil
- 4 large eggs, lightly beaten
- 1 cup matzo meal
- 1¾ tsp. kosher salt

1. Whisk together oil, eggs, and ¼ cup water. Add matzo meal and 1¾ tsp. kosher salt; whisk until well blended. Cover and chill 30 minutes.

2. Shape batter into 18 (1-inch) balls (about 1 Tbsp. each), using wet hands. Bring 2½ qt. water to a boil in a large saucepan over medium-high heat. Drop matzo balls into boiling water; return to a boil. Cover and reduce heat to medium-low; simmer 30 minutes. Remove matzo balls from water with a slotted spoon.

Matzo Ball Soup

Chicken-Tasso-Andouille Sausage Gumbo

Hands-on Time: 45 min.
Total Time: 4 hr., 15 min.
Makes: about 20 servings

Tasso is a spicy smoked cut of pork or beef popular in many Cajun dishes.

     4 lb. skinned and boned chicken thighs
     1 lb. andouille or smoked sausage
     1 lb. tasso or smoked ham
     1 cup vegetable oil
     1 cup all-purpose flour
     4 medium onions, chopped
     2 large green bell peppers, chopped
     2 large celery ribs, chopped
     4 large garlic cloves, minced
     4 (32-oz.) containers chicken broth
  1½ tsp. dried thyme
     1 tsp. black pepper
     ½ tsp. ground red pepper
     ⅓ cup chopped fresh parsley
        Hot cooked rice
        Garnishes: sliced green onions, filé powder

1. Cut first 3 ingredients into bite-size pieces. Place in a large Dutch oven over medium heat; cook, stirring often, 20 minutes or until browned. Drain on paper towels. Wipe out Dutch oven with paper towels.
2. Heat oil in Dutch oven over medium heat; slowly whisk in flour, and cook, whisking constantly, 25 minutes or until mixture is a dark mahogany color.
3. Stir in onions and next 3 ingredients; cook, stirring often, 18 to 20 minutes or until tender. Gradually add broth. Stir in chicken, sausage, tasso, thyme, and black and red ground peppers.
4. Bring mixture to a boil over medium-high heat. Reduce heat to medium-low, and simmer, stirring occasionally, 2¹/₂ to 3 hours. Stir in parsley. Remove from heat, and serve over hot cooked rice. Garnish, if desired.

Shrimp-Tasso-Andouille Sausage Gumbo: Omit chicken thighs and proceed with Steps 1, 2, and 3. Proceed with Step 4, stirring in 4 lb. medium-size raw shrimp, peeled and, if desired, deveined, the last 15 minutes of cooking.

Chicken-Tasso-Andouille Sausage Gumbo

Hoppin' John Stew with White Cheddar Cheese Grits

Hands-on Time: 33 min.
Total Time: 48 min., including grits
Makes: 4 to 6 servings

This hearty, updated twist is served with grits instead of rice.

- 1 Tbsp. butter
- 1 cup chopped smoked ham
- 1 medium onion, chopped
- 2 (15-oz.) cans black-eyed peas, drained and rinsed
- 2 (10-oz.) cans diced tomatoes with green chiles, undrained
- 1 cup frozen corn kernels
- 1 tsp. sugar
- ¼ cup chopped fresh cilantro
- White Cheddar Cheese Grits
- Garnish: cilantro sprigs

1. Melt butter in a Dutch oven over medium heat; add ham and onion, and sauté 3 to 5 minutes or until onion is tender. Stir in black-eyed peas and next 3 ingredients. Cover, reduce heat to low, and cook, stirring occasionally, 15 minutes. Remove from heat, and stir in cilantro. Serve immediately over White Cheddar Cheese Grits. Garnish, if desired.

White Cheddar Cheese Grits

Hands-on Time: 10 min.
Total Time: 15 min.
Makes 4 to 6 servings

- 2 cups chicken broth
- 2 Tbsp. butter
- ½ cup uncooked quick-cooking grits
- 1 cup (4 oz.) shredded white Cheddar cheese

1. Bring chicken broth and butter to a boil in a medium saucepan over medium-high heat. Gradually whisk in grits, and return to a boil. Reduce heat to medium-low, and simmer, stirring occasionally, 5 minutes or until thickened. Stir in cheese until melted. Serve immediately.

Hoppin' John Stew with
White Cheddar Cheese Grits

MEATS & POULTRY

Whether you're looking for a perfect weeknight meal, or a special holiday dish, this collection of delicious main dishes will be your go-to source for any occasion.

Southern Stuffed Rosemary Chicken

Hands-on Time: 25 min.
Total Time: 55 min.
Makes: 8 servings

- 2 (6-oz.) packages cornbread stuffing mix
- 1 large egg, lightly beaten
- ½ cup finely chopped pecans, toasted
- 8 skinned and boned chicken breasts (about 3 lb.)
- ¼ cup olive oil, divided
- 1 Tbsp. chopped fresh rosemary
- 1 tsp. salt
- ½ tsp. pepper
- ¼ cup grated Parmesan cheese
- 1 (8-oz.) package sliced fresh mushrooms
- 4 green onions, sliced
- 1 (10¾-oz.) can reduced-fat cream of chicken soup
- 1 cup chicken broth
- Garnish: fresh rosemary sprigs

1. Preheat oven to 400°. Prepare stuffing mix according to package directions; let cool. Stir in egg and pecans.

2. Butterfly chicken breasts by making a lengthwise cut in one side, cutting to but not through the opposite side; unfold. Spoon stuffing mixture evenly down center of one side of each butterflied chicken breast; fold opposite side over stuffing, and place in a lightly greased baking dish. Stir together 3 Tbsp. olive oil and chopped rosemary; brush evenly over chicken. Sprinkle chicken evenly with salt, pepper, and Parmesan cheese.

3. Bake chicken, uncovered, at 400° for 20 minutes or until done.

4. Sauté mushrooms and green onions in remaining 1 Tbsp. oil in a large skillet over medium-high heat 5 minutes or until tender; stir in soup and chicken broth. Reduce heat, and simmer, stirring often, 5 minutes or until thoroughly heated. Spoon mushroom mixture evenly over chicken; garnish, if desired.

Note: We tested with Stove Top Cornbread Stuffing Mix.

Southern Stuffed Rosemary Chicken

Lemon Chicken

Hands-on Time: 30 min.
Total Time: 30 min.
Makes: 8 servings

- 4 skinned and boned chicken breasts (about 1½ lb.)
- 1 tsp. salt
- ½ tsp. pepper
- ⅓ cup all-purpose flour
- 4 Tbsp. butter, divided
- 2 Tbsp. olive oil, divided
- ¼ cup chicken broth
- ¼ cup lemon juice
- 8 lemon slices
- ¼ cup chopped fresh flat-leaf parsley
- Garnish: lemon slices

1. Cut each chicken breast in half lengthwise. Place chicken between 2 sheets of heavy-duty plastic wrap; flatten to ¼-inch thickness, using a rolling pin or flat side of a meat mallet. Sprinkle chicken with salt and pepper and lightly dredge chicken in flour, shaking off excess.

2. Melt 1 Tbsp. butter with 1 Tbsp. olive oil in a large nonstick skillet over medium-high heat. Cook half of chicken in skillet 2 to 3 minutes on each side or until golden brown and done. Transfer chicken to a serving platter; keep warm. Repeat procedure with 1 Tbsp. butter and remaining olive oil and chicken.

3. Add broth and lemon juice to skillet; cook 1 to 2 minutes or until sauce is slightly thickened, stirring to loosen particles from bottom of skillet. Add 8 lemon slices.

4. Remove skillet from heat. Add parsley and remaining 2 Tbsp. butter; stir until butter melts. Pour sauce over chicken. Serve immediately. Garnish, if desired.

Lemon Chicken

Grilled Chicken with Corn and Slaw

Hands-on Time: 30 min.
Total Time: 30 min.
Makes: 4 servings

- 1 cup mayonnaise
- ¼ cup chopped fresh cilantro
- 6 Tbsp. white wine vinegar, divided
- ¾ tsp. salt, divided
- ⅛ tsp. pepper
- 4 skinned and boned chicken breasts (about 1 lb.)
- 4 ears fresh corn, husks removed
- ¼ cup melted butter
- 1 (10-oz.) package shredded coleslaw mix
- 3 Tbsp. olive oil
- ½ tsp. sugar
- ¼ tsp. pepper

1. Combine mayonnaise, cilantro, 3 Tbsp. vinegar, $^1/_4$ tsp. salt, and $^1/_8$ tsp. pepper in a small bowl. Reserve $^3/_4$ cup mayonnaise mixture. Brush chicken with remaining $^1/_4$ cup mayonnaise mixture.
2. Preheat grill to 350° to 400° (medium-high) heat. Grill chicken and corn at the same time, covered with grill lid. Grill chicken 7 minutes on each side or until done; grill corn 14 minutes or until done, turning every 4 to 5 minutes and basting with melted butter.
3. Toss coleslaw mix with oil, sugar, $^1/_4$ tsp. pepper, and remaining 3 Tbsp. vinegar and $^1/_2$ tsp. salt. Season chicken and corn with salt and pepper to taste. Serve with coleslaw and reserved mayonnaise mixture.

Grilled Chicken with Corn and Slaw

fix it!

Problem: Your grilled chicken turns out dry.

Solution: Always allow the meat to rest before cutting into it. That way, the meat has time to seal in all the flavorful juices. You may also want to invest in a meat thermometer to ensure properly cooked meats.

Grilled Chicken Thighs with White Barbecue Sauce

Hands-on Time: 31 min.
Total Time: 4 hr., 31 min., including sauce
Makes: 5 servings

- 1 Tbsp. dried thyme
- 1 Tbsp. dried oregano
- 1 Tbsp. ground cumin
- 1 Tbsp. paprika
- 1 tsp. onion powder
- ½ tsp. salt
- ½ tsp. pepper
- 10 skin-on, bone-in chicken thighs (about 3 lb.)
- White Barbecue Sauce
- Garnishes: cherry tomatoes, fresh parsley sprigs

1. Combine first 7 ingredients until blended. Rinse chicken, and pat dry; rub seasoning mixture over chicken. Place chicken in a zip-top plastic freezer bag. Seal and chill 4 hours.
2. Preheat grill to 350° to 400° (medium-high) heat. Remove chicken from bag, discarding bag.
3. Grill chicken, covered with a grill lid, 8 to 10 minutes on each side. Serve with White Barbecue Sauce. Garnish, if desired.

White Barbecue Sauce

Hands-on Time: 10 min.
Total Time: 10 min.
Makes: 1³/₄ cups

This versatile sauce received our highest rating and is also good over baked potatoes or as a condiment for burgers.

- 1½ cups mayonnaise
- ¼ cup white wine vinegar
- 1 garlic clove, minced
- 1 Tbsp. coarse ground pepper
- 1 Tbsp. spicy brown mustard
- 1 tsp. sugar
- 1 tsp. salt
- 2 tsp. horseradish

1. Stir together all ingredients until well blended. Store in an airtight container in refrigerator up to 1 week.

Grilled Chicken Thighs with White Barbecue Sauce

Pan-Fried Chicken-and-Ham Parmesan

Hands-on Time: 18 min.
Total Time: 26 min., including pasta, butter, and tomatoes
Makes: 4 servings

- 4 (6-oz.) skinned and boned chicken breasts
- 1 tsp. salt
- ½ tsp. pepper
- 1 large egg
- ¼ cup all-purpose flour
- ⅔ cup Italian-seasoned breadcrumbs
- 2 Tbsp. olive oil
- 8 thinly sliced smoked deli ham slices (about ¼ lb.)
- 4 (1-oz.) fresh mozzarella cheese slices
- Garlic-Herb Pasta
- Sautéed Grape Tomatoes

1. Preheat oven to 350°. Sprinkle chicken with salt and pepper. Whisk together egg and 2 Tbsp. water. Dredge chicken in flour; dip in egg mixture, and dredge in breadcrumbs, shaking off excess.
2. Cook chicken in hot oil in a large ovenproof skillet over medium-high heat 3 to 4 minutes on each side or until golden. Top chicken with ham and cheese.
3. Bake chicken in skillet at 350° for 8 minutes or until cheese is melted. Serve over Garlic-Herb Pasta; top with Sautéed Grape Tomatoes.

Garlic-Herb Pasta

Hands-on Time: 5 min.
Total Time: 15 min.
Makes: 4 servings

- 8 oz. vermicelli
- ¼ cup Garlic-Herb Butter
- Salt to taste

1. Cook vermicelli according to package directions; drain. Toss with Garlic-Herb Butter. Season with salt to taste.

Garlic-Herb Butter

Hands-on Time: 15 min.
Total Time: 15 min.
Makes: ½ cup

- ½ cup butter, softened
- 1 large garlic clove, pressed
- ⅔ cup chopped fresh basil
- ¼ cup chopped fresh parsley
- ¼ tsp. salt

1. Stir together softened butter, garlic clove, basil, parsley, and salt until well blended. Use immediately, or cover and chill up to 3 days. For longer storage, form into a log or press into ice cube trays, and wrap tightly with plastic wrap; freeze up to 1 month.

Sautéed Grape Tomatoes

Hands-on Time: 10 min.
Total Time: 13 min.
Makes: 4 servings

Grape tomatoes deliver a sweet taste of summer and cook in minutes. They make a delicious stand-alone side dish as well as a salsa-like topping for poultry and seafood.

- 1 pt. grape tomatoes, halved
- 1 Tbsp. light brown sugar
- 3 Tbsp. balsamic vinegar
- ¼ tsp. salt
- 1 tsp. olive oil
- 2 Tbsp. thinly sliced fresh basil

1. Sauté tomatoes and next 3 ingredients in hot oil in a small skillet over medium-high heat 2 to 3 minutes or until thoroughly heated. Remove from heat, and stir in basil.

Classic Chicken Tetrazzini

Hands-on Time: 20 min.
Total Time: 55 min.
Makes: 8 to 10 servings

Use leftover diced cooked turkey after your holiday meal in place of the chicken as a variation.

- 1½ (8-oz.) packages vermicelli
- ½ cup butter
- ½ cup all-purpose flour
- 4 cups milk
- ½ cup dry white wine
- 2 Tbsp. chicken bouillon granules
- 1 tsp. seasoned pepper
- 2 cups freshly grated Parmesan cheese, divided
- 4 cups diced cooked chicken
- 1 (6-oz.) jar sliced mushrooms, drained
- ¾ cup slivered almonds

1. Preheat oven to 350°. Prepare pasta according to package directions.
2. Meanwhile, melt butter in a Dutch oven over low heat; whisk in flour until smooth. Cook 1 minute, whisking constantly. Gradually whisk in milk and wine; cook over medium heat, whisking constantly, 8 to 10 minutes or until mixture is thickened and bubbly. Whisk in bouillon granules, seasoned pepper, and 1 cup Parmesan cheese.
3. Remove from heat; stir in diced cooked chicken, sliced mushrooms, and hot cooked pasta.
4. Spoon mixture into a lightly greased 13- x 9-inch baking dish; sprinkle with slivered almonds and remaining 1 cup Parmesan cheese.
5. Bake at 350° for 35 minutes or until bubbly.

Spice-Rubbed Grilled Turkey Tenderloins

Hands-on Time: 30 min.
Total Time: 40 min.
Makes: 4 to 6 servings

- 2 Tbsp. light brown sugar
- 1 tsp. salt
- 1 tsp. ground cumin
- ¼ to ½ tsp. ground red pepper
- ⅛ tsp. ground ginger
- ⅛ tsp. ground coriander
- 1½ lb. turkey tenderloin
- 2 Tbsp. olive oil

1. Preheat grill to 350° to 400° (medium-high) heat. Stir together first 6 ingredients. Brush turkey with olive oil, and rub with brown sugar mixture.
2. Grill turkey, covered with grill lid 10 minutes on each side or until a meat thermometer inserted into thickest portion registers 165°. Let stand 10 minutes before serving.

Classic Chicken Tetrazzini

Spicy Grilled Pork Tenderloin with Blackberry Sauce

Hands-on Time: 15 min.
Total Time: 40 min.
Makes: 6 to 8 servings

2	(¾-lb.) pork tenderloins
1	Tbsp. olive oil
1½	Tbsp. Caribbean jerk seasoning
1	tsp. salt
⅔	cup seedless blackberry preserves
¼	cup Dijon mustard
1	Tbsp. orange zest
2	Tbsp. rum or orange juice
1	Tbsp. grated fresh ginger

1. Preheat grill to 350° to 400° (medium-high) heat. Remove silver skin from tenderloins, leaving a thin layer of fat. Brush tenderloins with oil, and rub with seasoning and salt.

2. Grill tenderloins, covered with grill lid, 10 minutes on each side or until a meat thermometer inserted into thickest portion registers 155°. Remove from grill, and let stand 10 minutes.

3. Meanwhile, whisk together blackberry preserves and next 4 ingredients in a small saucepan, and cook over low heat, whisking constantly, 5 minutes or until thoroughly heated.

4. Cut pork diagonally into thin slices, and arrange on a serving platter; drizzle with warm sauce.

Spicy Grilled Pork Tenderloin with Blackberry Sauce

fix it!

Problem: You forgot to clean the grill grates after the last cookout.

Solution: Rub the cut side of an onion on the hot grill grates to remove any leftover residue.

Pork Roast with Carolina Gravy

Hands-on Time: 25 min.
Total Time: 4 hr., 18 min.
Makes: 8 servings

  4 medium leeks
  1 (5- to 6-lb.) bone-in pork shoulder
     roast (Boston butt)
  Kitchen string
  2 tsp. salt
  2 tsp. pepper
  3 thick bacon slices, chopped
  1 Tbsp. vegetable oil
 10 garlic cloves, halved
  3 medium onions, halved and sliced
 2½ cups low-sodium fat-free chicken broth
  ½ cup dry white wine
 10 fresh thyme sprigs
  4 bay leaves
  1 Tbsp. butter

1. Preheat oven to 350°. Remove and discard root ends and dark green tops of leeks. Thinly slice leeks; rinse well, and drain.
2. Tie pork roast with kitchen string, securing at 2-inch intervals. Season with salt and pepper.
3. Cook bacon in hot oil in an ovenproof Dutch oven or large, deep cast-iron skillet over medium-high heat 3 minutes. Add leeks, garlic, and onion, and cook, stirring frequently, 15 to 17 minutes or until mixture is golden brown; transfer to a bowl.
4. Add pork roast, fat side down, to Dutch oven; and cook 2 minutes on all sides or until browned. Remove pork.
5. Return leek mixture to Dutch oven; top with pork. Add broth and next 3 ingredients. Reduce heat to medium, and bring to a light boil. Remove from heat, and cover with heavy-duty aluminum foil.
6. Bake at 350° for 3 to 3¹/₂ hours or until a meat thermometer inserted into thickest portion registers 180° to 185°. Remove pork from Dutch oven, cover with foil, and let stand 20 minutes before slicing.
7. Meanwhile, pour pan juices through a wire mesh strainer into a saucepan to equal 4 cups, discarding solids. Add equal parts broth and white wine to pan

juices to equal 4 cups. Let stand 5 minutes; skim fat from surface of pan juices.
8. Bring to a boil over medium-high heat, and cook 20 to 25 minutes or until liquid is reduced to 1 cup and slightly thickened. Remove from heat, and stir in butter until melted. Serve with pork.

Shredded Pork With Carolina Gravy: Prepare recipe as directed through Step 5. Bake at 350° for 4 to 5 hours or until a meat thermometer inserted into thickest portion registers 195°. Remove pork from Dutch oven, and cover with foil; let stand 20 minutes. Shred pork with 2 forks. Proceed with recipe as directed.

> ## kitchen secret:
>
> If you don't own an instant-read thermometer, it's worth purchasing one for this recipe. Cooking this budget-friendly roast to between 180° and 185° ensures incredibly tender slices for a pretty presentation.

Pork Roast with Carolina Gravy

Apricot-Pineapple Sweet Ribs

Hands-on Time: 20 min.
Total Time: 3 hr., 50 min.
Makes: 4 to 6 servings

   2 slabs baby back ribs (about 2 lb. each)
Rib Dry Rub
Rib Liquid Seasoning
Sweet Barbecue Glaze

1. Remove thin membrane from back of each slab by slicing into it and then pulling it off. (This will make ribs more tender.) Generously apply Rib Dry Rub on both sides of ribs, pressing gently to adhere.
2. Light one side of grill, heating to 250° (low) heat; leave other side unlit. Place slabs, meat sides up, over unlit side, and grill, covered with grill lid, 2 hours and 15 minutes, maintaining temperature inside grill between 225° and 250°. Remove slabs from grill. Place each slab, meat side down, on a large piece of heavy-duty aluminum foil. (Foil should be large enough to completely wrap slab.) Pour ¹/₂ cup of Rib Liquid Seasoning over each slab. Tightly wrap each slab in foil. Return slabs to unlit side of grill. Grill, covered with grill lid, 1 hour.
3. Remove slabs; unwrap and discard foil. Brush Sweet Barbecue Glaze on both sides of slabs. Grill slabs, covered with grill lid, on unlit side of grill 15 minutes or until caramelized.

Rib Dry Rub

Hands-on Time: 5 min.
Total Time: 5 min.
Makes: about ¹/₂ cup

  ¼ cup firmly packed dark brown sugar
  4 tsp. garlic salt
  4 tsp. chili powder
  2 tsp. salt
  1 tsp. ground black pepper
  ½ tsp. celery salt
  ¼ tsp. ground white pepper
  ¼ tsp. ground red pepper
  ¼ tsp. ground cinnamon

1. Stir together all ingredients. Store in an airtight container up to 1 month.

Rib Liquid Seasoning

Hands-on Time: 5 min.
Total Time: 5 min.
Makes: about 1 cup

  ½ cup pineapple juice
  ½ cup apricot nectar
  1 Tbsp. Rib Dry Rub
  1½ tsp. balsamic vinegar
  1½ tsp. minced garlic

1. Stir together all ingredients. Store in an airtight container in refrigerator up to 2 weeks.

Sweet Barbecue Glaze

Hands-on Time: 5 min.
Total Time: 5 min.
Makes: about 1¹/₂ cups

  ¼ cup tomato-based barbecue sauce
  ¼ cup honey

1. Stir together all ingredients. Store in an airtight container in refrigerator up to 2 weeks.

Note: We tested with Big Bob Gibson Bar-B-Q Championship Red Sauce.

Apricot-Pineapple Sweet Ribs

Pork Chops with Pepper Jelly Sauce

Hands-on Time: 39 min.
Total Time: 39 min.
Makes: 6 servings

Pepper jelly adds a perfect balance of sweet and hot to these chops.

- 4 (¾-inch-thick) bone-in pork loin chops (about 2¼ lb.)
- 1 tsp. salt
- ¾ tsp. freshly ground black pepper
- 3 Tbsp. butter, divided
- 3 Tbsp. olive oil
- 1 Tbsp. all-purpose flour
- 1 large jalapeño pepper, seeded and minced
- ⅓ cup dry white wine
- 1 cup chicken broth
- ½ cup red pepper jelly

1. Sprinkle pork with salt and pepper. Melt 1 Tbsp. butter with oil in a 12-inch cast-iron skillet over medium-high heat. Add pork chops; cook 8 minutes. Turn and cook 10 minutes or until a meat thermometer inserted into thickest portion registers 150°. Remove from skillet, and keep warm.
2. Add flour and jalapeño to skillet. Cook, stirring constantly, 1 to 2 minutes or until flour is golden brown. Add wine, stirring to loosen particles from bottom of skillet; cook 1 minute or until almost completely reduced.
3. Add chicken broth, and cook 2 to 3 minutes or until mixture begins to thicken. Whisk in pepper jelly until melted and smooth. Cook 3 to 4 minutes or until thickened. Remove from heat. Whisk in remaining 2 Tbsp. butter. Season with salt and freshly ground pepper to taste. Return pork to skillet; turn to coat. Serve pork with sauce.

Note: We tested with Braswell's Red Pepper Jelly.

Honey-Bourbon Glazed Ham

Hands-on Time: 20 min.
Total Time: 3 hr., 20 min.
Makes: 15 servings

- 1 (9¼-lb.) fully cooked, bone-in ham
- 40 whole cloves
- ½ cup firmly packed light brown sugar
- ½ cup honey
- ½ cup bourbon
- ⅓ cup Creole mustard
- ⅓ cup molasses
- Garnishes: sliced kiwifruit, red grapes, fresh parsley

1. Preheat oven to 350°. Remove skin from ham, and trim fat to ¼-inch thickness. Make shallow cuts in fat 1 inch apart in a diamond pattern; insert cloves in centers of diamonds. Place ham in an aluminum foil-lined 13- x 9-inch pan.
2. Stir together brown sugar and next 4 ingredients; spoon over ham. Bake at 350° on lowest oven rack 2 hours and 30 minutes, basting with pan juices every 30 minutes. Shield ham with foil after 1 hour to prevent excessive browning. Remove ham from oven, and let stand 30 minutes. Garnish, if desired.

Honey-Bourbon Glazed Ham

Fennel-Crusted Rib Roast

Hands-on Time: 20 min.
Total Time: 3 hr., 5 min.
Makes: 8 servings

1   (7- to 9-lb.) 4-rib prime rib roast, trimmed
2   tsp. black peppercorns
2   tsp. fennel seeds
1½   tsp. coriander seeds
1   Tbsp. olive oil
4   tsp. kosher salt
Garnishes: fresh cranberries, oranges, gray
      sea salt

1. Preheat oven to 400°. Let roast stand at room temperature 30 minutes.
2. Pulse peppercorns, fennel, and coriander in a spice grinder 5 times or until coarsely ground. (Or place spices in a zip-top plastic freezer bag, and crush using a rolling pin or skillet.) Rub roast with oil, and sprinkle with salt. Press spice mixture onto all sides of roast. Place on a rack in a roasting pan.
3. Bake roast at 400° for 2 hours or until a meat thermometer inserted into thickest portion registers 120° to 125° (medium-rare) or to desired degree of doneness. Let roast stand 15 minutes to 1 hour before slicing. Garnish, if desired.

Fennel-Crusted
Rib Roast

Herb-and-Potato Chip-Crusted
Beef Tenderloin

Herb-and-Potato Chip-Crusted Beef Tenderloin

Hands-on Time: 40 min.
Total Time: 2 hr., 20 min.
Makes: 6 to 8 servings

Herb-and-Potato Chip-Crusted Beef Tenderloin gets added crunch with a flavorful coating of fresh herbs, panko breadcrumbs, and kettle-cooked potato chips.

  1 (4- to 5-lb.) beef tenderloin, trimmed
  3 tsp. kosher salt, divided
  ¾ cup panko (Japanese breadcrumbs)
  3 garlic cloves, pressed
  2 tsp. coarsely ground pepper, divided
  3 Tbsp. olive oil, divided
1¼ cups crushed, plain kettle-cooked
      potato chips
  ¼ cup finely chopped fresh parsley
  1 Tbsp. finely chopped fresh thyme
  1 bay leaf, crushed
  1 egg white, lightly beaten
  1 Tbsp. Dijon mustard
Garnish: fresh sage

1. Preheat oven to 400°. Sprinkle beef with 2 tsp. salt. Let stand 30 to 45 minutes.

2. Meanwhile, sauté panko, garlic, 1 tsp. pepper, and remaining 1 tsp. salt in 1 Tbsp. hot oil in a skillet over medium heat 2 to 3 minutes or until deep golden brown. Let cool completely (about 10 minutes). Stir in potato chips and next 4 ingredients.

3. Pat beef dry with paper towels, and sprinkle with remaining 1 tsp. pepper. Brown beef in remaining 2 Tbsp. hot oil in a roasting pan over medium-high heat until browned on all sides (about 2 to 3 minutes per side). Transfer beef to a wire rack in an aluminum foil-lined jelly-roll pan. Let stand 10 minutes.

4. Spread mustard over beef. Press panko mixture onto top and sides.

5. Bake at 400° for 40 to 45 minutes or until coating is crisp and a meat thermometer inserted into thickest portion registers 130° (rare). Let stand 10 minutes. Garnish, if desired.

Note: For medium-rare, cook tenderloin to 135°; for medium, cook to 150°.

Braised Beef Brisket

Hands-on Time: 15 min.
Total Time: 4 hr., 35 min., plus 1 day for chilling
Makes: 16 servings

- 2 (14.5-oz.) cans low-sodium fat-free beef broth
- 1 cup low-sodium soy sauce
- ¼ cup lemon juice
- 5 garlic cloves, chopped
- 1 Tbsp. hickory liquid smoke (optional)
- 1 (7- to 9-lb.) beef brisket

1. Stir together first 4 ingredients and, if desired, liquid smoke in a large roasting pan. Place brisket in pan, fat side up. Spoon broth mixture and liquid smoke over brisket. Cover tightly with aluminum foil, and chill 24 hours.

2. Preheat oven to 300°. Bake brisket, covered, 4 to 4¹⁄₂ hours or until fork-tender. Uncover and let stand 20 minutes.

3. Transfer brisket to a cutting board. Trim fat from brisket. Cut brisket across the grain into thin slices. (Or cut brisket into large pieces, and shred with two forks.) Pour pan drippings through a wire-mesh strainer, discarding solids. Serve brisket with drippings.

kitchen secret:

Can't find a large brisket? Substitute 2 smaller ones that equal the same weight.

Braised Beef Brisket

Bev's Famous Meatloaf

Hands-on Time: 30 min.
Total Time: 2 hr., 5 min.
Makes: 10 servings

- 2 lb. lean ground beef
- 1 lb. ground pork sausage
- 18 saltine crackers, crushed
- ½ green bell pepper, diced
- ½ onion, finely chopped
- 2 large eggs, lightly beaten
- 1 Tbsp. Worcestershire sauce
- 1 tsp. yellow mustard
- ½ cup firmly packed brown sugar, divided
- ½ cup ketchup

1. Preheat oven to 350°. Combine first 8 ingredients and ¼ cup brown sugar in a medium bowl until blended. Place mixture in a lightly greased 11- x 7-inch baking dish, and shape mixture into a 10- x 5-inch loaf.
2. Bake at 350° for 1 hour. Remove from oven, and drain. Stir together ketchup and remaining ¼ cup brown sugar; pour over meatloaf. Bake 15 more minutes or until a meat thermometer inserted into thickest portion registers 160°. Remove from oven; let stand 20 minutes. Remove from baking dish before slicing.

Bev's Famous Meatloaf

Tomato 'n' Beef Casserole with Polenta Crust

Hands-on Time: 55 min.
Total Time: 1 hr., 5 min.
Makes: 6 servings

- 1 tsp. salt
- 1 cup plain yellow cornmeal
- 1 cup (4 oz.) shredded sharp Cheddar cheese, divided
- ½ tsp. Montreal steak seasoning
- 1 lb. ground chuck
- 1 cup chopped onion
- 1 medium zucchini, cut in half lengthwise and sliced (about 2 cups)
- 1 Tbsp. olive oil
- 2 (14½-oz.) cans petite diced tomatoes, drained
- 1 (6-oz.) can tomato paste
- 2 Tbsp. chopped fresh flat-leaf parsley

1. Preheat oven to 350°. Bring 3 cups water and 1 tsp. salt to a boil in a 2-qt. saucepan over medium-high heat; whisk in cornmeal. Reduce heat to low; simmer, whisking constantly, 3 minutes or until thickened. Remove from heat, and stir in ¼ cup Cheddar cheese and steak seasoning. Spread cornmeal mixture into a lightly greased 11- x 7-inch baking dish.
2. Brown ground chuck in a large nonstick skillet over medium-high heat, stirring often, 10 minutes or until meat crumbles and is no longer pink; drain and transfer to a bowl.
3. Sauté onion and zucchini in hot oil in skillet over medium heat 5 minutes or until crisp-tender. Stir in beef, tomatoes, and tomato paste; simmer, stirring often, 10 minutes. Pour beef mixture over cornmeal crust. Sprinkle with remaining ¾ cup cheese.
4. Bake at 350° for 30 minutes or until bubbly. Sprinkle casserole with parsley just before serving.

Italian Sausage Casserole with Polenta Crust:
Substitute Italian sausage for ground chuck and Italian six-cheese blend for Cheddar cheese. Prepare recipe as directed, sautéing 1 medium-size green bell pepper, chopped, with onion and zucchini in Step 3.

Picadillo Tacos

Hands-on Time: 15 min.
Total Time: 31 min.
Makes: 8 tacos

This meaty mixture is also great served as a taco salad or wrapped in enchiladas and burritos.

- 1 lb. ground round
- 1 Tbsp. vegetable oil
- 2 carrots, diced
- 1 small onion, diced
- ½ tsp. salt
- 2 plum tomatoes, diced
- 1 to 2 canned chipotle peppers in adobo sauce, minced
- 8 (8-inch) soft taco-size corn or flour tortillas, warmed
- Garnish: fresh cilantro sprigs, lime wedges

1. Cook ground round in hot oil in a large skillet over medium-high heat, stirring often, 7 minutes or until meat crumbles and is browned. Stir in carrots, onion, and salt; sauté 5 minutes. Add tomatoes and chipotle peppers; cook, stirring occasionally, 3 to 4 minutes or until tomatoes begin to soften. Serve mixture with warm tortillas. Garnish, if desired.

Vegetarian Picadillo Tacos: Substitute 1 (12-oz.) package frozen meatless burger crumbles for ground round. Proceed with recipe as directed, sautéing crumbles in hot oil 3 to 4 minutes.

Picadillo Tacos

FISH & SHELLFISH

Enjoy the fresh catch any time of year with these favorite seafood recipes.

Blackened Salmon with Hash Browns and Green Onions

Hands-on Time: 15 min.
Total Time: 41 min.
Makes: 4 servings

All fillets are not equal in thickness, so cooking times will vary. Plan on about 10 minutes total cooking time for 1-inch-thick pieces and 15 minutes for 1½ inches thick, and so on. Place the largest piece on the heat first.

- 3 bunches green onions
- 6 cups frozen shredded hash browns
- 1 Tbsp. chopped fresh or 1 tsp. dried dill
- ½ to ¾ tsp. salt
- 4 Tbsp. olive oil, divided
- 2 tsp. blackened seasoning
- 4 (6- to 8-oz.) salmon fillets
- Garnish: fresh dill sprigs

1. Preheat oven to 300°. Remove and discard root ends and 1 inch of top green portions of green onions, and set green onions aside.
2. Toss together hash browns, dill, and salt in a large bowl.

3. Heat 2 Tbsp. oil in a large nonstick skillet over medium heat. Add hash brown mixture in an even layer, and cook 5 minutes or until lightly browned. (Do not stir.) Place a lightly greased baking sheet, greased side down, onto skillet; invert hash browns onto baking sheet. Place skillet back on heat. Slide hash browns back into skillet, cooked side up, and cook 5 more minutes or until golden brown.
4. Press hash browns down with a spatula to flatten. Remove from skillet onto same baking sheet, and keep warm in oven at 300°. Sprinkle blackened seasoning evenly over fillets.
5. Cook salmon in 1 Tbsp. hot oil in same nonstick skillet over medium heat 4 to 6 minutes on each side or just until fish begins to flake with a fork. Remove from skillet onto serving plates.
6. Sauté green onions in remaining 1 Tbsp. hot oil in same nonstick skillet over medium heat 4 minutes or until tender; remove from skillet, and serve with salmon and hash browns. Garnish, if desired.

Note: We tested with Old Bay Blackened Seasoning. Use a skillet with flared sides so that the cooked hash browns slide out of the pan easily.

fix it!

Problem: The salmon stuck to the pan when you tried to sauté it.

Solution: Be sure that the oil is very hot before you add the fish to the pan. Let it cook a minute or 2 before trying to move it—the bottom will create a crust that helps prevent sticking.

Blackened Salmon with Hash Browns and Green Onions

Poached Salmon

scrape down sides as needed. With processor running, pour oil through food chute in a slow, steady stream, processing until smooth. Smash remaining 6 garlic cloves, using flat side of a knife.
2. Pour water to a depth of 2$\frac{1}{2}$ inches into a large skillet over medium-high heat. Add smashed garlic, $\frac{1}{2}$ bunch fresh parsley, and lemon slices; bring to a boil. Add salmon fillets; return liquid to a boil, reduce heat to low, and simmer 7 to 10 minutes or until fish flakes with a fork. Remove salmon from skillet; and discard liquid in skillet. Serve salmon with garlic-parsley mixture. Garnish, if desired.

Lemon-Grilled Salmon

Hands-on Time: 15 min.
Total Time: 8 hr., 35 min.
Makes: 4 servings

   2   (15- x 6-inch) cedar grilling planks
   3   Tbsp. chopped fresh dill
   3   Tbsp. chopped fresh parsley
   2   tsp. lemon zest
   3   Tbsp. fresh lemon juice
   1   Tbsp. olive oil
   1   garlic clove, pressed
   ½   tsp. salt
   ¼   tsp. pepper
   4   (6-oz.) salmon fillets

1. Weigh down cedar planks with a heavier object in a large container. Add water to cover, and soak at least 8 hours.
2. Combine dill and next 5 ingredients; set aside.
3. Sprinkle salt and pepper evenly on salmon.
4. Remove cedar planks from water, and place planks on cooking grate on grill.
5. Grill soaked planks, covered with grill lid, over medium-high heat (350° to 400°) 2 minutes or until the planks begin to lightly smoke. Place 2 fillets on each cedar plank, and grill, covered with grill lid, 15 to 18 minutes or until fish flakes with a fork. Remove fish from planks to individual serving plates using a spatula. (Carefully remove planks from grill using tongs.) Spoon reserved herb mixture over fish, and serve immediately.

Poached Salmon

Hands-on Time: 10 min.
Total Time: 20 min.
Makes: 6 servings

If you can boil water, then you can poach salmon. First, create a flavorful poaching liquid by adding garlic, herbs, and lemon to water in a large skillet. Then simply bring the water to a slight boil, add the salmon fillets, and reduce heat to a simmer. You'll have a heart-healthy main dish in minutes.

   8   garlic cloves, divided
   ½   cup loosely packed fresh parsley leaves
   ¼   cup loosely packed fresh mint leaves
   ½   tsp. salt
   3   Tbsp. extra virgin olive oil
   ½   bunch fresh parsley
   3   lemons, sliced
   6   (6-oz.) 1-inch-thick salmon fillets
   Garnish: lemon slices

1. Combine 2 garlic cloves, $\frac{1}{2}$ cup parsley leaves, $\frac{1}{4}$ cup mint leaves, and $\frac{1}{2}$ tsp. salt in the bowl of a food processor; pulse until smooth, stopping to

Classic Fried Catfish

Classic Fried Catfish

Hands-on Time: 20 min.
Total Time: 8 hr., 20 min.
Makes: 6 servings

For an extra-crispy crust, use stone-ground yellow cornmeal, if available. Serve with lemon slices and your favorite tartar sauce.

1½ cups buttermilk
¼ tsp. hot sauce
6 (4- to 6-oz.) catfish fillets
⅓ cup plain yellow cornmeal
⅓ cup masa harina (corn flour)*
⅓ cup all-purpose flour
2 tsp. salt
1 tsp. ground black pepper
1 tsp. ground red pepper
¼ tsp. garlic powder
Peanut oil
Garnishes: lemon slices, fresh parsley sprigs

1. Whisk together buttermilk and hot sauce.
2. Place catfish in a single layer in a 13- x 9-inch baking dish; pour buttermilk mixture over fish. Cover and chill 8 hours, turning once.
3. Combine cornmeal and next 6 ingredients in a shallow dish.
4. Let fish stand at room temperature 10 minutes. Remove fish from buttermilk mixture, allowing excess to drip off. Dredge fish in cornmeal mixture, shaking off excess.
5. Pour oil to a depth of 2 inches into a large, deep cast-iron or heavy-duty skillet; heat to 360°.
6. Fry fish, in batches, 2 minutes on each side or until golden brown. Transfer to a wire rack on a paper towel-lined jelly-roll pan. Keep warm in a 225° oven until ready to serve. Garnish, if desired.

*All-purpose flour or plain yellow cornmeal may be substituted.

Pecan-Crusted Tilapia

Hands-on Time: 18 min.
Total Time: 34 min., including sauce
Makes: 4 servings

If you don't have a skillet large enough to hold all the fillets easily, we recommend cooking them in batches and keeping them warm in a 200° oven.

- ½ cup pecan halves
- 4 (6-oz.) fresh tilapia fillets
- 1 tsp. salt
- ½ tsp. garlic powder
- ¼ tsp. pepper
- 3 Tbsp. butter
- Golden Rum Butter Sauce
- Garnishes: lemon wedge, fresh parsley sprig

1. Process pecans in a food processor until finely chopped. Sprinkle fillets with salt, garlic powder, and pepper. Dredge fish in finely chopped pecans.
2. Melt butter in a large nonstick skillet over medium-high heat. Add fish; cook 3 to 4 minutes on each side or until well browned and fish flakes with a fork. Serve with Golden Rum Butter Sauce. Garnish, if desired.

Golden Rum Butter Sauce

Hands-on Time: 16 min.
Total Time: 16 min.
Makes: ⅓ cup

This sauce also tastes great on shrimp or scallops.

- 3 Tbsp. butter
- 1 shallot, minced
- 1 garlic clove, minced
- 2 Tbsp. rum*
- 2 Tbsp. fresh lemon juice
- 2 Tbsp. fresh orange juice
- 1 tsp. honey
- ½ tsp. salt

1. Melt 1 Tbsp. butter in a small skillet over medium-high heat; add shallot and garlic, and cook, stirring occasionally, 5 minutes or until shallot is tender. Reduce heat to low, and slowly whisk in rum, next 4 ingredients, and remaining 2 Tbsp. butter. Cook, stirring occasionally, 1 minute; serve warm.

*Fresh lemon juice may be substituted.

Pecan-Crusted Tilapia

Bayou Fish Fillets with Sweet-Hot Pecan Sauce

Hands-on Time: 36 min.
Total Time: 36 min., including sauce
Makes: 6 servings

  1 (6-oz.) package cornbread mix
1½ tsp. Creole seasoning
 ½ tsp. salt
 ½ tsp. pepper
  6 (6-oz.) cod or tilapia fillets
Canola oil
Sweet-Hot Pecan Sauce

1. Stir together cornbread mix and Creole seasoning until blended.
2. Sprinkle salt and pepper over fillets. Dredge fillets in cornbread mixture.
3. Pour oil to a depth of 4 inches into a large Dutch oven; heat to 375°. Fry fillets, in batches, 1 to 1½ minutes on each side or until golden. Drain on a wire rack over paper towels. Serve with Sweet-Hot Pecan Sauce.

Sweet-Hot Pecan Sauce

Hands-on Time: 20 min.
Total Time: 20 min.
Makes: 1 cup

 ¼ cup butter
 ¼ cup chopped red onion
  1 tsp. minced garlic
 ½ cup pecan pieces, chopped
 ½ cup firmly packed light brown sugar
  2 Tbsp. lemon juice
  2 Tbsp. Worcestershire sauce
  1 Tbsp. hot sauce

1. Melt butter in a medium saucepan over medium heat. Add onion, and sauté 3 minutes or until tender. Add garlic, and cook 1 minute. Stir in pecans and next 4 ingredients. Cook, stirring constantly, until sugar is dissolved. Store in an airtight container in refrigerator up to 1 week.

Bayou Fish Fillets with
Sweet-Hot Pecan Sauce

Crispy Baked Cod

Hands-on Time: 10 min.
Total Time: 27 min.
Makes: 6 servings

You can substitute mahi-mahi, grouper, catfish, salmon, or tilapia for cod.

- 1 cup panko (Japanese breadcrumbs)*
- 2 Tbsp. chopped fresh parsley
- 2 tsp. lemon zest
- 1 tsp. minced garlic
- 6 (6-oz.) cod fillets
- 1 tsp. salt
- 2 Tbsp. melted butter

1. Preheat oven to 400°. Combine first 4 ingredients in a small bowl.
2. Place fillets on a lightly greased wire rack in a baking pan; sprinkle evenly with salt. Spoon panko mixture evenly onto fillets, pressing down gently. Drizzle evenly with 2 Tbsp. melted butter.
3. Bake at 400° for 17 minutes or until breadcrumbs are golden and fish flakes with a fork.

*1 cup fine, dry breadcrumbs may be substituted.

Sizzling Flounder

Hands-on Time: 10 min.
Total Time: 31 min.
Makes: 4 servings

While flounder is a favorite, use any firm-fleshed fish, such as tilapia, grouper, or catfish. Adjust the cooking time according to the thickness of the fish.

- ¼ cup grated Parmesan cheese
- 1 tsp. paprika
- 4 (6-oz.) flounder fillets
- ¾ tsp. salt
- ¼ tsp. pepper
- ½ cup butter
- 2 Tbsp. fresh lemon juice

Sizzling Flounder

1. Place 1 oven rack 5 inches from heat; place a second rack in middle of oven. Combine Parmesan cheese and paprika. Season fish with salt and pepper.
2. Preheat oven to 450°. Heat butter in a broiler-safe 13- x 9-inch baking dish in oven 8 minutes or until butter is melted and beginning to brown. Place fish in hot butter, skin sides up.
3. Bake at 450° on middle oven rack 10 minutes. Carefully flip fish; baste with pan juices. Sprinkle with lemon juice and Parmesan cheese mixture. Bake 5 more minutes or just until fish flakes with a fork. Remove from oven; increase oven temperature to broil.
4. Broil fish on oven rack 5 inches from heat 2 to 3 minutes or until bubbly and golden brown.

Seared Halibut with Herbed Tomato Sauce

Hands-on Time: 31 min.
Total Time: 31 min.
Makes: 4 servings

- 4 (6-oz.) halibut fillets (½ inch thick)*
- ½ tsp. salt, divided
- ¼ tsp. pepper
- 2 tsp. extra virgin olive oil
- ½ medium onion, chopped
- 2 garlic cloves, minced
- 1 Tbsp. drained capers
- ¼ tsp. dried basil
- ¼ tsp. dried oregano
- 1 (14.5-oz.) can petite diced tomatoes

1. Pat fish dry with paper towels. Season fish with ¼ tsp. salt and ¼ tsp. pepper. Cook fish in hot oil in a large skillet over medium-high heat 3 to 4 minutes on each side or until fish flakes with a fork and is opaque throughout. Transfer fish to a serving platter, and keep warm.

2. Add onion and garlic to skillet; sauté 1 to 2 minutes or until onion is tender. Stir in capers, basil, oregano, and remaining ¼ tsp. salt. Cook 1 minute. Reduce heat to low, add tomatoes, and cook, stirring occasionally, 10 minutes. Top fish with tomato sauce.

*Frozen halibut or fresh or frozen cod may be substituted.

Seared Halibut with Herbed Tomato Sauce

Tuna Cornbread Cakes

Hands-on Time: 27 min.
Total Time: 47 min., including aioli
Makes: 4 servings

  1 (6-oz.) package buttermilk cornbread mix
  ⅔ cup milk
  2 Tbsp. mayonnaise
  3 green onions, thinly sliced
  3 large eggs, lightly beaten
  2 Tbsp. chopped fresh parsley
  1 tsp. Old Bay seasoning
  1 tsp. Worcestershire sauce
  2 (5-oz.) aluminum foil pouches herb-and-
     garlic-flavored light tuna chunks
  3 Tbsp. butter
  3 Tbsp. vegetable oil
  Lemon Aioli

1. Preheat oven to 425°. Stir together cornbread mix
and ⅔ cup milk. Pour batter into a lightly greased
8-inch square pan.
2. Bake at 425° for 15 minutes or until golden brown.
Cool on a wire rack 5 minutes or just until warm.
3. Stir together mayonnaise and next 5 ingredients in
a large bowl.
4. Crumble cornbread to equal 2 cups. Reserve
remaining cornbread for another use. Fold cornbread
crumbs and tuna chunks into mayonnaise mixture
until well blended. Shape tuna mixture into 8 (3- to
3½-inch) patties.
5. Melt 3 Tbsp. butter with vegetable oil in a large
skillet over medium-high heat. Add tuna patties, and
cook, in batches, 2 to 3 minutes on each side or until
golden brown; drain on paper towels. Serve cakes
with Lemon Aioli.

Note: We tested with Martha White Buttermilk
Cornbread & Muffin Mix and StarKist Tuna
Creations Herb & Garlic Chunk Light Tuna.

Lemon Aioli

Hands-on Time: 10 min.
Total Time: 10 min.
Makes: ¾ cup

  ¾ cup mayonnaise
  2 garlic cloves, minced
  1 tsp. lemon zest
  1 Tbsp. fresh lemon juice
  ¼ tsp. salt
  ¼ tsp. pepper

1. Stir together ¾ cup mayonnaise and remaining
ingredients. Cover and chill mixture up to 3 days.

Tuna Cornbread Cakes

Beach Shrimp

Crawfish Jambalaya

Hands-on Time: 15 min.
Total Time: 55 min.
Makes: 4 to 6 servings

     1   cup uncooked long-grain rice
     2   cups chicken broth
    ¼   cup butter
     1   medium onion, chopped
    ½   cup chopped green bell pepper
    ½   cup chopped celery
     4   garlic cloves, minced
     1   (14.5-oz.) can stewed tomatoes, undrained
     1   tsp. Cajun seasoning
     1   lb. frozen crawfish tails, thawed, drained,
         and rinsed
     1   cup chopped green onions
    ⅛   tsp. black pepper

1. Prepare rice according to package directions, substituting 2 cups chicken broth for water; set aside.
2. Melt butter in a Dutch oven over medium-high heat; sauté onion, bell pepper, and celery 8 minutes or until vegetables are tender. Add garlic; sauté 1 minute.
3. Stir in stewed tomatoes and Cajun seasoning; reduce heat to low, and simmer, uncovered, 15 to 20 minutes. Add crawfish tails, and cook 5 minutes. Stir in 1 cup chopped green onions, cooked rice, and black pepper.

Beach Shrimp

Hands-on Time: 10 min.
Total Time: 35 min.
Makes: 6 to 8 servings

Serve with toasty French bread to sop up the sauce. To bake this when you are on vacation at the beach, purchase a large disposable roasting pan for easy cleanup.

     3   lb. unpeeled, large raw shrimp (21/25 count)
     1   (16-oz.) bottle Italian dressing
    1½   Tbsp. freshly ground pepper
     2   garlic cloves, pressed
     2   lemons, halved
    ¼   cup chopped fresh parsley
    ½   cup butter, cut up

1. Preheat oven to 375°. Place first 4 ingredients in a 13- x 9-inch baking dish, tossing to coat. Squeeze juice from lemons over shrimp mixture, and stir. Add lemon halves to pan. Sprinkle evenly with parsley; dot with butter.
2. Bake at 375° for 25 minutes, stirring after 15 minutes. Serve in pan.

fake it!

3 lb. frozen peeled, large raw shrimp, thawed according to package directions, may be substituted. Prepare recipe as directed, reducing pepper to ½ tsp.

Coconut Shrimp

Hands-on Time: 20 min.
Total Time: 35 min., including sauce
Makes: 4 servings

1½ lb. unpeeled, large raw shrimp (21/25 count)
Vegetable cooking spray
2 egg whites
¼ cup cornstarch
1 Tbsp. Caribbean jerk seasoning
1 cup sweetened flaked coconut
1 cup panko (Japanese breadcrumbs)
1 tsp. paprika
Honey-Mustard Sauce

1. Preheat oven to 425°. Peel shrimp, leaving tails on; devein shrimp, if desired.
2. Place a wire rack coated with cooking spray in a 15- x 10-inch jelly-roll pan.
3. Whisk egg whites in a bowl just until foamy.
4. Combine cornstarch and Caribbean jerk seasoning in a shallow dish.
5. Combine coconut, breadcrumbs, and paprika in another shallow dish.

6. Dredge shrimp, one at a time, in cornstarch mixture; dip in egg whites, and dredge in coconut mixture, pressing gently with fingers. Lightly coat shrimp with cooking spray; arrange shrimp on wire rack.
7. Bake at 425° for 10 to 12 minutes or just until shrimp turn pink, turning after 8 minutes. Serve with Honey-Mustard Sauce.

Honey-Mustard Sauce

Hands-on Time: 5 min.
Total Time: 5 min.
Makes: about 1¼ cups

½ cup plain fat-free yogurt
¼ cup coarse-grained mustard
¼ cup honey
2 Tbsp. horseradish

1. Stir together all ingredients. Serve immediately, or cover and chill up to 3 days.

Coconut Shrimp

kitchen secrets:

- Vegetable cooking spray is the secret to oven-fried crispiness. Lightly spraying the panko-coated shrimp allows the breading to brown evenly, keeping it low in fat but still crunchy. Be sure to turn the shrimp after 8 minutes of baking so that both sides get crisp.

- Choose shrimp that are slightly firm in texture, avoiding soft and limp ones. Shelled shrimp should be moist and translucent. If purchasing unshelled shrimp, make sure shells are tightly attached. Avoid dark spots, which mean shrimp are past their peak.

Southwest Shrimp Tacos

Hands-on Time: 34 min.
Total Time: 34 min.
Makes: 8 servings

Serve with hot sauce, Mexican crema or regular sour cream, and chopped radishes.

- 10 to 12 (10-inch) wooden skewers
- 2 lb. unpeeled, large raw shrimp (21/25 count)
- 2 Tbsp. hot sauce
- 1 Tbsp. olive oil
- 1½ tsp. ancho chile powder
- 1½ tsp. ground cumin
- ¾ tsp. salt
- 16 to 20 (8-inch) soft taco-size corn or flour tortillas
- 3 cups shredded cabbage
- 1 cup grated carrots
- Lime wedges

1. Soak skewers in water 20 minutes.
2. Meanwhile, peel shrimp; devein, if desired. Coat cold cooking grate of grill with cooking spray, and place on grill. Preheat grill to 350° to 400° (medium-high) heat.
3. Toss shrimp with hot sauce and next 4 ingredients. Thread shrimp onto skewers. Grill shrimp, covered with grill lid, 1 to 2 minutes on each side or just until shrimp turn pink. Grill tortillas 1 minute on each side or until warmed.
4. Combine cabbage and carrots. Remove shrimp from skewers just before serving. Serve in warm tortillas with cabbage mixture and lime wedges.

Roasted Tomato-and-Feta Shrimp

Hands-on Time: 10 min.
Total Time: 35 min.
Makes: 6 servings

- 2 pt. grape tomatoes
- 3 garlic cloves, sliced
- 3 Tbsp. olive oil
- 1 tsp. kosher salt
- ½ tsp. black pepper
- 1½ lb. peeled and deveined, medium-size raw shrimp (31/40 count)
- ½ cup chopped jarred roasted red bell peppers
- ½ cup chopped fresh parsley
- 1 (4-oz.) package crumbled feta cheese
- 2 Tbsp. fresh lemon juice
- Crusty French bread, sliced

1. Preheat oven to 450°. Place tomatoes and next 4 ingredients in a 13- x 9-inch baking dish, tossing gently to coat. Bake 15 minutes. Stir in shrimp and bell peppers. Bake 10 to 15 minutes or just until shrimp turn pink. Toss with parsley, feta cheese, and lemon juice. Serve immediately with crusty French bread.

Roasted Tomato-and-Feta Shrimp

Bayou Fried Shrimp

Hands-on Time: 42 min.
Total Time: 57 min.
Makes: 6 to 8 servings

As an alternative to fish fry mix, try using self-rising flour to dredge shrimp. It gives the shrimp a nice, puffy outside.

  3 lb. unpeeled, large raw shrimp
  2 cups milk
  1 large egg
  1 Tbsp. yellow mustard
  1 tsp. Cajun seasoning
  1 (12-oz.) package fish fry mix
  1 Tbsp. Cajun seasoning
Vegetable oil

1. Peel shrimp, leaving tails on. Butterfly shrimp by making a deep slit down back of each from large end to tail, cutting to but not through inside curve of shrimp. Devein shrimp, and place in a large bowl.
2. Whisk together milk and next 3 ingredients. Pour mixture over shrimp. Let stand at least 15 minutes or up to 1 hour.
3. Combine fish fry mix and 1 Tbsp. Cajun seasoning. Dredge shrimp in fish fry mixture, and shake off excess. Arrange on baking sheets.
4. Pour oil to a depth of 3 inches into a Dutch oven; heat to 325°. Fry shrimp, in batches, 1¹/₂ minutes on each side or until golden brown; drain on wire racks over paper towels.

Bayou Fried Shrimp

Grilled Shrimp-and-Green Bean Salad

Hands-on Time: 38 min.
Total Time: 1 hr., 18 min., including vinaigrette
Makes: 4 to 6 servings

- 8 (12-inch) wooden skewers
- 2 lb. peeled, medium-size raw shrimp (21/25 count)
- Basil Vinaigrette, divided
- 1½ lb. fresh green beans, trimmed
- 6 cooked bacon slices, crumbled
- 1⅓ cups (5½ oz.) shredded Parmesan cheese
- ¾ cup chopped roasted, salted almonds
- Cornbread (optional)

1. Soak wooden skewers in water to cover 30 minutes.
2. Meanwhile, combine shrimp and ¾ cup Basil Vinaigrette in a large zip-top plastic bag; seal and chill 15 minutes, turning occasionally.
3. Preheat grill to 350° to 400° (medium-high) heat. Cook green beans in boiling salted water to cover 4 minutes or until crisp-tender; drain. Plunge into ice water to stop the cooking process; drain, pat dry, and place in a large bowl.
4. Remove shrimp from marinade, discarding marinade. Thread shrimp onto skewers.
5. Grill shrimp, covered with grill lid, 2 minutes on each side or just until shrimp turn pink. Remove shrimp from skewers, and toss with green beans, crumbled bacon, Parmesan cheese, roasted almonds, and remaining ¾ cup Basil Vinaigrette. Serve over hot cooked cornbread, if desired.

Basil Vinaigrette

Hands-on Time: 10 min.
Total Time: 10 min.
Makes: about 1½ cups

- ½ cup chopped fresh basil
- ½ cup balsamic vinegar
- 4 large shallots, minced
- 3 garlic cloves, minced
- 1 Tbsp. brown sugar
- 1 tsp. seasoned pepper
- ½ tsp. salt
- 1 cup olive oil

1. Whisk together first 7 ingredients in a bowl. Gradually add olive oil, whisking constantly until blended.

Grilled Shrimp-and-Green Bean Salad

Shrimp-Pesto Pizza

Hands-on Time: 37 min.
Total Time: 37 min., including pesto
Makes: 6 servings

1	lb. unpeeled, large raw shrimp (31/35 count)
1	large yellow onion, chopped
1	red bell pepper, chopped
¼	tsp. salt
¼	tsp. black pepper
1½	tsp. olive oil
1½	lb. bakery pizza dough
	All-purpose flour
	Plain yellow cornmeal
½	cup Garden Pesto
¾	cup freshly grated Parmesan cheese

1. Coat cold cooking grate of grill with cooking spray, and place on grill. Preheat grill to 350° (medium) heat.
2. Peel shrimp, and slice in half lengthwise; devein, if desired. Set aside.
3. Sauté onion, bell pepper, salt, and black pepper in $^1/_2$ tsp. hot oil in a large skillet over medium heat 5 minutes or until tender. Transfer onion mixture to a large bowl. Sauté shrimp in remaining 1 tsp. hot oil 3 minutes or just until shrimp turn pink. Add shrimp to onion mixture, and toss.
4. Divide dough into 6 equal portions. Lightly sprinkle flour on a large surface. Roll each portion into a 6-inch round (about $^1/_4$ inch thick). Carefully transfer pizza dough rounds to a cutting board or baking sheet sprinkled with cornmeal.
5. Slide pizza dough rounds onto cooking grate of grill. Spread Garden Pesto over rounds; top with shrimp mixture. Sprinkle each with 2 Tbsp. Parmesan cheese.
6. Grill, covered with grill lid, 4 minutes. Rotate pizzas one-quarter turn, and grill, covered with grill lid, 5 to 6 more minutes or until pizza crusts are cooked. Serve immediately.

Garden Pesto

Hands-on Time: 10 min.
Total Time: 23 min.
Makes: 1¼ cups

¼	cup pine nuts
¼	cup chopped pecans
2½	cups firmly packed fresh basil leaves
½	cup chopped fresh parsley
2	garlic cloves, chopped
⅔	cup olive oil, divided
¾	cup (3 oz.) shredded Parmesan cheese

1. Preheat oven to 350°. Bake pine nuts and pecans in a single layer in a shallow pan 8 minutes or until toasted and fragrant. Let cool 5 minutes.
2. Process basil leaves, parsley, garlic, and $^1/_3$ cup olive oil in a food processor until a coarse paste forms. Add nuts and Parmesan cheese, and process until blended. With processor running, pour remaining $^1/_3$ cup olive oil through food chute in a slow, steady stream; process until smooth. Cover and chill up to 5 days.

fake it!
Refrigerated store-bought pesto may be substituted for Garden Pesto.

Shrimp-Pesto Pizza

Shrimp Burgers with Sweet 'n' Spicy Tartar Sauce

Hands-on Time: 37 min.
Total Time: 2 hr., 7 min., including sauce
Makes: 4 servings

The recipes for shrimp burgers, a favorite food of Southern shrimping towns, are often a big secret. Here we divulge our version, which is chunky and spicy with some Cajun flair.

1¼ lb. unpeeled, medium-size raw shrimp (31/40 count)
1 large egg, lightly beaten
1 Tbsp. mayonnaise
2 tsp. lemon juice
½ tsp. salt
⅛ tsp. ground red pepper
3 Tbsp. finely chopped celery
2 Tbsp. chopped green onion
1 Tbsp. chopped fresh parsley
1¼ cups crushed cornbread crackers (about 1 sleeve or 24 crackers)
4 kaiser rolls with poppy seeds, split
Sweet 'n' Spicy Tartar Sauce
4 Bibb lettuce leaves
Garnish: grilled lemon halves

1. Peel shrimp; devein, if desired. Cut each shrimp into thirds.
2. Line a 15- x 10-inch jelly-roll pan with aluminum foil. Coat with cooking spray.
3. Combine egg and next 4 ingredients until blended; stir in celery, green onion, and parsley. Fold in shrimp and cracker crumbs. (Mixture will be very thick.) Shape into 4 (4-inch-wide, 1-inch-thick) patties. Place patties on prepared pan. Cover and chill 1 to 24 hours. Transfer to freezer, and freeze 30 minutes.
4. Coat cold cooking grate of grill with cooking spray; place on grill. Preheat grill to 350° to 400° (medium-high) heat. Grill burgers, covered with grill lid, 4 to 5 minutes or until burgers lift easily from cooking grate using a large spatula. Turn burgers, and grill 4 to 5 minutes or until shrimp turn pink and burgers are cooked through and lightly crisp.
5. Grill rolls, cut sides down, 1 to 2 minutes or until lightly toasted. Serve burgers on rolls with Sweet 'n' Spicy Tartar Sauce and lettuce. Garnish, if desired.

Sweet 'n' Spicy Tartar Sauce

Hands-on Time: 5 min.
Total Time: 35 min.
Makes: about 1 cup

1 cup mayonnaise
2 Tbsp. chopped fresh parsley
2 Tbsp. horseradish
1½ tsp. Cajun seasoning
1½ tsp. lemon juice
¼ tsp. paprika

1. Stir together all ingredients in a bowl. Cover and chill 30 minutes to 24 hours.

Note: We tested with McCormick Cajun Seasoning.

Shrimp Burgers with Sweet 'n' Spicy Tartar Sauce

SIDE DISHES

Serve up the perfect side kick to any meal, or create a Southern veggie plate with these delicious dishes.

Green Bean Casserole

Hands-on Time: 5 min.
Total Time: 4 hr., 45 min.
Makes: 10 servings

- 2 (16-oz.) packages frozen french-cut green beans, thawed
- 1 (10-oz.) container refrigerated Alfredo sauce
- 1 (8-oz.) can diced water chestnuts, drained
- 1 (6-oz.) jar sliced mushrooms, drained
- 1 cup (4 oz.) shredded Parmesan cheese
- ½ tsp. freshly ground pepper
- 1 (6-oz.) can french fried onions, divided
- ½ cup chopped pecans

1. Stir together first 6 ingredients and half of french fried onions; spoon mixture into a lightly greased 4-qt. slow cooker.
2. Cover and cook on LOW 4½ hours or until bubbly.
3. Heat pecans and remaining half of french fried onions in a small nonstick skillet over medium-low heat, stirring often, 1 to 2 minutes or until toasted and fragrant; sprinkle over casserole just before serving.

Green Bean Casserole

Butterbeans and Bacon

Hands-on Time: 20 min.
Total Time: 1 hr., 50 min.
Makes: 6 servings

- 3 thick-cut bacon slices, chopped
- 1 cup diced onion (1 medium onion)
- 3 garlic cloves, minced
- 1 bay leaf
- ¾ cup chopped green bell pepper
- 2 plum tomatoes, seeded and chopped (optional)
- 1 (32-oz.) container chicken broth
- 4 cups fresh or thawed frozen butterbeans
- 1 tsp. black pepper
- 1 tsp. Worcestershire sauce
- ½ tsp. salt
- ½ tsp. hot sauce

1. Cook bacon in a skillet over medium heat, stirring often, 8 minutes or until crisp. Remove bacon, and drain on paper towels, reserving drippings in skillet. Add onion, garlic, and bay leaf; cook, stirring often, 3 minutes or until onion is tender.
2. Add bell pepper; cook, stirring often, 3 minutes. Add tomatoes, if desired, and cook, stirring often, 3 minutes.
3. Add chicken broth and butterbeans; bring to a boil. Cover, reduce heat, and simmer, stirring occasionally, 30 minutes.
4. Uncover and simmer 30 minutes, stirring often. Stir in black pepper and next 3 ingredients. Cook, stirring often, 5 minutes. Remove and discard bay leaf. Sprinkle with cooked bacon.

kitchen secret:

Cooked beans freeze beautifully, so you can make a double batch to enjoy later.

Sautéed Greens

Hands-on Time: 26 min.
Total Time: 26 min.
Makes: 4 to 6 servings

- ½ cup chopped onion
- 3 garlic cloves, minced
- 1 Tbsp. chopped fresh ginger
- 1 serrano pepper, split*
- 1 Tbsp. sesame oil
- 1 tsp. salt
- ½ tsp. pepper
- 1 (1-lb.) package fresh collard greens, washed, trimmed, and coarsely chopped
- 1 Tbsp. sugar
- 1 Tbsp. rice vinegar

1. Sauté onion and next 3 ingredients in hot oil in a large skillet or wok 1 minute. Stir in salt and pepper. Add greens; sauté 2 minutes. Add sugar and vinegar; cover and cook 3 minutes or until wilted. Remove and discard serrano pepper before serving.

*¹/₂ jalapeño pepper, split, may be substituted.

Sautéed Greens with Pork: Stir in ¹/₂ lb. chopped smoked pork with greens.

Baked Grits and Greens

Hands-on Time: 28 min.
Total Time: 58 min.
Makes: 8 to 10 servings

To make ahead, prepare through Step 2 up to a day before; cover and chill. Remove from the fridge, add the crushed croutons, and let stand 30 minutes before baking.

- 1 tsp. garlic salt
- 1 cup uncooked quick-cooking grits
- ⅓ cup finely chopped red onion
- 5 Tbsp. butter, divided
- 2 large eggs
- 1 (10-oz.) package frozen chopped spinach, thawed and drained
- 1½ cups (6 oz.) shredded Parmesan cheese
- ½ cup bottled creamy Caesar dressing
- ½ tsp. freshly ground pepper
- 1¼ cups coarsely crushed garlic-flavored croutons

1. Preheat oven to 350°. Bring 4 cups water and garlic salt to a boil in a large saucepan over medium-high heat; gradually stir in grits. Reduce heat to medium; cook, stirring often, 5 minutes or until thickened. Remove from heat, and stir in onion and 3 Tbsp. butter.
2. Combine eggs and next 4 ingredients in a large bowl. Stir about one-fourth of grits mixture gradually into egg mixture; add remaining grits mixture, stirring constantly. Pour into a lightly greased 13- x 9-inch baking dish.
3. Melt remaining 2 Tbsp. butter; toss with coarsely crushed croutons; sprinkle over grits mixture.
4. Bake at 350° for 30 to 35 minutes or until mixture is set and croutons are golden brown.

Baked Grits and Greens with Bacon: Prepare recipe as directed, stirring 1 (3-oz.) package bacon bits into egg mixture.

Note: We tested with Oscar Mayer Real Bacon Bits.

Sautéed Greens

Asparagus-New Potato Hash

Hands-on Time: 27 min.
Total Time: 1 hr., 2 min.
Makes: 8 servings

- 1 lb. small red potatoes
- 1 lb. fresh asparagus
- 2 shallots, minced
- 2 Tbsp. olive oil
- 1 tsp. chopped fresh thyme
- 1 tsp. salt
- ½ tsp. pepper
- 2 tsp. fresh lemon juice
- ⅓ cup (1½ oz.) crumbled farmer's cheese or queso fresco
- Garnish: lemon slices

1. Bring potatoes and salted water to cover to a boil in a Dutch oven over medium-high heat. Cook 15 minutes or just until tender; drain well. Cool 15 minutes; cut into quarters.
2. Snap off and discard tough ends of asparagus. Cut asparagus into ½-inch pieces.
3. Sauté shallots in hot oil in a large nonstick skillet 1 minute. Add asparagus, thyme, salt, pepper, and lemon juice; sauté 2 to 3 minutes or until asparagus is crisp-tender. Add potatoes, and sauté 3 minutes or until mixture is thoroughly heated. Remove from heat, and sprinkle with cheese. Garnish, if desired.

Note: We tested with Chapel Hill Creamery farmer's cheese.

Broccoli, Grape, and Pasta Salad

Hands-on Time: 30 min.
Total Time: 3 hr., 30 min.
Makes: 6 to 8 servings

If you're a broccoli salad fan, you will love this combination of colorful ingredients. Cook the pasta al dente so it's firm enough to hold its own when tossed with the tangy-sweet salad dressing.

- 1 cup chopped pecans
- ½ (16-oz.) package farfalle (bow-tie) pasta
- 1 lb. fresh broccoli
- 1 cup mayonnaise
- ⅓ cup sugar
- ⅓ cup diced red onion
- ⅓ cup red wine vinegar
- 1 tsp. salt
- 2 cups seedless red grapes, halved
- 8 cooked bacon slices, crumbled

1. Preheat oven to 350°. Bake pecans in a single layer in a shallow pan 5 to 7 minutes or until lightly toasted and fragrant, stirring halfway through.
2. Prepare pasta according to package directions.
3. Meanwhile, cut broccoli florets from stems, and separate florets into small pieces using the tip of a paring knife. Peel away tough outer layer of stems, and finely chop stems.
4. Combine mayonnaise and next 4 ingredients in a large bowl; add broccoli, hot cooked pasta, and grapes, and stir to coat. Cover and chill 3 hours. Stir bacon and pecans into salad just before serving.

Asparagus-New Potato Hash

Two-Cheese Squash Casserole

Hands-on Time: 25 min.
Total Time: 1 hr., 8 min.
Makes: 10 to 12 servings

For a tasty and colorful twist, substitute sliced zucchini for half of the yellow squash.

- 4 lb. yellow squash, sliced
- 1 large sweet onion, finely chopped
- 2½ cups soft, fresh breadcrumbs, divided
- 1¼ cups (5 oz.) freshly shredded Parmesan cheese, divided
- 1 cup (4 oz.) shredded Cheddar cheese
- ½ cup chopped fresh chives
- 1 (8-oz.) container sour cream
- 1 tsp. garlic salt
- 1 tsp. freshly ground pepper
- 2 large eggs, lightly beaten
- 2 Tbsp. melted butter

1. Preheat oven to 350°. Cook yellow squash and onion in boiling water to cover in a Dutch oven 8 minutes or until tender; drain squash mixture well.
2. Combine squash mixture, 1 cup breadcrumbs, ³/₄ cup Parmesan cheese, and next 6 ingredients. Spoon into a lightly greased 13- x 9-inch baking dish.

Two-Cheese
Squash Casserole

3. Combine melted butter and remaining 1¹/₂ cups breadcrumbs and ¹/₂ cup Parmesan cheese. Sprinkle breadcrumb mixture over top of casserole.
4. Bake at 350° for 35 to 40 minutes or until set.

Church-Style Lemon-Roasted Potatoes

Hands-on Time: 28 min.
Total Time: 1 hr., 8 min.
Makes: 6 to 8 servings

Any leftover potatoes are great for potato salad the next day.

- 3 Tbsp. olive oil
- 1½ Tbsp. butter
- 3 lb. small Yukon gold or red potatoes, peeled
- ¼ cup lemon juice
- 4 tsp. chopped fresh thyme
- ¾ tsp. salt
- ½ tsp. pepper

1. Preheat oven to 400°. Cook olive oil and butter in a skillet over medium heat, stirring constantly, 3 to 4 minutes or until butter begins to turn golden brown. Remove butter mixture from heat, and add peeled potatoes, tossing gently to coat.
2. Spread potatoes in a single layer in a 15- x 10-inch jelly-roll pan.
3. Bake at 400° for 40 to 45 minutes or until potatoes are golden brown and tender, stirring twice. Transfer potatoes to a large serving bowl, and toss with lemon juice, chopped fresh thyme, salt, and pepper until well coated. Serve potatoes immediately.

kitchen secret:

If you don't want to peel little potatoes, you can use larger peeled Yukons. Simply cut into large chunks, and bake as directed.

Cornbread Stuffing with Sweet Potato and Squash

Hands-on Time: 47 min.
Total Time: 1 hr., 57 min.
Makes: 10 servings

- 1 cup frozen diced onion, red and green bell peppers, and celery
- 2 small garlic cloves, pressed
- 1 Tbsp. canola oil
- 1½ lb. butternut squash, peeled, seeded, and cut into ¼-inch cubes
- 2 medium-size sweet potatoes, peeled and cut into ¼-inch cubes
- 1 Granny Smith apple, peeled and cut into ¼-inch cubes
- 3 Tbsp. melted butter
- 2 Tbsp. brown sugar
- 1 Tbsp. chopped fresh sage
- 2 tsp. Creole seasoning, divided
- 2 (14-oz.) cans low-sodium fat-free chicken broth, divided
- 1 (8-oz.) package cornbread stuffing mix
- 1 large egg, lightly beaten
- ⅓ cup chopped pecans
- Garnish: fresh or dried sage leaves

1. Preheat oven to 375°. Sauté frozen onion mixture and garlic in 1 Tbsp. hot oil in a large, deep skillet over medium-high heat 2 minutes or until vegetables are tender.

2. Stir in squash, next 5 ingredients, 1 tsp. Creole seasoning, and ¼ cup water. Cover, reduce heat to medium, and cook, stirring occasionally, 15 minutes or until squash and potatoes are tender. Stir in 1 can chicken broth.

3. Remove from heat; cool 15 minutes. Stir together stuffing mix, egg, and remaining 1 can chicken broth and 1 tsp. Creole seasoning in a medium bowl. Fold into cooled squash mixture. Spoon mixture into a lightly greased 13- x 9-inch baking dish.

4. Bake, covered with aluminum foil, at 375° for 25 minutes. Uncover and sprinkle with pecans; bake 20 minutes or until dressing is thoroughly heated and pecans are toasted. Let stand 10 minutes before serving. Garnish, if desired.

Cornbread Stuffing with
Sweet Potato and Squash

Sweet Potato Soufflé

Hands-on Time: 13 min.
Total Time: 53 min.
Makes: 10 to 12 servings

Guests won't even know this sweet potato soufflé is lightened with brown sugar, cinnamon, and a hint of orange; it endows the common sweet potato with decadence.

- 1 (14½-oz.) can mashed sweet potato
- 1 cup sugar
- ⅔ cup all-purpose flour, divided
- ½ cup melted butter, divided
- ¼ cup milk
- 1 tsp. orange zest
- 2 Tbsp. fresh orange juice
- 1 tsp. vanilla extract
- 2 large eggs, lightly beaten
- 1 cup chopped pecans
- 1 cup firmly packed brown sugar

1. Preheat oven to 350°. Stir together potato, sugar, ⅓ cup flour, ¼ cup butter, and next 5 ingredients; pour into a lightly greased 13- x 9-inch baking dish.

2. Combine chopped pecans, brown sugar, and remaining ⅓ cup flour and ¼ cup butter; sprinkle over potato mixture.

3. Bake at 350° for 40 minutes or until bubbly.

Salt-and-Pepper Oven Fries

Hands-on Time: 5 min.
Total Time: 32 min.
Makes: 8 to 10 servings

You can serve these fries with plain ketchup, but be sure to try them the French way at least once—with Lemon-Garlic Mayo.

- 1 (26-oz.) package frozen extra-crispy french fried potatoes
- ¾ tsp. freshly ground pepper
- ½ tsp. kosher salt

1. Preheat oven to 425°. Arrange potatoes in a single layer on 2 lightly greased 15- x 10-inch jelly-roll pans. Bake 15 minutes, placing one pan on middle oven rack and other on lower oven rack. Switch pans, and bake 12 to 15 more minutes or until lightly browned. Sprinkle with pepper and salt, tossing lightly. Serve immediately.

Note: We tested with Ore-Ida Extra Crispy Fast Food Fries.

Italian Oven Fries: Prepare recipe as directed. Sprinkle potatoes with ⅔ cup (2½ oz.) grated Parmesan cheese and ½ tsp. garlic powder, tossing lightly. Serve with warm marinara sauce.

Lemon-Garlic Mayo

Hands-on Time: 5 min.
Total Time: 10 min.
Makes: about 1 cup

- 1 Tbsp. lemon juice
- 2 garlic cloves, minced
- 1 cup mayonnaise
- 2 Tbsp. chopped fresh parsley
- Salt and pepper to taste

1. Combine lemon juice and minced garlic in a small bowl; let stand 5 minutes. Stir in mayonnaise and parsley. Season with salt and pepper to taste.

Salt-and-Pepper Oven Fries

Beer-Battered Onion Rings

Hands-on Time: 22 min.
Total Time: 1 hr., 7 min.
Makes: 8 servings

3	large Vidalia, Spanish, or Bermuda onions
2¼	cups all-purpose flour
¼	cup plain yellow cornmeal
2	tsp. baking powder
1	tsp. salt
2	cups beer
1	large egg, lightly beaten

Vegetable oil

1. Peel onions; cut into ¹/₂-inch-thick slices, and separate into rings. Place rings in a large bowl of ice water; let stand 30 minutes. Drain on paper towels.
2. Combine flour and next 3 ingredients; stir well. Add beer and egg, stirring until thoroughly blended and smooth. Chill batter 15 minutes.
3. Dip onion rings into batter, coating both sides well. Pour oil to a depth of 2 to 3 inches into a Dutch oven; heat to 375°. Fry onion rings, a few at a time, 3 to 5 minutes or until golden on both sides. Drain well on paper towels. Serve immediately.

Fried Green Tomatoes

Fried Green Tomatoes

Hands-on Time: 24 min.
Total Time: 24 min.
Makes: 4 to 6 servings

The cornmeal-and-flour crust is what sets this recipe apart from others.

1	large egg, lightly beaten
½	cup buttermilk
½	cup all-purpose flour, divided
½	cup cornmeal
1	tsp. salt
½	tsp. pepper
3	medium-size green tomatoes, cut into ¹/₃-inch slices

Vegetable oil
Salt to taste

1. Combine egg and buttermilk; set aside.
2. Combine ¹/₄ cup all-purpose flour, cornmeal, 1 tsp. salt, and pepper in a shallow bowl or pan.
3. Dredge tomato slices in remaining ¹/₄ cup flour; dip in egg mixture, and dredge in cornmeal mixture.
4. Pour oil to a depth of ¹/₂ inch in a large cast-iron skillet; heat to 375°. Drop tomatoes, in batches, into hot oil, and cook 2 minutes on each side or until golden. Drain on paper towels or a rack. Sprinkle hot tomatoes with salt.

Curried Cauliflower

Hands-on Time: 19 min.
Total Time: 19 min.
Makes: 4 servings

- 1 tsp. curry powder
- ¼ tsp. dried crushed red pepper
- 2 Tbsp. vegetable oil
- 2 (10-oz.) packages fresh cauliflower florets
- 1 medium onion, chopped
- ¾ tsp. salt

1. Cook curry powder and red pepper in hot oil in a large skillet over medium heat, stirring often, 1 minute. Add cauliflower, onion, and salt, and cook, stirring constantly, 2 to 3 minutes or until onion is crisp-tender. Reduce heat to low; add 6 Tbsp. water. Cover and cook, stirring occasionally, 8 to 10 minutes or just until cauliflower is tender.

Curried Cauliflower

Hoppin' John Salad

Hands-on Time: 11 min.
Total Time: 4 hr., 11 min.
Makes: 7 cups

Be sure to share this savory side dish with family and friends on New Year's Day for good luck.

- 2 celery ribs, diced
- 1 yellow bell pepper, diced
- 1 red bell pepper, diced
- ½ medium onion, diced
- 4 (15-oz.) cans black-eyed peas, drained and rinsed
- 2 jalapeño peppers, seeded and diced
- 2 Tbsp. chopped fresh parsley
- 1 garlic clove, minced
- 1 tsp. salt
- 1 tsp. freshly ground pepper
- ½ tsp. ground cumin
- ½ cup red wine vinegar
- 2 Tbsp. balsamic vinegar
- ¼ cup olive oil
- 4 bacon slices, cooked and crumbled
Garnish: fresh chopped parsley

Southern foodlore

The first published recipe for Hoppin' John appeared in The Carolina Housewife in 1847. This Southern specialty is thought to bring good luck for the New Year. Originally, a dime was buried among the black-eyed peas, and whoever found it was guaranteed good luck during the coming year. It is also often served with collard greens, which are considered a token for hoped riches.

1. Combine diced vegetables, peas, and next 6 ingredients in a large bowl.
2. Combine vinegars in a small bowl; whisk in oil in a slow, steady stream, blending well. Add to vegetable mixture, tossing gently to coat. Cover and chill 3 to 4 hours. Stir in bacon. Garnish, if desired.

Hot Slaw à la Greyhound Grill

Hands-on Time: 31 min.
Total Time: 36 min.
Makes: 6 servings

This tangy slaw is a favorite of award-winning cookbook authors Matt and Ted Lee. Pair it with broiled fish or pulled pork.

- ½ large red cabbage (about 1½ lb.), shredded
- ½ large green cabbage (about 1½ lb.), shredded
- 4 thick bacon slices, diced
- ½ cup cider vinegar
- ½ tsp. celery seeds
- ¼ tsp. dried crushed red pepper
- 2 tsp. salt
- 1 tsp. freshly ground pepper
Pepper vinegar to taste (optional)

1. Bring 3½ qt. water to a boil in a large stockpot. Cook shredded cabbage in boiling water 4 minutes or just until it turns a dull gray purple. Remove from heat; drain well.
2. Cook bacon in a skillet over medium-low heat 8 minutes or just until crisp; remove bacon, and drain on paper towels, reserving drippings in skillet.
3. Stir cider vinegar, celery seeds, and red pepper into hot drippings, stirring to loosen particles from bottom of skillet. Stir in cabbage, salt, black pepper, and bacon; cook, stirring occasionally, 4 minutes or until cabbage is tender and red cabbage turns a bright magenta color. Place mixture in a serving dish, and, if desired, sprinkle with pepper vinegar to taste.

Heirloom Tomatoes with Fresh
Peaches, Goat Cheese, and Pecans

Heirloom Tomatoes with Fresh Peaches, Goat Cheese, and Pecans

Hands-on Time: 20 min.
Total Time: 20 min.
Makes: 6 servings

⅓ cup white balsamic vinegar
1 garlic clove, minced
2 Tbsp. light brown sugar
2 Tbsp. olive oil
⅛ tsp. salt
1 large fresh peach, peeled and diced
2 Tbsp. chopped fresh basil
About 2 lb. heirloom tomatoes, sliced
¾ cup (3 oz.) crumbled goat cheese
½ cup coarsely chopped toasted pecans
Freshly ground pepper to taste

1. Whisk together balsamic vinegar, minced garlic, brown sugar, olive oil, and salt. Stir in diced peach and chopped fresh basil. Spoon over sliced tomatoes; top with crumbled goat cheese and chopped toasted pecans. Sprinkle with freshly ground pepper to taste.

Big Daddy's Grilled Blue Cheese -and-Bacon Potato Salad

Hands-on Time: 30 min.
Total Time: 1 hr., 5 min.
Makes: 6 servings

Grilling the potatoes in an easy-to-fold aluminum foil packet adds a subtle note of smoky flavor—plus it makes cleanup a breeze.

- 3 lb. baby red potatoes, cut in half
- 2 Tbsp. olive oil
- 1 tsp. salt
- 1 tsp. freshly ground pepper
- 1 cup mayonnaise
- ¼ cup chopped fresh parsley
- ¼ cup white balsamic vinegar*
- 2 tsp. sugar
- 2 tsp. Dijon mustard
- 1 cup thinly sliced red onion
- 1 cup (4 oz.) crumbled blue cheese
- 6 bacon slices, cooked and crumbled

1. Preheat grill to 350° to 400° (medium-high) heat. Place potatoes in a single layer in center of a large piece of heavy-duty aluminum foil. Drizzle with olive oil; sprinkle with salt and pepper. Bring up foil sides over potatoes; double-fold top and side edges to seal, making 1 large packet.
2. Grill potatoes, in foil packet, covered with grill lid, 15 minutes on each side. Remove packet from grill. Carefully open packet, using tongs, and let potatoes cool 5 minutes.
3. Whisk together mayonnaise and next 4 ingredients in a large bowl; add potatoes, tossing gently to coat. Stir in onion, blue cheese, and bacon.

*Balsamic vinegar may be substituted but will darken the color of the dressing.

Big Daddy's Grilled Blue Cheese-and-Bacon Potato Salad

Tomato-and-Watermelon Salad

Hands-on Time: 16 min.
Total Time: 2 hr., 31 min.
Makes: 4 to 6 servings

Combine sweet, juicy watermelon chunks with fresh tomato, onion and a red wine vinaigrette for a salad that is the essence of summer.

- 5 cups (¾-inch) seeded watermelon cubes
- 1½ lb. ripe tomatoes, cut into ¾-inch cubes
- 3 tsp. sugar
- ½ tsp. salt
- 1 small red onion, quartered and thinly sliced
- ½ cup red wine vinegar
- ¼ cup extra virgin olive oil
  Romaine lettuce leaves (optional)
  Cracked pepper to taste

1. Combine watermelon and tomatoes in a large bowl; sprinkle with sugar and salt, tossing to coat. Let stand 15 minutes.
2. Stir in onion, vinegar, and oil. Cover and chill 2 hours. Serve chilled with lettuce leaves, if desired. Sprinkle with cracked pepper to taste.

Tomato-and-Watermelon Salad

Layered Southwestern Salad

Hands-on Time: 17 min.
Total Time: 17 min.
Makes: 8 to 10 servings

The perfect party dish or grilling side dish, this salad has cooling flavors and none of the heat typical of Southwestern dishes.

- ½ cup lime juice
- ½ cup olive oil
- ½ cup sour cream
- ⅓ cup chopped fresh cilantro
- 1 tsp. sugar
- ½ tsp. salt
- ½ tsp. pepper
- 1 (16-oz.) package romaine lettuce, shredded
- 5 plum tomatoes, chopped
- 1 (15-oz.) can black beans, drained and rinsed
- 1 small red onion, chopped
- 1 (8-oz.) package shredded Mexican four-cheese blend
- 1 (15-oz.) can whole kernel corn with red and green peppers, drained
- 1 (6-oz.) can sliced ripe olives, drained
- 2 cups crushed tortilla chips

1. Combine first 7 ingredients in a blender or food processor; pulse until smooth, stopping to scrape down sides.
2. Layer lettuce and next 7 ingredients in a 3-qt. glass bowl. Pour vinaigrette over salad just before serving, and gently toss. Serve immediately.

Hearts of
Romaine Salad

Hearts of Romaine Salad

Hands-on Time: 15 min.
Total Time: 45 min.
Makes: 8 servings

- ¼ cup extra virgin olive oil
- ¼ cup Champagne vinegar or white wine vinegar
- 2 Tbsp. minced shallots
- 1 Tbsp. whole grain Dijon mustard
- 2 tsp. honey
- ¾ tsp. salt
- ¼ tsp. freshly ground pepper
- 4 romaine lettuce hearts
- 8 radishes, halved and thinly sliced

Salt and pepper to taste
Garnishes: freshly shaved Parmesan cheese, chopped fresh chives

1. Whisk together first 7 ingredients until blended. Cover and chill 30 minutes. (Dressing may be stored in refrigerator up to 3 days.)

2. Cut romaine hearts in half lengthwise, keeping leaves intact. Arrange halves on individual serving plates. Sprinkle with radishes. Drizzle evenly with vinaigrette. Season with salt and pepper to taste. Garnish, if desired.

Grilled Shrimp Gumbo Salad

Hands-on Time: 52 min.
Total Time: 1 hr., 40 min., including vinaigrette
Makes: 6 to 8 servings

Terrific flavors from the garden and grill come together in this summery twist on a New Orleans favorite. Served in smaller portions, it also makes a great first course.

- 6 (12-inch) wooden skewers
- 1 lb. unpeeled, large raw shrimp (36/40 count)
- 2 Tbsp. olive oil, divided
- 2½ tsp. Cajun seasoning, divided
- 1 lb. fresh okra
- 6 (½-inch-thick) sweet onion slices
- 1 green bell pepper, quartered
- 2 (16-oz.) packages baby heirloom tomatoes, cut in half

Fresh Corn Vinaigrette

1. Soak wooden skewers in water 30 minutes.
2. Preheat grill to 350° to 400° (medium-high) heat. Peel shrimp; devein, if desired. Drizzle shrimp with 1 Tbsp. olive oil, and sprinkle with ½ tsp. Cajun seasoning. Thread shrimp onto skewers.
3. Drizzle remaining 1 Tbsp. olive oil over okra, onion, and bell pepper; sprinkle with remaining 2 tsp. Cajun seasoning.
4. Grill okra, covered with grill lid, 4 minutes on each side or until tender. Grill onion slices and bell pepper, covered with grill lid, 6 minutes on each side or until tender. Grill shrimp, covered with grill lid, 2 minutes on each side or just until shrimp turn pink.
5. Cut okra in half lengthwise; coarsely chop bell pepper. Toss together okra, bell pepper, and onion in a large bowl.
6. Remove shrimp from skewers, and toss with okra mixture, tomatoes, and Fresh Corn Vinaigrette.

Grilled Shrimp Gumbo Salad

Fresh Corn Vinaigrette

Hands-on Time: 10 min.
Total Time: 10 min.
Makes: 1¹/₂ cups

- 1 cup fresh corn kernels
- ²⁄₃ cup olive oil
- ¼ cup fresh lemon juice
- 1 garlic clove, minced
- 2 Tbsp. balsamic vinegar
- 1 Tbsp. Creole mustard
- 1 tsp. chopped fresh thyme

Salt and freshly ground pepper to taste

1. Whisk together fresh corn kernels, olive oil, fresh lemon juice, minced garlic clove, balsamic vinegar, Creole mustard, and chopped fresh thyme. Season with salt and freshly ground pepper to taste.

Avocado Fruit Salad

Hands-on Time: 15 min.
Total Time: 1 hr., 15 min.
Makes: 6 cups

You can prepare this salad a day ahead, but don't cut up the avocado or add garnishes until just before you serve it.

 1 (24-oz.) jar refrigerated orange and grapefruit sections, drained, rinsed, and patted dry
 1 (24-oz.) jar refrigerated tropical mixed fruit in light syrup, drained, rinsed, and patted dry
 2 cups cubed fresh cantaloupe
 1 medium-size ripe avocado, halved and cut into chunks
 ¼ cup chopped fresh mint
 2 Tbsp. lime juice
 Garnishes: reduced-fat sour cream, crushed pistachios

1. Toss together first 6 ingredients. Cover and chill 1 hour. Garnish, if desired.

Note: We tested with Del Monte SunFresh Citrus Salad and Del Monte SunFresh Tropical Mixed Fruit in Light Syrup With Passion Fruit Juice.

kitchen secret:

Take advantage of fresh winter citrus and substitute sectioned oranges and grapefruit for the jarred version. 1 (24-oz.) jar equals about 1½ to 2 cups of sections.

Avocado Fruit Salad

DESSERTS

From cakes to pies to cookies and bars, everyone will want to save room for these sweet endings.

Sour Cream Pound Cake

Hands-on Time: 20 min.
Total Time: 1 hr., 50 min.
Makes: 10 to 12 servings

  1½ cups butter, softened
    3 cups sugar
    6 large eggs
    3 cups all-purpose flour
   ½ tsp. salt
   ¼ tsp. baking soda
    1 (8-oz.) container sour cream
    1 tsp. lemon extract
   ¼ tsp. almond extract
     Garnishes: fresh peach slices, fresh mint sprigs

1. Preheat oven to 325°. Beat butter at medium speed with an electric mixer until creamy. Gradually add sugar, beating at medium speed until light and fluffy. Add eggs, one at a time, beating just until the yolk disappears.
2. Sift together flour, salt, and baking soda. Add flour mixture to butter mixture alternately with sour cream, beginning and ending with flour mixture. Beat batter at low speed just until blended after each addition. Stir in extracts. Pour into a greased and floured 12-cup tube pan.
3. Bake at 325° for 1 hour and 20 minutes or until a long wooden pick inserted in center of cake comes out clean. Cool in pan on a wire rack 10 minutes. Remove cake from pan, and cool completely on wire rack. Garnish, if desired.

Coca-Cola Cake

Hands-on Time: 23 min.
Total Time: 1 hr., 8 min., including frosting
Makes: 12 servings

The magical brew of carbonated cola is the secret to the tender texture.

    1 cup Coca-Cola
   ½ cup buttermilk
    1 cup butter, softened
  1¾ cups sugar
    2 large eggs, lightly beaten
    2 tsp. vanilla extract
    2 cups all-purpose flour
   ¼ cup cocoa
    1 tsp. baking soda
  1½ cups miniature marshmallows
     Coca-Cola Frosting
     Garnish: ¾ cup chopped pecans, toasted

1. Preheat oven to 350°. Combine Coca-Cola and buttermilk; set aside.
2. Beat butter at low speed with an electric mixer until creamy. Gradually add sugar; beat until blended. Add egg and vanilla; beat at low speed until blended.
3. Combine flour, cocoa, and baking soda. Add flour mixture to butter mixture alternately with cola mixture; beginning and ending with flour mixture. Beat at low speed just until blended.
4. Stir in marshmallows. Pour batter into a greased and floured 13- x 9-inch pan. Bake at 350° for 30 to 35 minutes. Remove from oven; cool 10 minutes. Pour Coca-Cola Frosting over warm cake; garnish, if desired.

kitchen secret:

Don't make the frosting ahead—you need to pour it over the cake shortly after baking.

Sour Cream Pound Cake

Coca-Cola Frosting

Hands-on Time: 7 min.
Total Time: 7 min.
Makes: 2¼ cups

- ½ cup butter
- ⅓ cup Coca-Cola
- 3 Tbsp. cocoa
- 1 (16-oz.) package powdered sugar
- 1 Tbsp. vanilla extract

1. Bring first 3 ingredients to a boil in a large saucepan over medium heat, stirring until butter melts. Remove from heat; whisk in sugar and vanilla.

Classic Strawberry Shortcake

Hands-on Time: 33 min.
Total Time: 2 hr., 48 min.
Makes: 8 servings

With juicy strawberries spooned over sweet and tender biscuits, old-fashioned strawberry shortcakes are the perfect springtime dessert. If the berries are very sweet, decrease the sugar to suit your taste. Drop the dough easily by using a lightly greased ⅓ cup dry measure.

- 2 (16-oz.) containers fresh strawberries, quartered
- ¾ cup sugar, divided
- ¼ tsp. almond extract (optional)
- 2¾ cups all-purpose flour
- 4 tsp. baking powder
- ¾ cup cold butter, cut up
- 2 large eggs, lightly beaten
- 1 (8-oz.) container sour cream
- 1 tsp. vanilla extract
- 2 cups sweetened whipped cream
Garnish: fresh mint sprigs

1. Combine strawberries, ½ cup sugar, and, if desired, almond extract. Cover berry mixture, and let stand 2 hours.
2. Preheat oven to 450°. Combine flour, remaining ¼ cup sugar, and baking powder in a large bowl; cut butter into flour mixture with a pastry blender or fork until crumbly.
3. Whisk together eggs, sour cream, and vanilla until blended; add to flour mixture, stirring just until dry ingredients are moistened. Drop dough by lightly greased ⅓ cupfuls onto a lightly greased baking sheet. (Coat cup with vegetable cooking spray after each drop.)
4. Bake at 450° for 12 to 15 minutes or until golden.
5. Split shortcakes in half horizontally. Spoon about ½ cup berry mixture onto each shortcake bottom; top each with a rounded tablespoon sweetened whipped cream, and cover with tops. Serve with remaining whipped cream. Garnish, if desired.

Strawberry Jam Shortcakes: Prepare recipe as directed. Before topping shortcake bottoms with strawberry mixture, stir together ¼ cup strawberry jam and 2 Tbsp. chopped fresh mint. Spread cut sides of bottom shortcake halves evenly with jam mixture. Proceed with recipe as directed.

Classic Strawberry Shortcake

Caramel Cream Cake

Hands-on Time: 20 min.
Total Time: 5 hr., 31 min., including batter, filling, and frosting
Makes: 12 servings

- 1 cup finely chopped sweetened flaked coconut
- 1 recipe Pecan Pie Cake Batter
- 1 recipe Pecan Pie Filling
- 1 recipe Cream Cheese Frosting
- 1 cup finely chopped pecans, toasted
- 1 cup sweetened flaked coconut, toasted

1. Preheat oven to 350°. Stir 1 cup finely chopped coconut into Pecan Pie Cake Batter; spoon batter into 3 greased and floured 9-inch cake pans.
2. Bake at 350° for 25 minutes or until a wooden pick inserted in center comes out clean. Cool in pans on wire racks 10 minutes; remove from pans, and cool completely on wire racks.
3. Spread Pecan Pie Filling between layers. Spread Cream Cheese Frosting on top and sides of cake. Sprinkle top and sides with toasted pecans and toasted coconut.

Pecan Pie Cake Batter

Hands-on Time: 20 min.
Total Time: 20 min.
Makes about 6 cups

- ½ cup butter, softened
- ½ cup shortening
- 2 cups sugar
- 5 large eggs, separated
- 1 Tbsp. vanilla extract
- 2 cups all-purpose flour
- 1 tsp. baking soda
- 1 cup buttermilk
- 1 cup finely chopped pecans, toasted

1. Beat ½ cup butter and shortening at medium speed with an electric mixer until fluffy; gradually add sugar, beating until well blended. Add egg yolks, one at a time, beating just until blended after each addition. Stir in vanilla. Combine flour and baking soda; add to butter mixture alternately with buttermilk, beginning and ending with flour mixture. Beat at low speed until blended after each addition. Stir in pecans.
2. Beat egg whites at medium speed until stiff peaks form; fold one-third of egg whites into batter. Gently fold in remaining beaten egg whites just until blended. Use immediately.

Pecan Pie Filling

Hands-on Time: 14 min.
Total Time: 4 hr., 14 min.
Makes: about 3 cups

- ½ cup firmly packed dark brown sugar
- ¾ cup dark corn syrup
- ⅓ cup cornstarch
- 4 egg yolks
- 1½ cups half-and-half
- ⅛ tsp. salt
- 3 Tbsp. butter
- 1 tsp. vanilla extract

1. Whisk together first 6 ingredients in a heavy 3-qt. saucepan until smooth. Bring mixture to a boil over medium heat, whisking constantly; boil 1 minute or until thickened. Remove from heat; whisk in butter and vanilla. Place a sheet of wax paper directly on surface, and chill 4 hours.

Cream Cheese Frosting

Hands-on Time: 12 min.
Total Time: 12 min.
Makes: about 3 cups

- ½ cup butter, softened
- 1 (8-oz.) package cream cheese, softened
- 1 (16-oz.) package powdered sugar
- 1 tsp. vanilla extract

1. Beat butter and cream cheese at medium speed with an electric mixer until creamy. Gradually add powdered sugar, beating at low speed until blended; stir in vanilla.

Mocha Latte Cupcakes

Hands-on Time: 1 hr., 14 min.
Total Time: 2 hr., 12 min., including frosting
Makes: 6½ dozen miniature cupcakes

> 1   (12-oz.) package dark chocolate morsels
> ½   cup butter, softened
> ½   (8-oz.) package cream cheese, softened
> 2   cups sugar
> 4   large eggs
> 1   tsp. vanilla extract
> 3   cups all-purpose flour
> 1   tsp. baking powder
> ½   tsp. baking soda
> ½   tsp. salt
> 1   (8-oz.) container sour cream
> Double Shot Latte Buttercream Frosting
> Garnish: chocolate shavings

1. Preheat oven to 350°. Microwave dark chocolate morsels at HIGH 1½ minutes or until melted and smooth, stirring at 30-second intervals.
2. Beat butter and cream cheese at medium speed with an electric mixer until creamy. Beat in sugar until light and fluffy. Add eggs, one at a time, beating until blended after each addition. Stir in vanilla.
3. Combine flour and next 3 ingredients. Gradually add to butter mixture alternately with sour cream, beating until blended. Stir melted chocolate into batter. (Batter will be very thick.) Spoon batter by rounded tablespoonfuls into 4 lightly greased 24-cup miniature muffin pans.
4. Bake at 350° for 11 to 13 minutes or until a wooden pick inserted in centers comes out clean. Cool in pans on wire racks 5 minutes. Remove from pans to wire racks, and cool completely (about 30 minutes). Spread cupcakes with Double Shot Latte Buttercream Frosting. Garnish, if desired.

Note: To prepare regular-size cupcakes, spoon batter into 2 lightly greased 12-cup muffin pans, filling two-thirds full. Bake at 350° for 22 to 24 minutes or until a wooden pick inserted in centers comes out clean. Cool and decorate as desired.

Double Shot Latte Buttercream Frosting

Hands-on Time: 10 min.
Total Time: 10 min.
Makes: about 3 cups

> ½   cup butter, softened
> 1   (3-oz.) package cream cheese, softened
> 1½   Tbsp. instant espresso
> 2   tsp. vanilla extract
> 1   (16-oz.) package powdered sugar
> 3   to 4 Tbsp. milk

1. Beat first 4 ingredients at medium speed with an electric mixer until creamy.
2. Gradually add powdered sugar alternately with 3 Tbsp. milk, beating at low speed until blended and smooth after each addition.
3. If desired, beat in remaining 1 Tbsp. milk, 1 tsp. at a time, until desired consistency.

Mocha Latte Cupcakes

Brandy Alexander Cheesecake

Hands-on Time: 20 min.
Total Time: 11 hr., 8 min.
Makes: 10 to 12 servings

- 1 (10-oz.) box chocolate-flavored bear-shaped graham crackers, crushed (about 2¼ cups)
- 6 Tbsp. melted butter
- 2 Tbsp. sugar, divided
- 4 (8-oz.) packages cream cheese, softened
- 1¼ cups sugar
- 3 Tbsp. cornstarch
- 4 large eggs, at room temperature
- 4 Tbsp. brandy, divided
- 4 Tbsp. crème de cacao, divided*
- 1 (16-oz.) container sour cream
- Garnishes: blackberries, currants, raspberries, strawberries

1. Preheat oven to 325°. Stir together crushed graham crackers, butter, and 1 Tbsp. sugar. Press mixture on bottom and halfway up sides of a 9-inch springform pan. Freeze 10 minutes.
2. Beat cream cheese, 1¼ cups sugar, and cornstarch at medium speed with an electric mixer 2 to 3 minutes or until smooth. Add eggs, one at a time, beating at low speed just until yellow disappears after each addition. Add 3 Tbsp. brandy and 3 Tbsp. crème de cacao, and beat just until blended. Pour into prepared crust.

Brandy Alexander Cheesecake

3. Bake at 325° for 1 hour or just until center is almost set.
4. During last 2 minutes of baking, stir together sour cream and remaining 1 Tbsp. sugar, 1 Tbsp. brandy, and 1 Tbsp. crème de cacao.
5. Spread sour cream mixture over cheesecake. Bake at 325° for 8 more minutes. Remove cheesecake from oven; gently run a knife along outer edge of cheesecake, and cool completely in pan on a wire rack (about 1½ hours). Cover and chill 8 to 24 hours.
6. Remove sides of springform pan, and place cheesecake on a serving plate. Garnish, if desired.

*Coffee liqueur may be substituted. We tested with Kahlúa.

Note: We tested with Nabisco Teddy Grahams chocolate graham snacks.

Hummingbird Cake

Hands-on Time: 43 min.
Total Time: 1 hr., 53 min., including frosting
Makes: 16 servings

This is the ultimate recipe for Hummingbird Cake. It's the most requested recipe in Southern Living magazine history and frequents covered dish dinners all across the South, always receiving rave reviews.

- 3 cups all-purpose flour
- 2 cups sugar
- 1 tsp. baking soda
- 1 tsp. salt
- 1 tsp. ground cinnamon
- 3 large eggs, beaten
- 1 cup vegetable oil
- 1½ tsp. vanilla extract
- 1 (8-oz.) can crushed pineapple, undrained
- 1 cup chopped pecans
- 2 cups chopped bananas
- Cream Cheese Frosting
- ½ cup chopped pecans

1. Preheat oven to 350°. Combine first 5 ingredients in a large bowl; add eggs and oil, stirring until dry ingredients are moistened. (Do not beat.) Stir in vanilla, pineapple, 1 cup pecans, and bananas.

2. Pour batter into 3 greased and floured 9-inch round cake pans. Bake at 350° for 25 to 30 minutes or until a wooden pick inserted in center comes out clean. Cool in pans on wire racks 10 minutes; remove from pans, and cool completely on wire racks.

3. Spread Cream Cheese Frosting between layers and on top and sides of cake; sprinkle ¹/₂ cup chopped pecans on top. Store in refrigerator.

Cream Cheese Frosting

Hands-on Time: 12 min.
Total Time: 12 min.
Makes: 3 cups

  1 (8-oz.) package cream cheese, softened
  ½ cup butter, softened
  1 (16-oz.) package powdered sugar, sifted
  1 tsp. vanilla extract

1. Beat cream cheese and butter at medium speed with an electric mixer until smooth. Gradually add powdered sugar, beating at low speed until light and fluffy. Stir in vanilla.

Blackberry-Apple
Upside-Down Cake

Blackberry-Apple Upside-Down Cake

Hands-on Time: 30 min.
Total Time: 1 hr., 15 min.
Makes: 8 servings

If using frozen berries, add them straight from the freezer so that they hold their shape.

  ¾ cup butter, softened and divided
  ½ cup firmly packed light brown sugar
  ¼ cup honey
  2 large Gala apples, peeled and cut into
      ¼-inch-thick slices
  1 cup fresh or frozen blackberries*
  1 cup granulated sugar
  2 large eggs
  1½ cups all-purpose flour
  1 tsp. baking powder
  ½ cup milk
  1 tsp. vanilla extract

1. Preheat oven to 350°. Melt ¹/₄ cup butter in a lightly greased 9-inch round cake pan (with sides that are at least 2 inches high) over low heat. Remove from heat. Sprinkle with brown sugar; drizzle honey over brown sugar. Arrange apple slices in concentric circles over brown sugar mixture, overlapping as needed; sprinkle with blackberries.

2. Beat granulated sugar and remaining ¹/₂ cup butter at medium speed with an electric mixer until blended. Add eggs, one at a time, beating until blended after each addition.

3. Stir together flour and baking powder. Add flour mixture to sugar mixture alternately with milk, beginning and ending with flour mixture. Beat at low speed just until blended after each addition. Stir in vanilla. Spoon batter over blackberries in pan.

4. Bake at 350° for 45 minutes or until a wooden pick inserted in center comes out clean. Cool in pan on a wire rack 10 minutes. Carefully run a knife around edge of cake to loosen. Invert cake onto a serving plate, spooning any topping in pan over cake.

*1 cup fresh or frozen cranberries may be substituted.

Scrumptious Apple Pie

Scrumptious Apple Pie

Hands-on Time: 30 min.
Total Time: 1 hr., 55 min.
Makes: 8 servings

- 7 cups peeled and sliced Granny Smith apples (about 5 medium)
- ½ cup granulated sugar
- 2 tsp. fresh lemon juice
- ¾ cup all-purpose flour, divided
- ½ tsp. salt, divided
- ¾ cup butter
- 1 cup firmly packed light brown sugar
- ½ cup uncooked quick-cooking oats
- ½ (14.1-oz.) package refrigerated piecrusts
- ½ cup chopped pecans
  Jarred caramel topping, vanilla ice cream

1. Preheat oven to 375°. Stir together first 3 ingredients, ¼ cup flour, and ¼ tsp. salt until well blended.
2. Cut butter into remaining ½ cup flour with a pastry blender or fork until mixture resembles small peas. Stir in brown sugar, oats, and remaining ¼ tsp. salt.

3. Fit piecrust into a 9-inch pie plate according to package directions; fold edges under, and crimp. Place apple mixture in piecrust; top with brown sugar mixture, pressing gently to adhere. Shield edges of crust with aluminum foil. Place pie on a foil-lined baking sheet.
4. Bake at 375° for 25 minutes. Remove foil from crust, and bake 25 more minutes or until golden brown. Sprinkle with pecans, and bake 5 to 7 minutes or until pecans are toasted. Let pie stand 30 minutes to 2 hours before serving. Serve with caramel topping and ice cream.

Heavenly Key Lime Pie

Hands-on Time: 15 min.
Total Time: 2 hr., 30 min.
Makes: 6 to 8 servings

This pie is great with fresh or bottled Key lime juice.

- 1 (14-oz.) can sweetened condensed milk
- 3 egg yolks
- 2 tsp. Key lime zest*
- ½ cup Key lime juice
- 1 (9-inch) graham cracker piecrust
- 1 cup whipping cream
- 3 Tbsp. powdered sugar

1. Preheat oven to 350°. Whisk together condensed milk and next 3 ingredients until well blended. Pour mixture into piecrust.
2. Bake at 350° for 15 minutes or until pie is set. Cool completely on a wire rack (about 1 hour). Chill 1 hour before serving.
3. Beat whipping cream at high speed with an electric mixer 2 to 3 minutes or until soft peaks form, gradually adding powdered sugar. Top cooled pie with whipped cream.

*Regular lime zest and juice may be substituted.

Note: We tested with Nellie & Joe's Famous Key West Lime Juice.

Orange-Sweet Potato Pie with Rosemary-Cornmeal Crust

Hands-on Time: 35 min.
Total Time: 4 hr., 35 min.
Makes: 8 servings

Rosemary-Cornmeal Crust:
- ¾ cup all-purpose flour
- ½ cup plain white cornmeal
- ¼ cup powdered sugar
- 2 tsp. chopped fresh rosemary
- ¼ tsp. salt
- ½ cup cold butter, cut into pieces
- ¼ cup very cold water

Orange-Sweet Potato Filling:
- 1½ lb. sweet potatoes
- 3 large eggs
- ¾ cup granulated sugar
- 1 cup evaporated milk
- 3 Tbsp. melted butter
- 2 tsp. orange zest
- 1 Tbsp. fresh orange juice
- ½ tsp. ground cinnamon
- ¼ tsp. ground nutmeg
- 1½ tsp. vanilla extract

1. Prepare Rosemary-Cornmeal Crust: Whisk together first 5 ingredients in a medium bowl until well blended. Cut butter into flour mixture with a pastry blender or fork until mixture resembles small peas and is crumbly.

2. Sprinkle cold water, 1 Tbsp. at a time, over surface of mixture in bowl; stir with a fork until dry ingredients are moistened. Place dough on a plastic wrap-lined flat surface, and shape into a disc. Wrap in plastic wrap, and chill 30 minutes.

3. Unwrap dough, and roll between 2 new sheets of lightly floured plastic wrap into a 12-inch circle. Fit into a 9-inch pie plate. Fold edges under, and crimp. Chill 30 minutes.

4. Preheat oven to 400°. Bake crust 20 minutes, shielding edges with aluminum foil to prevent excessive browning. Cool completely on a wire rack (about 1 hour).

5. Meanwhile, prepare Orange-Sweet Potato Filling: Bake sweet potatoes at 400° on a baking sheet 50 to 55 minutes or until tender. Let stand 5 minutes. Cut potatoes in half lengthwise; scoop out pulp into a bowl. Mash pulp. Discard skins.

6. Whisk together eggs and granulated sugar until well blended. Add milk, next 6 ingredients, and sweet potato pulp, stirring until blended. Pour mixture into Rosemary-Cornmeal Crust.

7. Bake at 400° for 20 minutes. Reduce temperature to 325°, and bake 20 to 25 minutes or until center is set. Let cool completely on a wire rack (about 1 hour).

Orange-Sweet Potato Pie with Rosemary-Cornmeal Crust.

bake it!

Substitute ½ (14.1-oz.) package of refrigerated piecrusts for cornmeal crust ingredients. Unroll on a lightly floured surface. Sprinkle with 1 Tbsp. plain white cornmeal and 2 tsp. chopped fresh rosemary. Lightly roll cornmeal and rosemary into crust. Fit into a 9-inch pie plate according to package directions. Fold edges under; crimp. Proceed as directed, beginning with Step 5.

Pecan-Peach Cobbler

Hands-on Time: 45 min.
Total Time: 1 hr., 41 min.
Makes: 10 to 12 servings

- 12 to 15 fresh peaches, peeled and sliced (about 16 cups)
- ⅓ cup all-purpose flour
- ½ tsp. ground nutmeg
- 3 cups sugar
- ⅔ cup butter
- 1½ tsp. vanilla extract
- 2 (14.1-oz.) packages refrigerated piecrusts
- ½ cup chopped pecans, toasted and divided
- 5 Tbsp. sugar, divided

Sweetened whipped cream

1. Preheat oven to 475°. Stir together peaches, flour, nutmeg, and 3 cups sugar in a Dutch oven. Bring mixture to a boil over medium heat; reduce heat to low, and simmer 10 minutes. Remove from heat; stir in butter and vanilla. Spoon half of mixture into a lightly greased 13- x 9-inch baking dish.

2. Unroll 2 piecrusts. Sprinkle ¼ cup pecans and 2 Tbsp. sugar over 1 piecrust; top with other piecrust. Roll to a 14- x 10-inch rectangle. Trim sides to fit baking dish. Place pastry over peach mixture in dish.

3. Bake at 475° for 20 to 25 minutes or until lightly browned. Unroll remaining 2 piecrusts. Sprinkle 2 Tbsp. sugar and remaining ¼ cup pecans over 1 piecrust; top with remaining piecrust. Roll into a 12-inch circle. Cut into 1-inch strips, using a fluted pastry wheel. Spoon remaining peach mixture over baked pastry. Arrange pastry strips over peach mixture; sprinkle with remaining 1 Tbsp. sugar. Bake 15 to 18 minutes or until lightly browned. Serve warm or cold with whipped cream.

Pecan-Peach Cobbler

Profiteroles with Coffee Whipped Cream

Hands-on Time: 20 min.
Total Time: 1 hr., 10 min., including whipped cream
Makes: about 2 dozen

These small cream puffs are surprisingly easy to make. Store cooled, unfilled puffs in an airtight container up to two days.

- ¾ cup all-purpose flour
- 1½ tsp. sugar
- ⅓ cup butter
- 3 large eggs, beaten
- Parchment paper
- Coffee Whipped Cream
- Hot fudge topping

1. Preheat oven to 400°. Stir together flour and sugar.
2. Bring butter and ¾ cup water to a boil in a 3-qt. saucepan over medium-high heat, stirring occasionally. Immediately remove from heat, and quickly stir in flour mixture all at once. Beat with a wooden spoon until mixture is smooth and leaves sides of pan, forming a ball of dough. Gradually add eggs, beating until mixture is smooth and glossy.
3. Drop dough by rounded tablespoonfuls onto a parchment paper-lined baking sheet.
4. Bake at 400° for 20 minutes or until puffy and golden brown. Remove from oven to a wire rack. Pierce one side of each cream puff with a knife to allow steam to escape. Cool completely on baking sheet (about 20 minutes).
5. Cut each cream puff in half horizontally. Dollop Coffee Whipped Cream onto bottom halves; top with remaining halves. Cover and chill until ready to serve. Drizzle with hot fudge topping just before serving.

kitchen secret:
Use a 1-inch scoop coated with cooking spray to drop dough onto the baking sheet.

Coffee Whipped Cream

Hands-on Time: 5 min.
Total Time: 5 min.
Makes: about 2 cups

- 2 Tbsp. coffee liqueur
- 1 tsp. instant espresso
- 1 cup heavy cream
- 2 Tbsp. powdered sugar

1. Stir together coffee liqueur and instant espresso until blended. Beat heavy cream at medium-high speed with an electric mixer until foamy. Add liqueur mixture and powdered sugar, and beat until soft peaks form.

Note: We tested with Kahlúa coffee liqueur.

Profiteroles with Coffee Whipped Cream

Pavlova with Lemon Cream and Berries

Hands-on Time: 30 min.
Total Time: 14 hr.
Makes: 8 servings

Assemble this dessert just before serving, but you can make the meringue up to two days ahead; store in an airtight container.

- 1 cup sugar
- 1 Tbsp. cornstarch
- 4 egg whites, at room temperature
- ¼ tsp. cream of tartar
- Pinch of salt
- ¼ tsp. vanilla extract
- Parchment paper
- 1 (10-oz.) jar lemon curd
- ⅓ cup sour cream
- Assorted fresh berries
- Garnish: fresh lemon zest

1. Preheat oven to 225°. Whisk together sugar and cornstarch. Beat egg whites at medium-high speed with a heavy-duty electric stand mixer 1 minute; add cream of tartar and salt, beating until blended. Gradually add sugar mixture, 1 Tbsp. at a time, beating at medium-high speed until mixture is glossy, stiff peaks form, and sugar dissolves. (Do not overbeat.) Beat in vanilla. Gently spread mixture into a 7-inch round on a parchment paper-lined baking sheet, making an indentation in center of meringue to hold filling.
2. Bake at 225° for 1 hour and 30 minutes or until pale golden and outside has formed a crust. Turn oven off; let meringue stand in oven, with door closed and light on, 12 hours.
3. Meanwhile, whisk together lemon curd and sour cream until smooth. Cover and chill.
4. Spoon lemon mixture into center of meringue, and top with berries. (Center of meringue may fall after the lemon mixture and berries have been added.) Garnish, if desired.

Pavlova with Lemon Cream and Berries

Banana Pudding

Hands-on Time: 1 hr.
Total Time: 2 hr., 15 min.
Makes: 8 servings

This is definitely a cookie lover's version. Serve right away if you like crispy cookies, or chill overnight for a softer texture. It's delicious served warm, at room temperature, or chilled. If you omit the meringue, you won't need to bake the pudding.

Pudding:
- 1 (12-oz.) package vanilla wafers
- 5 ripe bananas, sliced
- 2 cups milk
- ½ cup sugar
- ⅓ cup all-purpose flour
- 3 egg yolks
- ⅛ tsp. salt
- ½ tsp. vanilla extract

Meringue:
- 3 egg whites
- ¼ cup sugar

1. Prepare Pudding: Preheat oven to 325°. Arrange one-third of vanilla wafers in a medium-size

Banana Pudding

Raspberry Tiramisù Bites

Hands-on Time: 30 min.
Total Time: 2 hr., 30 min.
Makes: 8 servings

There are crisp Italian cookies also called ladyfingers, but be sure to use soft ones in this recipe. Look for them in the bakery or produce section of your supermarket.

- 3 Tbsp. seedless raspberry preserves
- 1 Tbsp. orange liqueur
- 1 (3-oz.) package cream cheese, softened
- ¼ cup sugar
- ½ cup heavy cream
- 8 ladyfingers, halved crosswise
- 8 fresh raspberries
Garnish: fresh mint sprigs

1. Microwave raspberry preserves in a small microwave-safe bowl at HIGH 20 seconds. Stir in liqueur.
2. Beat cream cheese and sugar at medium speed with an electric mixer until creamy (about 1 minute).
3. Beat heavy cream at medium speed with an electric mixer until soft peaks form. Fold into cream cheese mixture. Spoon into a zip-top plastic bag. (Do not seal.) Snip 1 corner of bag with scissors to make a hole (about ½ inch in diameter).
4. Press 1 ladyfinger half onto bottom of 1 (1½-oz.) shot glass. Repeat procedure with 7 more shot glasses. Drizzle about ½ tsp. raspberry mixture into each glass. Pipe a small amount of cream cheese mixture evenly into each glass. Repeat procedure with remaining ladyfingers, raspberry mixture, and cream cheese mixture. Top each glass with 1 raspberry. Cover and chill 2 hours. Garnish, if desired.

ovenproof bowl (about 2 qt.); cover with one-third of banana slices. Repeat layers twice with remaining vanilla wafers and bananas.
2. Whisk together milk and next 4 ingredients in a heavy saucepan. Cook over medium-low heat, whisking constantly, 15 minutes or until pudding-like thickness. Remove from heat, and stir in vanilla. Pour over vanilla wafers and bananas in bowl.
3. Prepare Meringue: Beat egg whites at medium speed with an electric mixer until foamy. Gradually add sugar, beating until sugar dissolves and stiff peaks form. Spread meringue over pudding, sealing to edge of bowl.
4. Bake at 325° for 15 minutes or until golden. Serve immediately, or let cool completely (about 30 minutes), and cover and chill 1 hour before serving.

Raspberry Tiramisù Bites

Caramel-Pecan-Pumpkin Bread Puddings

Caramel-Pecan-Pumpkin Bread Puddings

Hands-on Time: 27 min.
Total Time: 9 hr., 22 min.
Makes: 11 servings

Bread Puddings:
4   large eggs
2   (15-oz.) cans pumpkin
1   cup granulated sugar
1½ cups milk
1   cup half-and-half
1   tsp. ground cinnamon
½   tsp. salt
½   tsp. ground nutmeg
½   tsp. vanilla extract
1   (12-oz.) French bread loaf, cut into
    1-inch pieces (about 10 cups)

Caramel-Pecan Sauce:
1   cup pecans, chopped
1   cup firmly packed light brown sugar
½   cup butter
1   Tbsp. light corn syrup
1   tsp. vanilla extract

1. Prepare Bread Puddings: Whisk together eggs and next 8 ingredients in a large bowl until well blended. Add bread pieces, stirring to coat thoroughly. Cover with plastic wrap, and chill 8 to 24 hours.
2. Preheat oven to 350°. Spoon bread mixture into 11 (6-oz.) lightly greased ramekins. (Ramekins will be completely full, and mixture will mound slightly.) Place on an aluminum foil-lined jelly-roll pan.
3. Bake at 350° for 50 minutes, shielding with foil after 30 minutes.
4. During last 15 minutes of baking, prepare Caramel-Pecan Sauce: Heat pecans in a medium skillet over medium-low heat, stirring often, 3 to 5 minutes or until lightly toasted and fragrant.
5. Cook brown sugar, butter, and corn syrup in a saucepan over medium heat, stirring occasionally, 3 to 4 minutes or until sugar is dissolved. Remove from heat; stir in vanilla and pecans.
6. Remove bread puddings from oven; drizzle with Caramel-Pecan Sauce. Bake 5 minutes or until sauce is thoroughly heated and begins to bubble.

Coconut Cream Tarts with Macadamia Nut Crusts

Hands-on Time: 48 min.
Total Time: 5 hr., 3 min.
Makes: 1 dozen

The crisp, sturdy crust perfectly complements the creamy custard in these stellar tarts.

¾   cup sugar
⅓   cup all-purpose flour
4   large eggs
2   cups milk
1   Tbsp. vanilla extract
1½ cups flaked coconut, divided
2½ cups all-purpose flour
¾   cup cold butter, cut up
1½ cups macadamia nuts, chopped
1   cup whipping cream
3   Tbsp. sugar

1. Stir together ¾ cup sugar and ⅓ cup flour; whisk in eggs.

2. Cook milk in a heavy saucepan over medium heat until hot. Gradually whisk about one-fourth of hot milk into egg mixture; add to remaining hot milk, whisking constantly.

3. Cook over medium-high heat, whisking constantly, 5 to 6 minutes or until thickened. Remove from heat; stir in vanilla and 1 cup coconut. Cover and chill 3 hours.

4. Preheat oven to 350°. Bake remaining ¹/₂ cup coconut in a shallow pan, stirring occasionally, 5 to 6 minutes or until toasted; set aside. Increase oven temperature to 375°.

5. Pulse 2¹/₂ cups flour and butter in a food processor until crumbly. Add 2 Tbsp. water, and pulse 30 seconds or until dough forms a ball. Turn out onto a lightly floured surface; knead in nuts.

6. Divide dough into 12 equal portions; press each portion into a (3- to 4-inch) tart pan. Prick bottoms with a fork, and place on a 15- x 10-inch jelly-roll pan. Cover and freeze 30 minutes.

7. Bake on jelly-roll pan at 375° for 15 to 20 minutes or until golden. Cool in tart pans 5 minutes; remove from pans, and cool completely on a wire rack.

8. Spoon coconut custard mixture into tart shells.

9. Beat whipping cream and 3 Tbsp. sugar at high speed with an electric mixer until soft peaks form; dollop or pipe onto tarts. Sprinkle tarts with toasted coconut; chill.

Luscious Lemon Bars

Hands-on Time: 20 min.
Total Time: 2 hr., 5 min.
Makes: about 2 dozen

2¼ cups all-purpose flour, divided
½ cup powdered sugar
1 cup cold butter, cut into pieces
4 large eggs
2 cups granulated sugar
1 tsp. lemon zest
⅓ cup fresh lemon juice
½ tsp. baking powder
Powdered sugar

1. Preheat oven to 350°. Line bottom and sides of a 13- x 9-inch pan with heavy-duty aluminum foil or parchment paper, allowing 2 to 3 inches to extend over sides; lightly grease foil.

2. Combine 2 cups flour and ¹/₂ cup powdered sugar. Cut in butter using a pastry blender or 2 forks until crumbly. Press mixture onto bottom of prepared pan.

3. Bake at 350° for 20 to 25 minutes or until lightly browned.

4. Meanwhile, whisk eggs in a large bowl until smooth; whisk in granulated sugar, lemon zest, and lemon juice. Stir together baking powder and remaining ¹/₄ cup flour; whisk into egg mixture. Pour mixture over hot baked crust.

5. Bake at 350° for 25 minutes or until filling is set. Let cool in pan on a wire rack 30 minutes. Lift from pan, using foil sides as handles. Cool completely on a wire rack (about 30 minutes). Remove foil, and cut into bars; sprinkle with powdered sugar.

Note: To make ahead, prepare as directed. Cover tightly, and freeze up to 1 month.

Luscious Lemon Bars

So-Good Brownies

Hands-on Time: 12 min.
Total Time: 52 min.
Makes: 16 servings

This is our adaptation of a recipe many of our foodies use from Baker's Chocolate.

  4 (1-oz.) unsweetened chocolate baking squares
  ¾ cup butter
 1½ cups granulated sugar
  ½ cup firmly packed light brown sugar
  3 large eggs
  1 cup all-purpose flour
  1 tsp. vanilla extract
  ⅛ tsp. salt

1. Preheat oven to 350°. Line bottom and sides of an 8-inch pan with aluminum foil, allowing 2 to 3 inches to extend over sides; lightly grease foil.

So-Good Brownies

2. Microwave chocolate squares and butter in a large microwave-safe bowl at HIGH 1½ to 2 minutes or until melted and smooth, stirring at 30-second intervals. Whisk in granulated and brown sugars. Add eggs, one at a time, whisking just until blended after each addition. Whisk in flour, vanilla, and salt.
3. Pour mixture into prepared pan.
4. Bake at 350° for 40 to 44 minutes or until a wooden pick inserted in center comes out with a few moist crumbs. Cool completely on a wire rack (about 1 hour). Lift brownies from pan, using foil sides as handles. Gently remove foil, and cut brownies into 16 squares.

Candy-and-Pretzel Brownies: Sprinkle 1 cup pretzel sticks, broken into pieces, and 2 (3.7-oz.) king-size chocolate-coated caramel-peanut nougat bars, coarsely chopped, over batter. Increase bake time to 52 to 54 minutes.

Note: Be sure to insert wooden pick into brownies, not candy bar pieces, when testing for doneness. We tested with Snickers King Size candy bars.

White Chocolate-Blueberry Brownies: A taste of chocolate-covered blueberries gave our Food staff this idea. Stir 1 (3.5-oz.) package dried blueberries and 1 (4-oz.) white chocolate bar, coarsely chopped, into batter. Increase bake time to 44 to 46 minutes.

Praline Bars

Hands-on Time: 25 min.
Total Time: 35 min.
Makes: 60 bars

A sheet of graham crackers is a whole perforated (but unbroken) cracker that is stacked and wrapped.

 15 graham cracker sheets
  ¾ cup chopped pecans
 1¾ cups firmly packed light brown sugar
  1 cup butter
  ½ cup semisweet chocolate morsels
  ½ cup white chocolate morsels

Praline Bars

1. Preheat oven to 350°. Separate each graham cracker sheet into 4 crackers; place in a lightly greased 15- x 10-inch jelly-roll pan. Sprinkle chopped pecans over graham crackers.
2. Bring brown sugar and butter to a boil in a saucepan over medium-high heat. Boil 2 minutes. Pour brown sugar mixture evenly over graham crackers in pan.
3. Bake at 350° for 10 minutes. Quickly remove graham crackers to wax paper, using a spatula, and let cool completely.
4. Microwave semisweet chocolate morsels in a microwave-safe bowl at HIGH 30 seconds. Stir and microwave at HIGH 30 more seconds or until smooth. Drizzle chocolate evenly over cooled bars. Repeat procedure with white chocolate morsels.

Carrot Cake Sandwich Cookies

Hands-on Time: 15 min.
Total Time: 1 hr., 18 min., including frosting
Makes: 1 dozen sandwiches

- ¾   cup grated carrots (about 2 medium carrots)
- 2   Tbsp. firmly packed dark brown sugar
- ½   tsp. ground ginger
- ½   tsp. ground cinnamon
- ⅓   cup raisins
- 1   (16.5-oz.) package refrigerated sugar cookie dough
- Cream Cheese Frosting

1. Preheat oven to 350°. Toss together first 4 ingredients in a large bowl. Stir raisins into carrot mixture.
2. Tear cookie dough into pieces, and stir into carrot mixture until well combined.
3. Drop cookie dough mixture by tablespoonfuls, 2 inches apart, onto lightly greased baking sheets. (Dough should make 24 cookies.)
4. Bake at 350° for 15 to 18 minutes or until edges are crisp. Cool on baking sheets 5 minutes. Remove to wire racks, and cool 10 minutes or until completely cool.
5. Turn half of cookies over, bottom sides up. Spread each with 1 Tbsp. chilled Cream Cheese Frosting. Top with remaining cookies, bottom sides down, and press gently to spread filling to edges of cookies.

Note: We tested with Pillsbury Create 'n Bake refrigerated sugar cookie dough.

Cream Cheese Frosting

Hands-on Time: 10 min.
Total Time: 40 min.
Makes: about 1 cup

- 5   oz. cream cheese, softened
- ¼   cup unsalted butter, softened
- 1   cup powdered sugar
- ½   tsp. fresh lemon juice
- ¼   tsp. vanilla extract

1. Beat cream cheese and butter at medium speed with an electric mixer until creamy.
2. Add remaining ingredients, beating until smooth. Cover and chill 30 minutes or until spreading consistency.

Chocolate Sugar Cookies

Hands-on Time: 1 hr.
Total Time: 2 hr., 15 min.
Makes: about 1 dozen

Create fun shapes for an outstanding twist on traditional sugar cookies.

1	cup butter, softened
1	cup sugar
1	large egg
2¼	cups all-purpose flour
¾	cup unsweetened cocoa
¼	tsp. salt

1. Preheat oven to 350°. Beat butter and sugar at medium speed with an electric mixer until fluffy. Add egg, beating until blended.
2. Combine flour, cocoa, and salt; gradually add to butter mixture, beating just until blended.
3. Divide dough into 2 equal portions; flatten each portion into a disk. Cover and chill 10 minutes.
4. Place 1 portion of dough on a lightly floured surface, and roll to ⅛-inch thickness. Cut with a 4¹/₂-inch butterfly-shaped cutter. Place cookies 2 inches apart on lightly greased baking sheets. Repeat procedure with remaining dough portion.
5. Bake, in batches, at 350° for 15 to 17 minutes or until edges are lightly browned. Let cool on baking sheets 5 minutes; remove to wire racks, and let cool 30 minutes or until completely cool. Decorate baked cookies as desired.

Vanilla Sugar Cookies: Omit unsweetened cocoa. Increase flour to 3 cups. Beat in 1 tsp. vanilla extract with butter in Step 1. Proceed with recipe as directed.

Lemon Thumbprint Cookies

Hands-on Time: 31 min.
Total Time: 1 hr., 2 min.
Makes: about 7 dozen

1	cup butter, softened
1	cup powdered sugar
1	cup granulated sugar
2	large eggs
1	cup vegetable oil
¼	cup fresh lemon juice
5¼	cups all-purpose flour
1	tsp. cream of tartar
1	tsp. baking soda
1	tsp. lemon zest
¼	tsp. salt
¾	cup plus 2 Tbsp. raspberry jam

1. Preheat oven to 350°. Beat butter at medium speed with an electric mixer until fluffy; add powdered and granulated sugars, beating well. Add eggs, oil, and lemon juice, beating until blended.
2. Combine flour and next 4 ingredients; gradually add to sugar mixture, beating until blended.
3. Shape dough into 1-inch balls, and place about 2 inches apart on lightly greased baking sheets. Press thumb in center of each cookie to make an indentation.
4. Bake, in batches, at 350° for 9 to 11 minutes or until set. (Do not brown.) Remove to wire racks to cool. Spoon ¹/₂ tsp. raspberry jam into each indentation.

Chocolate Sugar Cookies

Vanilla Bean Ice Cream

Hands-on Time: 20 min.
Total Time: 9 hr., 20 min.
Makes: about 1 qt.

- ¾ cup sugar
- 2 Tbsp. cornstarch
- ⅛ tsp. salt
- 2 cups milk
- 1 cup heavy whipping cream
- 1 egg yolk
- 1½ tsp. vanilla bean paste*

1. Whisk together first 3 ingredients in a large heavy saucepan. Gradually whisk in milk and cream. Cook over medium heat, stirring constantly, 10 to 12 minutes or until mixture thickens slightly. Remove from heat.
2. Whisk egg yolk until slightly thickened. Gradually whisk about 1 cup hot cream mixture into yolk. Add yolk mixture to remaining cream mixture, whisking constantly. Whisk in vanilla bean paste. Cool 1 hour, stirring occasionally.
3. Place plastic wrap directly on cream mixture, and chill 8 to 24 hours.
4. Pour mixture into freezer container of a 1½-qt. electric ice-cream maker, and freeze according to manufacturer's instructions. (Instructions and times may vary.)

*Vanilla extract may be substituted.

Chocolate-Raspberry Ice Cream: Before transferring ice cream to a container for further freezing, stir in 4 oz. finely chopped semisweet chocolate, and gently fold in ¼ cup melted seedless raspberry preserves.

Coconut Cream Pie Ice Cream: Reduce milk to 1 cup. Stir 1 cup coconut milk into sugar mixture with milk. Before transferring ice cream to a container for further freezing, stir in ¾ cup toasted, sweetened flaked coconut.

Vanilla Bean Ice Cream

Peach-and-Toasted Pecan Ice Cream

Hands-on Time: 32 min.
Total Time: 10 hr., 32 min.
Makes: about 1 qt.

- ¾ cup sugar
- 2 Tbsp. cornstarch
- ⅛ tsp. table salt
- 2 cups milk
- 1 cup heavy whipping cream
- 1 egg yolk
- 1½ tsp. vanilla bean paste*
- 1 cup peeled and coarsely chopped peaches
- 2 Tbsp. light corn syrup
- 1½ Tbsp. butter
- 1 cup coarsely chopped pecans
- ¼ tsp. kosher salt

1. Whisk together first 3 ingredients in a large heavy saucepan. Gradually whisk in milk and whipping cream. Cook over medium heat, stirring constantly, 10 to 12 minutes or until mixture thickens slightly. Remove from heat.
2. Whisk egg yolk until slightly thickened. Gradually whisk about 1 cup hot cream mixture into yolk. Add yolk mixture to remaining cream mixture, whisking constantly. Whisk in vanilla bean paste. Cool 1 hour, stirring occasionally.
3. Meanwhile, cook peaches and corn syrup in a small saucepan over medium heat, stirring often, 4 to 5 minutes. Coarsely mash, and let cool 30 minutes. Stir peach mixture into cooled cream mixture.
4. Place plastic wrap directly on cream mixture, and chill 8 to 24 hours.

5. Meanwhile, melt butter in a small skillet over medium heat. Add pecans; cook, stirring constantly, 8 to 9 minutes or until toasted and fragrant. Remove from heat, and sprinkle with ¼ tsp. kosher salt. Cool completely (about 30 minutes).
6. Pour chilled cream mixture into freezer container of a 1½-qt. electric ice-cream maker, and freeze according to manufacturer's instructions. (Instructions and times may vary.) Before transferring ice cream to an airtight container for further freezing, stir in pecan mixture.

*Vanilla extract may be substituted.

Peach-and-Toasted Pecan Ice Cream

Strawberry-Buttermilk Sherbet

Hands-on Time: 15 min.
Total Time: 3 hr., 15 min.
Makes: about 4½ cups

- 2 cups fresh strawberries*
- 2 cups buttermilk
- 1 cup sugar
- 1 tsp. vanilla extract
  Garnish: fresh mint sprigs

1. Process strawberries in a blender or food processor 30 seconds or until smooth, stopping to scrape down sides. Pour puree through a fine wire-mesh strainer into a large bowl, pressing with back of a spoon. Discard solids. Add buttermilk, sugar, and vanilla to puree; stir until well blended. Cover and chill 1 hour.
2. Pour strawberry mixture into freezer container of a 1½-qt. electric ice-cream maker; freeze according to manufacturer's instructions. (Instructions and times may vary.) Garnish, if desired.

*1 (16-oz.) package frozen strawberries, thawed, may be substituted.

Strawberry-Buttermilk Sherbet

Mint Tea Custard

Hands-on Time: 13 min.
Total Time: 1 hr., 53 min.
Makes: 6 servings

Baking these mini custards in a water bath ensures even temperatures when cooking.

1¼	cups low-fat evaporated milk
5	regular-size black tea bags
3	fresh mint sprigs, bruised
1	large lemon, quartered
½	cup sugar
4	large eggs
1	cup fat-free half-and-half

Garnishes: shaved chocolate, fresh mint sprigs

1. Preheat oven to 300°. Cook milk in a small non-aluminum saucepan over medium-low heat, stirring once, 2 to 3 minutes or just until bubbles appear. (Do not boil.) Remove from heat; add tea bags and next 2 ingredients. Cover and steep 20 minutes. Remove and discard tea bags, without squeezing; discard mint sprigs and lemon quarters. Reserve 1 cup tea mixture.

2. Whisk together sugar and eggs in a large bowl until mixture is thick and pale yellow. Gradually whisk in reserved 1 cup tea mixture and half-and-half until well blended. Pour mixture into 6 (4-oz.) custard cups or ramekins. Place custard cups in a roasting pan; add hot water halfway up sides of cups.

3. Bake at 300° for 40 to 50 minutes or until a knife inserted in center comes out clean. Carefully remove from oven, and let stand in pan in water bath 30 minutes. Remove from water bath. Serve immediately, or cover and chill at least 2 hours. Garnish, if desired.

kitchen secret:

Bruise mint sprigs by rolling them in your hands or pressing with the back of a spoon to release the flavorful oils.

Mint Tea Custard

White Chocolate-Cranberry Crème Brûlée

Hands-on Time: 18 min.
Total Time: 9 hr., 48 min., including sugared garnish
Makes: 6 servings

This elegant dessert is perfect for a holiday gathering.

    2   cups whipping cream
    4   oz. white chocolate
    1   tsp. vanilla extract
    5   egg yolks
    ½   cup sugar, divided
    ½   (15-oz.) can whole-berry cranberry sauce
Ice cubes
Garnish: Sugared Cranberries and Mint

1. Preheat oven to 300°. Combine ½ cup cream and white chocolate in a saucepan; cook over low heat, stirring constantly, 2 minutes or until chocolate is melted. Remove from heat; stir in vanilla and remaining 1½ cups cream.

2. Whisk together egg yolks and ¼ cup sugar until sugar is dissolved and mixture is thick and pale yellow. Add cream mixture, whisking until well blended. Pour mixture through a fine wire-mesh strainer into a large bowl.

3. Spoon 1½ Tbsp. cranberry sauce into each of 6 (4-oz.) ramekins. Pour cream-and-egg mixture evenly into ramekins; place ramekins in a large roasting pan. Add water to pan to depth of ½ inch.

4. Bake at 300° for 45 to 55 minutes or until edges are set. Cool custards in pan on a wire rack 25 minutes. Remove ramekins from water bath; cover and chill 8 hours.

5. Preheat broiler with oven rack 5 inches from heat. Sprinkle 1½ to 2 tsp. remaining sugar evenly over each ramekin. Fill a large roasting pan or 15- x 10- x 1-inch jelly-roll pan with ice; arrange ramekins in pan.

6. Broil 3 to 5 minutes or until sugar is melted and caramelized. Let stand 5 minutes. Garnish, if desired.

White Chocolate-Banana Crème Brûlée: Prepare recipe as directed through Step 2. Slice 2 bananas into ¼-inch-thick slices; toss bananas with ⅓ cup sugar. Melt 2 Tbsp. butter in a large nonstick skillet over medium-high heat. Add bananas, and cook 1 to 2 minutes on each side or until lightly browned. Line bottoms of 6 (4-oz.) ramekins evenly with banana slices. Pour cream mixture evenly into ramekins; place ramekins in a large roasting pan. Add water to pan to depth of ½ inch. Proceed with recipe as directed.

Sugared Cranberries and Mint

Hands-on Time: 15 min.
Total Time: 20 min.

    ¼   cup corn syrup
    ¼   cup dried cranberries
    1   bunch fresh mint sprigs
    ¼   cup sugar

1. Using a clean paintbrush, gently brush ¼ cup corn syrup onto the top side of dried cranberries and mint sprigs.

2. Sprinkle sugar over cranberries and mint. Let stand 5 minutes; sprinkle remaining sugar over cranberries and mint, gently shaking off excess.

White Chocolate-Cranberry Crème Brûlée

Southern-Style Caramel Apples

Hands-on Time: 15 min.
Total Time: 30 min.
Makes: 6 servings

6 apples
Food-safe branches, such as magnolia twigs,
or craft sticks
1 (14-oz.) package caramels
1 Tbsp. vanilla extract
Crushed peanut brittle or toasted pecans
(optional)

1. Remove stems from apples, and insert food-safe branches or craft sticks. Microwave caramels, vanilla extract, and 1 Tbsp. water at HIGH 1 minute or until melted, stirring every 30 seconds. Quickly dip or drizzle apples with caramel mixture; roll or sprinkle with crushed peanut brittle or toasted pecans, if desired. Stand apples on lightly greased wax paper, and chill 15 minutes before serving.

SAUCES & CONDIMENTS

Looking for an easy way to spice up your meal? Look no further than these fresh dressings, relishes, and sauces.

Honey-Balsamic Vinaigrette

Hands-on Time: 10 min.
Total Time: 10 min.
Makes: about 1 cup

Make this vinaigrette up to 2 days ahead, and refrigerate in an airtight container for up to 1 week. Allow it to come to room temperature, and whisk before serving.

- ½ cup olive oil
- ⅓ cup balsamic vinegar
- 1 Tbsp. chopped fresh parsley
- 1 Tbsp. chopped fresh thyme
- 2 Tbsp. honey
- Salt and pepper to taste

1. Whisk together first 5 ingredients until well blended. Whisk in salt and pepper to taste.

Pepper Jelly Vinaigrette

Hands-on Time: 10 min.
Total Time: 10 min.
Makes: ¾ cup

This vinaigrette is terrific drizzled over a summery trio of sliced tomatoes, cucumbers, and onion.

- ¼ cup rice wine vinegar
- ¼ cup pepper jelly
- 1 Tbsp. fresh lime juice
- 1 Tbsp. grated onion
- 1 tsp. salt
- ¼ tsp. pepper
- ¼ cup vegetable oil

1. Whisk together first 6 ingredients. Gradually add oil in a slow, steady stream, whisking until blended. Store in an airtight container in the refrigerator up to 1 week.

Warm Bacon Vinaigrette

Hands-on Time: 24 min.
Total Time: 24 min.
Makes: about 1½ cups

Serve this rich dressing over a simple spinach salad.

- 4 bacon slices
- 4 Tbsp. minced shallot
- 2 Tbsp. minced garlic
- 3 Tbsp. light brown sugar
- 6 Tbsp. orange juice
- 5 Tbsp. balsamic vinegar
- 3 Tbsp. coarse-grained mustard
- ⅓ cup olive oil
- ½ tsp. salt

1. Cook bacon in a large skillet over medium-high heat 8 to 10 minutes or until crisp. Remove bacon; drain on paper towels, reserving 2 Tbsp. drippings in skillet. Crumble bacon, and reserve for another use.
2. Cook shallots and garlic in hot drippings over medium heat, stirring occasionally, 3 minutes or until tender. Add brown sugar, and cook, stirring constantly, 1 minute or until sugar is dissolved.
3. Process garlic mixture, orange juice, and next 4 ingredients in a blender until combined. Store in an airtight container in the refrigerator up to 3 days.

Lemon-Mint Vinaigrette

Hands-on Time: 10 min.
Total Time: 10 min.
Makes: 1¹/₂ cups

Drizzle this vinaigrette over salad greens topped with fish or chicken, green peas, and shredded carrots.

- ½ cup olive oil
- ½ cup extra virgin olive oil
- 2 Tbsp. finely chopped fresh mint
- 2 Tbsp. finely chopped fresh parsley
- 6 Tbsp. fresh lemon juice
- 1 Tbsp. Dijon mustard
- 1 tsp. sugar
- ½ tsp. salt
- ½ tsp. pepper

1. Whisk together all ingredients until well blended. Store in an airtight container in the refrigerator up to 2 weeks. Let chilled vinaigrette come to room temperature before serving.

Soda Pop-and-Soy Marinade

Hands-on Time: 10 min.
Total Time: 10 min.
Makes: about 1¹/₃ cups

Don't use diet soft drink—the pork won't brown, and the aftertaste will be unpleasant. Tie the roast with kitchen string to create a shape that will cook evenly.

- 1 cup lemon-lime soft drink
- 1 Tbsp. light brown sugar
- 3 Tbsp. soy sauce
- 2 Tbsp. olive oil
- 1 Tbsp. Worcestershire sauce
- 2 garlic cloves, pressed
- ¾ tsp. ground ginger
- ⅛ tsp. ground cloves

1. Whisk together all ingredients until thoroughly blended. Use immediately.

Grilled Pork Loin Roast: Place Soda Pop-and-Soy Marinade in a shallow dish or large zip-top plastic freezer bag. Pierce 1 (2¹/₂-lb.) pork loin roast several times with a knife; add roast to marinade, and turn to coat. Cover or seal, and chill 4 to 6 hours, turning occasionally. Light one side of grill, heating to 350° to 400° (medium-high) heat; leave other side unlit. Remove roast from marinade, discarding marinade. Pat roast dry, and sprinkle with 1 tsp. salt and ¹/₂ tsp. pepper. Tie with kitchen string, securing at 2-inch intervals. Place roast over lit side of grill, and grill, covered with grill lid, 5 minutes on each side or until browned. Transfer roast to unlit side, and grill, covered with grill lid, 1 hour or until a meat thermometer inserted into thickest portion registers 150°. Remove from grill, and let stand 10 minutes before slicing. Garnish with fresh flat-leaf parsley sprigs, if desired.

Paul's Chicken Rub

Hands-on Time: 5 min.
Total Time: 5 min.
Makes: about 1²/₃ cups

This flavorful mix of spices is great rubbed on chicken. Let the chicken stand up to one hour in the refrigerator for maximum flavor.

- 1 cup Greek seasoning
- ¼ cup garlic powder
- ¼ cup paprika
- 3 Tbsp. dried oregano

1. Stir together all ingredients until well blended. Store in an airtight container.

Note: We tested with Cavender's All Purpose Greek Seasoning.

Hot Pepper Sauce

Hands-on Time: 15 min.
Total Time: 20 min., plus 3 weeks
Makes: 1 jar

A little bit of this spicy sauce goes a long way. Use it in place of your favorite hot sauce on dishes such as sautéed greens.

- 1 cup red and green Thai chile peppers, stemmed
- 1 cup cider vinegar
- 1 tsp. salt
- 1 tsp. sugar

1. Fill 1 (14-oz.) glass jar with red and green Thai chile peppers, filling to about 1 inch from top of jar. Bring vinegar, salt, and sugar to a boil in a small saucepan over medium heat, stirring until salt and sugar are dissolved (about 2 to 3 minutes). Remove from heat, and let stand 5 minutes. Pour hot mixture over peppers in jar. Cover and chill 3 weeks. Store in the refrigerator up to 6 months.

kitchen secret:

Chilling for 3 weeks allows the peppers to fire up the vinegar mixture. The longer it sits, the spicier it becomes. Remember to wear rubber gloves when filling the jars with peppers.

Hot Pepper Sauce

Spicy Rémoulade Sauce

Hands-on Time: 6 min.
Total Time: 6 min.
Makes: about 1¼ cups

Serve this sauce with boiled shrimp and shredded iceberg lettuce on toasted sourdough rolls.

- 1 cup mayonnaise
- ¼ cup sliced green onions
- 1 Tbsp. chopped fresh parsley
- 2 Tbsp. Creole mustard
- 2 tsp. lemon zest
- 2 garlic cloves, pressed
- ½ tsp. ground red pepper

1. Stir together all ingredients until well blended. Store in an airtight container in the refrigerator up to 3 days.

Spicy Rémoulade Sauce

Spicy Cocktail Sauce

Hands-on Time: 10 min.
Total Time: 10 min.
Makes: about 4 cups

This classic sauce is ideal for boiled shrimp and steamed oysters.

- 1½ cups chili sauce
- 1 cup ketchup
- ¾ cup prepared horseradish
- ⅓ cup fresh lemon juice
- 1½ Tbsp. Worcestershire sauce
- 2 to 3 tsp. hot sauce
- ½ tsp. salt
- ½ tsp. pepper

1. Combine all ingredients until well blended. Cover and chill until ready to serve. Store in an airtight container in the refrigerator up to 5 days.

Note: We tested with Heinz Chili Sauce.

Horseradish Sauce

Hands-on Time: 10 min.
Total Time: 10 min.
Makes: 3 cups

Serve a big dollop of this creamy sauce over roast beef.

- 1 cup whipping cream
- 1 cup mayonnaise
- ⅛ tsp. salt
- ¼ cup horseradish
- 1 tsp. lemon zest
- 1 tsp. fresh lemon juice

1. Beat whipping cream at medium speed with an electric mixer until soft peaks form. Add mayonnaise and salt, beating until blended; stir in horseradish, lemon zest, and lemon juice. Store in an airtight container in the refrigerator up to 3 days.

Creole Sauce

Hands-on Time: 8 min.
Total Time: 8 min.
Makes: 1¹/₄ cups

To lighten up this sauce, substitute ½ cup light mayonnaise and ½ cup yogurt for the mayonnaise.

- 1 cup mayonnaise
- 3 green onions, minced
- 2 garlic cloves, minced
- 2 Tbsp. Creole mustard
- 1 Tbsp. chopped fresh parsley
- ¼ tsp. ground red pepper

1. Stir together all ingredients until well blended. Store in an airtight container in the refrigerator up to 3 days.

Roasted Red Bell Pepper Sauce

Hands-on Time: 5 min.
Total Time: 5 min.
Makes: ³/₄ cup

This versatile and simple sauce starts with bottled roasted red peppers. Serve it with grilled scallops or over cheesy grits.

- 1 (7-oz.) jar roasted red bell peppers, drained
- 2 Tbsp. chopped fresh basil
- 1 Tbsp. olive oil
- 1 tsp. salt
- 2 tsp. fresh lemon juice
- ½ tsp. pepper
- ¼ tsp. sugar

1. Process all ingredients in a blender or food processor until smooth, stopping to scrape down sides as needed. Store in an airtight container in the refrigerator up to 3 days.

Basic Tomato Sauce

Hands-on Time: 30 min.
Total Time: 30 min.
Makes: 2²/₃ cups

Use a pasta shape that will capture your sauce, such as penne rigate, which has ridges.

- 4 to 5 garlic cloves, minced
- ½ tsp. dried crushed red pepper
- 2 Tbsp. extra virgin olive oil
- 1 (28-oz.) can crushed tomatoes
- ½ tsp. salt

1. Sauté garlic and crushed pepper in hot oil in a large saucepan over medium heat 1 minute. (Do not brown garlic.) Stir in tomatoes and salt. Bring sauce to a boil, reduce heat to low, and simmer, stirring occasionally, 15 minutes. Serve immediately.

Basic Tomato Sauce

Lemon-Caper Cream

Hands-on Time: 10 min.
Total Time: 10 min.
Makes: 1 cup

Serve this alongside crab cakes.

- ¾ cup reduced-fat sour cream
- 2 Tbsp. capers, drained
- 2 Tbsp. mayonnaise
- ½ tsp. lemon zest
- 1 tsp. fresh lemon juice
- Salt and pepper to taste

1. Stir together first 5 ingredients. Season with salt and pepper to taste. Store in an airtight container in the refrigerator up to 2 weeks.

Lemon-Caper Cream

Fresh Herb Mayonnaise

Hands-on Time: 10 min.
Total Time: 10 min.
Makes: about 2¼ cups

Slather this creamy mayo on your favorite sandwich.

- 2 cups mayonnaise
- 2 Tbsp. chopped fresh parsley
- 2 Tbsp. chopped fresh chives
- 1 Tbsp. chopped fresh basil
- 1 Tbsp. chopped fresh dill
- 1 Tbsp. chopped fresh oregano

1. Stir together all ingredients until well blended. Store in an airtight container in the refrigerator up to 2 days.

Sweet-Hot Ketchup

Hands-on Time: 5 min.
Total Time: 2 hr., 5 min.
Makes: 1⅓ cups

Update America's favorite condiment with spicy and sweet flavors.

- 1 cup ketchup
- 3 Tbsp. fresh lime juice
- 2 Tbsp. honey
- 1 tsp. lime zest
- 1 tsp. chipotle chile pepper seasoning

1. Stir together all ingredients until well blended. Cover and chill 2 hours. Store in an airtight container in the refrigerator up to 1 week.

Spicy Peach Ketchup

Hands-on Time: 10 min.
Total Time: 2 hr., 10 min.
Makes: 2 cups

1	cup ketchup
½	cup thick-and-spicy barbecue sauce
½	cup peach preserves

1. Stir together ketchup, barbecue sauce, and peach preserves until blended. Cover and chill 2 hours.

North Carolina Eastern-Style Barbecue Sauce

Hands-on Time: 5 min.
Total Time: 5 min.
Makes: 2 qt.

7	cups vinegar
1	cup ginger ale
3	Tbsp. plus 1 tsp. dried crushed red pepper
1	to 2 Tbsp. ground pepper

1. Stir together all ingredients until well blended. Serve sauce over pork barbecue or store in an airtight container in the refrigerator up to 1 week.

Southern foodlore

Pig Pickin's are a popular Southern tradition and are great for feeding a crowd. The whole pig is split and sloshed with sauce while it's roasted over an open-pit fire. After hours of slow cooking, the fall-off-the-bone meat is picked right off the pig.

Sausage Gravy

Hands-on Time: 16 min.
Total Time: 16 min.
Makes: 2 cups

This recipe is a Southern classic. Sausage gravy is most commonly served over buttermilk biscuits or grits.

8	oz. pork sausage
¼	cup all-purpose flour
2⅓	cups milk
½	tsp. salt
½	tsp. pepper

1. Cook sausage in a large skillet over medium heat, stirring until it crumbles and is no longer pink. Remove sausage, and drain on paper towels, reserving 1 Tbsp. drippings in skillet.
2. Whisk flour into hot drippings until smooth; cook, whisking constantly, 1 minute. Gradually whisk in milk, and cook, whisking constantly, 5 to 7 minutes or until thickened. Stir in sausage, salt, and pepper. Serve immediately.

Sausage Gravy

Brandy-Caramel Sauce

Hands-on Time: 10 min.
Total Time: 20 min.
Makes: about 2 cups

We suggest using the full amount of butter in this sauce, although half of our tasting table thought it was fine with 2 Tbsp. Try it with Scrumptious Apple Pie on page 356.

1	cup whipping cream
1½	cups firmly packed light brown sugar
2	Tbsp. to ¼ cup butter
2	Tbsp. brandy*
1	tsp. vanilla extract

1. Bring whipping cream to a light boil in a large saucepan over medium heat, stirring occasionally. Add sugar, and cook, stirring occasionally, 4 to 5 minutes or until sugar is dissolved and mixture is smooth. Remove from heat, and stir in butter, brandy, and vanilla. Let cool 10 minutes.

*Apple cider may be substituted.

Note: To make ahead, prepare recipe as directed. Store in an airtight container in the refrigerator up to 1 week. To reheat, let stand at room temperature 30 minutes. Place mixture in a microwave-safe bowl, and microwave at HIGH 1 minute, stirring after 30 seconds.

Hot Fudge Sauce

Hands-on Time: 17 min.
Total Time: 17 min.
Makes: 3 cups

3	(1-oz.) unsweetened chocolate squares
½	cup butter
1	(12-oz.) can evaporated milk
1	(16-oz.) package powdered sugar, sifted

1. Melt chocolate and butter in a heavy saucepan over low heat, stirring occasionally; add milk alternately with sugar, stirring well after each addition. Bring to a boil over medium heat, stirring constantly; reduce heat, and simmer 5 minutes or until thickened. Serve over ice cream. Store in an airtight container in the refrigerator up to 1 week.

Lemon Curd

Hands-on Time: 25 min.
Total Time: 55 min.
Makes: 2 cups

Use this recipe for Pavlova with Lemon Cream and Berries on page 360.

2	cups sugar
½	cup butter, coarsely chopped
¼	cup lemon zest
1	cup fresh lemon juice (about 6 lemons)
4	eggs, lightly beaten

1. Stir together sugar, chopped butter, lemon zest, and lemon juice in a large saucepan over medium heat and cook, stirring constantly, until sugar dissolves and butter melts.

Lemon Curd

Lemon-Herb Butter

Pecan-Honey Butter

Hands-on Time: 5 min.
Total Time: 5 min.
Makes: 1 cup

This subtly sweet butter is great served on dinner rolls or dolloped on a baked sweet potato.

- ½ cup butter, softened
- ½ cup finely chopped toasted pecans
- 2 Tbsp. honey

1. Stir together all ingredients until well blended. Store in an airtight container in the refrigerator up to 1 week, or freeze up to 1 month.

Note: Be sure to cool pecans completely after toasting.

2. Whisk about one-fourth of hot sugar mixture gradually into eggs; add egg mixture to remaining hot sugar mixture, whisking constantly.
3. Cook over medium-low heat, stirring constantly, 15 minutes or until mixture thickens and coats a spoon. Remove from heat; cool. Store in an airtight container in the refrigerator up to 2 weeks.

Lemon-Herb Butter

Hands-on Time: 5 min.
Total Time: 5 min.
Makes: about ¹/₂ cup

- ½ cup butter, softened
- 2 Tbsp. chopped fresh parsley
- 2 tsp. chopped fresh chives
- 2 tsp. lemon zest

1. Stir together softened butter, chopped fresh parsley, chopped fresh chives, and lemon zest until well blended. Store in an airtight container in the refrigerator up to 1 week.

Pecan-Honey Butter

Fresh Peach Salsa

Hands-on Time: 30 min.
Total Time: 30 min.
Makes: about 4 cups

This versatile salsa is equally delicious made with fresh nectarines. You'll need a 4- to 5-inch-long piece of ginger (about 1 inch thick) to yield 2 Tbsp. of grated ginger.

- 1 large sweet onion, chopped
- 1 jalapeño pepper, seeded and minced
- ¼ cup sugar
- 2 Tbsp. grated fresh ginger
- 2 Tbsp. olive oil
- 6 large firm peaches, peeled and chopped
- ¼ cup fresh lemon juice
- 2 Tbsp. chopped fresh cilantro
- ¼ tsp. salt

1. Sauté first 4 ingredients in hot oil in a large skillet over medium heat 5 minutes or until onion is tender. Stir in peaches and remaining ingredients, and cook, stirring gently, 5 minutes. Serve warm or at room temperature. Store leftovers in an airtight container in the refrigerator up to 2 days.

Fresh Peach Salsa

Watermelon Salsa (pictured on page 6)

Hands-on Time: 20 min.
Total Time: 20 min.
Makes: about 3 cups

This recipe doubles as a healthful and refreshing topping for grilled, baked, or broiled fish, shrimp, or chicken.

- 1½ tsp. lime zest
- ¼ cup fresh lime juice (about 3 limes)
- 1 Tbsp. sugar
- ¾ tsp. freshly ground black pepper
- 3 cups seeded and finely chopped watermelon
- 1 cucumber, peeled, seeded, and diced
- 2 jalapeño peppers, seeded and minced
- ¼ cup chopped red onion
- ¼ cup chopped fresh basil
- ½ tsp. salt
- Tortilla chips

1. Whisk together first 4 ingredients in a large bowl. Add watermelon and next 4 ingredients, gently tossing to coat. Chill until ready to serve. Stir in salt just before serving. Serve with tortilla chips. Store in an airtight container in the refrigerator up to 2 days.

Zesty Corn Salsa

Hands-on Time: 26 min.
Total Time: 36 min.
Makes: 2 cups

Serve as a dip with tortilla chips or as a relish for grilled chicken or pork.

- 6 ears fresh corn, shucked
- ¼ cup fresh lime juice
- 2 tsp. olive oil
- ½ tsp. lime zest
- 1 small jalapeño pepper, minced
- ¼ tsp. salt
- ¼ tsp. ground cumin

1. Grill corn, covered with grill lid, over medium-high heat (350° to 400°) 10 minutes on each side or until browned on all sides. Remove from grill; cool.

2. Cut corn from cob into a bowl; stir in lime juice and remaining ingredients. Store in an airtight container in the refrigerator up to 2 days.

Clementine-Cranberry Salsa

Hands-on Time: 15 min.
Total Time: 1 hr., 15 min.
Makes: about 2¼ cups

Serve this brightly flavored condiment alongside turkey fajitas, grilled chicken, or pork.

- 4 clementines, peeled and sectioned
- ½ cup fresh cranberries, coarsely chopped*
- ⅓ cup finely chopped red onion
- 1 Tbsp. sugar
- 1 Tbsp. fresh lime juice
- 1 Tbsp. olive oil
- ¼ tsp. salt
- 1 jalapeño pepper, seeded and finely chopped

1. Cut clementine sections in half. Combine all ingredients until well blended; cover and let stand 1 hour. Store in an airtight container in the refrigerator up to 2 days.

*Frozen cranberries, thawed, may be substituted.

Orange-Cranberry Salsa: Substitute 2 navel oranges for clementines. Makes 1½ cups.

> ## kitchen secret:
> Like your salsa hot? The seeds and veins of jalapeños and other peppers contain most of the heat. Don't remove them if you like a lot of spice.

Clementine-Cranberry Salsa

Orange Gremolata

Hands-on Time: 10 min.
Total Time: 10 min.
Makes: about ½ cup

Gremolata is a traditional herb garnish typically found in South American cuisine. It's great served over grilled meats.

- ½ cup minced fresh flat-leaf parsley
- 2 tsp. orange zest
- 2 tsp. minced fresh garlic
- ⅛ tsp. salt
- Pinch of pepper

1. Stir together all ingredients until well blended. Serve immediately, or cover and chill up to 3 days.

Olivata

1. Combine 1 Tbsp. water and first 3 ingredients in a small saucepan. Bring to a boil over medium-high heat. Reduce heat; simmer, stirring occasionally, 1 to 2 minutes or until liquid is absorbed and tomatoes are plump.

2. Process tomato mixture, olives, and next 5 ingredients in a food processor or blender until smooth, stopping to scrape down sides. Serve with French baguette slices. Store in an airtight container in the refrigerator up to 1 week.

Pecan Pesto

Hands-on Time: 10 min.
Total Time: 10 min.
Makes: about 3 cups

Traditional pesto gets a twist with pecans in place of pine nuts.

    4 cups loosely packed fresh basil leaves
    1 cup (4 oz.) freshly shredded Parmesan
       cheese
    1 cup toasted pecans
    1 cup olive oil
    4 garlic cloves
    2 Tbsp. fresh lemon juice
    ½ tsp. salt
    ½ tsp. pepper

1. Process all ingredients in a food processor until smooth. Store in an airtight container in the refrigerator up to 3 days.

Olivata

Hands-on Time: 14 min.
Total Time: 14 min.
Makes: about 1 cup

Olivata is a type of tapenade that is great served on bruschetta as an appetizer.

    ¼ cup sun-dried tomatoes
    1 Tbsp. balsamic vinegar
    1 Tbsp. red wine vinegar
    ½ cup pitted kalamata olives
    1 Tbsp. chopped fresh basil
    1 Tbsp. olive oil
    ½ tsp. chopped garlic
    ¼ tsp. pepper
    ⅛ tsp. salt
       French baguette slices

Pecan Pesto

Collard Green Pesto

Collard Green Pesto

Hands-on Time: 19 min.
Total Time: 19 min.
Makes: 4 cups

Here's a Southern twist on an old-world favorite. Use as a dip with fresh vegetables and pita chips or as a spread for a sandwich.

- 5 cups packaged fresh collard greens, washed, trimmed, and chopped
- 3 garlic cloves
- ¼ cup pecans
- ½ cup olive oil
- ⅓ cup grated Parmesan cheese
- ½ tsp. salt

1. Cook greens in boiling water to cover 3¹⁄₂ to 4 minutes or until tender; drain. Plunge into ice water to stop the cooking process; drain well.
2. Process garlic and pecans in a food processor until finely ground. Add greens, oil, cheese, salt, and ¹⁄₄ cup water; process 2 to 3 seconds or until smooth, stopping to scrape down sides. (Mixture will be thick.) Refrigerate leftovers up to 1 week. Cover tightly with plastic wrap to keep pesto a vibrant green.

Caramelized Sweet Onions

Hands-on Time: 55 min.
Total Time: 55 min.
Makes: about 2 cups

Georgia's Vidalia and Texas's 1015 sweet onions are available in spring and summer, but sweet onions are now available just about all year long. In fall and winter months, look for the South American OSO sweet onion.

- 4 lb. sweet onions, chopped (about 12 cups)
- 1 tsp. chopped fresh or ½ tsp. dried thyme
- 2 Tbsp. olive oil
- ½ tsp. salt

1. Cook onion and thyme in hot oil in a large deep skillet over medium heat, stirring often, 35 to 40 minutes or until caramel colored (a deep golden brown). Remove from heat; stir in salt.

Note: Store cooked onions in a zip-top plastic freezer bag or an airtight container in the refrigerator up to 1 week or freeze up to 2 months.

Caramelized Sweet Onions

Dilled Green Beans

Hands-on Time: 19 min.
Total Time: 44 min.
Makes: 7 pt.

- 2 lb. green beans
- 7 hot red peppers*
- 7 garlic cloves, quartered
- 3½ tsp. mustard seeds
- 3½ tsp. dill seeds
- 5 cups white vinegar (5% acidity)
- ½ cup pickling salt

1. Pack beans into hot jars, trimming to fit ½ inch from top. Add 1 pepper, 1 garlic clove (quartered), ½ tsp. mustard seeds, and ½ tsp. dill seeds to each of 7 (1-pt.) jars.
2. Bring vinegar, 5 cups water, and pickling salt to a boil; pour into each jar, filling to ½ inch from top. Remove air bubbles; wipe jar rims. Cover at once with metal lids; screw on bands.
3. Process in boiling-water bath 10 minutes.

*1¾ tsp. dried crushed red pepper may be substituted for hot red peppers. Add ¼ tsp. per jar.

Peppery Texas Pickles

Hands-on Time: 26 min.
Total Time: 8 hr., 29 min., plus 48 hr.
Makes: 3 qt.

- 2 lb. pickling cucumbers, sliced
- 1 cup chopped fresh cilantro
- 6 small dried red chile peppers
- 4 garlic cloves, thinly sliced
- 1 large sweet onion, sliced
- 3 cups white vinegar (5% acidity)
- ⅓ cup sugar
- 2 Tbsp. canning-and-pickling salt
- 1 Tbsp. pickling spices

1. Place first 5 ingredients in a large plastic bowl. (Do not use glass.)

Peppery Texas Pickles

2. Combine 1 cup water, vinegar, and remaining 3 ingredients in a 4-cup glass measuring cup. Microwave at HIGH 3 minutes; remove from microwave, and stir until sugar dissolves. Pour hot mixture evenly over cucumber mixture. Cover and chill 48 hours.
3. Spoon evenly into 3 (1-qt.) canning jars or freezer containers, leaving ½ inch of room at the top; seal, label, and freeze pickles 8 hours or up to 6 months. Thaw in refrigerator before serving; use thawed pickles within 1 week.

Green Tomato Pickles

Hands-on Time: 33 min.
Total Time: 1 hr., 19 min.
Makes: 7 pt.

     5 lb. green tomatoes, chopped
     1 large onion, chopped
     2 Tbsp. pickling salt
  1½ cups firmly packed light brown sugar
     2 cups cider vinegar (5% acidity)
     2 tsp. mustard seeds
     2 tsp. whole allspice
     2 tsp. celery seeds
  1½ tsp. whole cloves

1. Sprinkle tomato and onion with pickling salt; let stand 4 to 6 hours. Drain and pat dry with paper towels; set aside.
2. Combine brown sugar and vinegar in a Dutch oven; cook over medium heat, stirring constantly, until sugar dissolves.
3. Place mustard seeds and next 3 ingredients on 6-inch square of cheesecloth; tie with string. Add spice bag, tomato, onion, and 3 cups water to vinegar mixture.
4. Bring to a boil, stirring constantly; reduce heat, and simmer, stirring occasionally, 25 minutes or until tomato and onion are tender. Remove and discard spice bag.
5. Pour hot mixture into hot jars, filling to ½ inch from top. Remove air bubbles; wipe jar rims. Cover at once with metal lids, and screw on bands.
6. Process in boiling-water bath 10 minutes.

Pickled Grapes with Rosemary and Chiles

Hands-on Time: 10 min.
Total Time: 1 hr., 45 min.
Makes: 4 pt.

Add these gorgeous spicy-tart grapes to an antipasto platter or cheese plate, or stir them into chicken or mixed green salads. Guests will love the complex flavors. But the best part: Prep time is 10 minutes and "pickling" happens in the fridge in just a few hours.

     3 cups seedless green grapes (about 1 lb.)
     3 cups seedless red grapes (about 1 lb.)
     6 (4-inch-long) fresh rosemary sprigs, divided
     2 cups white wine vinegar
     3 garlic cloves, thinly sliced
     2 Tbsp. kosher salt
     2 tsp. sugar
     ½ tsp. dried crushed red pepper

1. Pack grapes into 4 (1-pt.) canning jars with lids. Add 1 rosemary sprig to each jar.
2. Bring vinegar, next 4 ingredients, 1 cup water, and remaining 2 rosemary sprigs to a simmer in a medium saucepan. Remove from heat, and discard rosemary sprigs. Pour hot vinegar mixture over grapes. Cover loosely, and let cool to room temperature (about 30 minutes). Seal and chill 1 hour before serving. Store in refrigerator up to 1 week.

Pickled Grapes with Rosemary and Chiles

Menus for All Occasions

Whether you're serving a crowd or a family of 4, these menus are sure to please.

Southern Picnic
Serves 8

Lemonade Iced Tea
(page 242)
Pork Roast with Carolina Gravy (page 312)
Heirloom Tomatoes with Fresh Peaches, Goat Cheese, and Pecans
(page 344)
Sweet-and-Tangy Braised Greens with Smoked Turkey
(page 165)
Banana Pudding
(page 360)

Holiday Open House
Serves 10 to 12

Simple Antipasto Platter
(page 109)
Warm Turnip Green Dip
(page 248)
Stuffed Mushrooms with Pecans (page 255)
Sweet Potato Squares with Lemon-Garlic Mayonnaise (page 258)
Easy Mini Muffulettas
(page 292)
Profiteroles with Coffee Whipped Cream
(page 359)
Luscious Lemon Bars
(page 363)

Pre-Game Tailgate
Serves 6 to 8

Raspberry Beer Cocktail
(page 245)
Fresh Peach Salsa
(page 382)
tortilla chips
Sweet and Savory Burgers (page 191)
baked beans
Layered Southwestern Salad (page 346)
Coca-Cola Cake (page 350)

Homestyle Brunch
Serves 8

Maple Coffee (page 244)
orange juice
One-Dish Blackberry French Toast (page 262)
bacon
Avocado Fruit Salad
(page 349)

Company Potluck
Serves 8

Simply Deviled Eggs
(page 140)
Classic Chicken Tetrazzini (page 310)
Hearts of Romaine Salad
(page 347)
Easy Three-Seed Pan Rolls (page 276)
So-Good Brownies
(page 364)

Summertime Cookout
Serves 4

Grilled Chicken Thighs with White Barbecue Sauce (page 308)
Big Daddy's Grilled Blue Cheese-and-Bacon Potato Salad (page 345)
Summer Vegetable Kabobs (page 182)
Pecan-Peach Cobbler (page 358)

Breakfast for Dinner
Serves 4

Spinach-and-Cheese Omelet* (page 269)
Buttermilk Biscuits (page 131)
Sausage Gravy (page 379)
grapefruit halves

*quadruple recipe

Simple Soup Supper
Serves 8 to 10

Grilled Pimiento Cheese Sandwiches (page 290)
Basil-Tomato Soup (page 298)
green salad with Pepper Jelly Vinaigrette (page 373)

Sunday Dinner Get-Together
Serves 10

Bev's Famous Meatloaf (page 318)
Perfect Mashed Potatoes (page 139)
green peas
Sour Cream Pound Cake (page 350)

Festive Family Feast
Serves 10

Fennel-Crusted Rib Roast (page 315)
Green Bean Casserole (page 335)
Sweet Potato Soufflé (page 339)
Double-Whammy Yeast Rolls (page 274)
Brandy Alexander Cheesecake (page 354)

Fish Fry
Serves 4 to 6

Bayou Fish Fillets with Sweet-Hot Pecan Sauce (page 324)
Hot Slaw à la Greyhound Grill (page 343)
Tomato-and-Watermelon Salad (page 346)
Sour Cream Cornbread (page 282)
Heavenly Key Lime Pie (page 356)

Ingredient	Substitution
BAKING PRODUCTS	
Baking Powder, 1 tsp.	• ½ tsp. cream of tartar plus ¼ tsp. baking soda
Chocolate	
semisweet, 1 oz.	• 1 oz. unsweetened chocolate plus 1 Tbsp. sugar
unsweetened, 1 oz. or square	• 3 Tbsp. cocoa plus 1 Tbsp. fat
chips, semisweet, 6-oz. package, melted	• 2 oz. unsweetened chocolate, 2 Tbsp. shortening plus ½ cup sugar
Cocoa, ¼ cup	• 1 oz. unsweetened chocolate (decrease fat in recipe by ½ Tbsp.)
Corn syrup, light, 1 cup	• 1 cup sugar plus ¼ cup water • 1 cup honey
Cornstarch, 1 Tbsp.	• 2 Tbsp. all-purpose flour or granular tapioca
Flour	
all-purpose, 1 Tbsp.	• 1½ tsp. cornstarch, potato starch, or rice starch • 1 Tbsp. rice flour or corn flour • 1½ Tbsp. whole wheat flour
all-purpose, 1 cup sifted	• 1 cup plus 2 Tbsp. sifted cake flour
cake, 1 cup sifted	• 1 cup minus 2 Tbsp. all-purpose flour
self-rising, 1 cup	• 1 cup all-purpose flour, 1 tsp. baking powder plus ½ tsp. salt
Shortening	
melted, 1 cup	• 1 cup cooking oil (don't use cooking oil unless recipe calls for melted shortening)
solid, 1 cup (used in baking)	• 1⅛ cups butter or margarine (decrease salt called for in recipe by ½ tsp.)
Sugar	
brown, 1 cup firmly packed	• 1 cup granulated white sugar
powdered, 1 cup	• 1 cup sugar plus 1 Tbsp. cornstarch (processed in food processor)
granulated white, 1 tsp.	• ⅛ tsp. noncaloric sweetener solution or follow manufacturer's directions
granulated white, 1 cup	• 1 cup corn syrup (decrease liquid called for in recipe by ¼ cup) • 1 cup honey (decrease liquid called for in recipe by ¼ cup)
Tapioca, granular, 1 Tbsp.	• 1½ tsp. cornstarch or 1 Tbsp. all-purpose flour

Ingredient | Substitution

DAIRY PRODUCTS

Butter, 1 cup
- ⅞ to 1 cup shortening or lard plus ½ tsp. salt

Cream

heavy (30% to 40% fat), 1 cup
- ¾ cup milk plus ⅓ cup butter or margarine (for cooking and baking; will not whip)

light (15% to 20% fat), 1 cup
- ¾ cup milk plus 3 Tbsp. butter or margarine (for cooking and baking)
- 1 cup evaporated milk, undiluted

half-and-half, 1 cup
- ⅞ cup milk plus ½ Tbsp. butter or margarine (for cooking and baking)
- 1 cup evaporated milk, undiluted

whipped, 1 cup
- 1 cup frozen whipped topping, thawed

Egg

1 large
- ¼ cup egg substitute

2 large
- 3 small eggs or ½ cup egg substitute
- 1 large egg plus 2 egg whites

1 egg white (2 Tbsp.)
- 2 Tbsp. egg substitute

Milk

buttermilk, 1 cup
- 1 Tbsp. vinegar or lemon juice plus whole milk to make 1 cup (let stand 10 minutes)
- 1 cup plain yogurt
- 1 cup whole milk plus 1¾ tsp. cream of tartar

fat-free, 1 cup
- 4 to 5 Tbsp. instant nonfat dry milk plus enough water to make 1 cup
- ½ cup fat-free evaporated milk plus ½ cup water

whole, 1 cup
- 4 to 5 Tbsp. instant nonfat dry milk plus enough water to make 1 cup
- ½ cup evaporated milk plus ½ cup water

sweetened condensed, 1 (14-oz.) can (about 1¼ cups)
- Heat the following ingredients until sugar and butter dissolve: ⅓ cup plus 2 Tbsp. evaporated milk, 1 cup sugar, 3 Tbsp. butter or margarine
- Add 1 cup plus 2 Tbsp. instant nonfat dry milk to ½ cup warm water. Mix well. Add ¾ cup sugar, and stir until smooth.

Ingredient

Substitution

DAIRY PRODUCTS (continued)

Sour Cream, 1 cup
- 1 cup plain yogurt plus 3 Tbsp. melted butter or 1 Tbsp. cornstarch
- 1 Tbsp. lemon juice plus evaporated milk to equal 1 cup

Yogurt, 1 cup (plain)
- 1 cup buttermilk

MISCELLANEOUS

Broth, beef or chicken canned broth, 1 cup
- 1 bouillon cube or 1 tsp. bouillon granules dissolved in 1 cup boiling water

Garlic

    1 small clove
- ⅛ tsp. garlic powder or minced dried garlic

    garlic salt, 1 tsp.
- ⅛ tsp. garlic powder plus ⅞ tsp. salt

Gelatin, flavored, 3-oz. package
- 1 Tbsp. unflavored gelatin plus 2 cups fruit juice

Herbs, fresh, chopped, 1 Tbsp.
- 1 tsp. dried herbs or ¼ tsp. ground herbs

Honey, 1 cup
- 1¼ cups sugar plus ¼ cup water

Mustard, dried, 1 tsp.
- 1 Tbsp. prepared mustard

Tomatoes, fresh, chopped, 2 cups
- 1 (16-oz.) can (may need to drain)

Tomato sauce, 2 cups
- ¾ cup tomato paste plus 1 cup water

ALCOHOL * Add water, white grape juice, or apple juice to get the specified amount of liquid (when liquid amount is crucial)

Amaretto, 2 Tbsp.
- ¼ to ½ tsp. almond extract*

Bourbon or Sherry, 2 Tbsp.
- 1 to 2 tsp. vanilla extract*

Brandy, fruit-flavored liqueur, port wine, rum, or sweet sherry, ¼ cup or more
- Equal amounts of unsweetened orange or apple juice plus 1 tsp. vanilla extract or corresponding flavor

Brandy or rum, 2 Tbsp.
- ½ to 1 tsp. brandy or rum extract*

Grand Marnier or other orange liqueur, 2 Tbsp.
- 2 Tbsp. unsweetened orange juice concentrate or 2 Tbsp. orange juice and ½ tsp. orange extract

Kahlúa or other coffee or chocolate liqueur, 2 Tbsp.
- ½ to 1 tsp. chocolate extract plus ½ to 1 tsp. instant coffee dissolved in 2 Tbsp. water

Marsala, ¼ cup
- ¼ cup white grape juice or ¼ cup dry white wine plus 1 tsp. brandy

Wine

    red, ¼ cup or more
- Equal measure of red grape juice or cranberry juice

    white, ¼ cup or more
- Equal measure of white grape juice or nonalcoholic white wine

Baking at High Altitudes

Liquids boil at lower temperatures (below 212°), and moisture evaporates more quickly at high altitudes. Both of these factors significantly impact the quality of baked goods. Also, leavening gases (air, carbon dioxide, water vapor) expand faster. If you live at 3,000 feet or below, first try a recipe as is. Sometimes few, if any, changes are needed. But the higher you go, the more you'll have to adjust your ingredients and cooking times.

A Few Overall Tips

- Use shiny new baking pans. This seems to help mixtures rise, especially cake batters.
- Use butter, flour, and parchment paper to prep your baking pans for nonstick cooking. At high altitudes, baked goods tend to stick more to pans.
- Be exact in your measurements (once you've figured out what they should be). This is always important in baking, but especially so when you're up so high. Tiny variations in ingredients make a bigger difference at high altitudes than at sea level.
- Boost flavor. Seasonings and extracts tend to be more muted at higher altitudes, so increase them slightly.
- Have patience. You may have to bake your favorite sea-level recipe a few times, making slight adjustments each time, until it's worked out to suit your particular altitude.

Ingredient/Temperature Adjustments

CHANGE	AT 3,000 FEET	AT 5,000 FEET	AT 7,000 FEET
Baking powder or baking soda	• Reduce each tsp. called for by up to ⅛ tsp.	• Reduce each tsp. called for by ⅛ to ¼ tsp.	• Reduce each tsp. called for by ¼ to ½ tsp.
Sugar	• Reduce each cup called for by up to 1 Tbsp.	• Reduce each cup called for by up to 2 Tbsp.	• Reduce each cup called for by 2 to 3 Tbsp.
Liquid	• Increase each cup called for by up to 2 Tbsp.	• Increase each cup called for by up to 2 to 4 Tbsp.	• Increase each cup called for by up to 3 to 4 Tbsp.
Oven temperature	• Increase 3° to 5°	• Increase 15°	• Increase 21° to 25°

fresh produce & herb primer

Spring

Bananas

select: Choose ripe bananas for immediate use and ones that are still slightly green for later use. They should be without bruises, full, and bright in color.

store: Store bananas at room temperature until ripe, then refrigerate. The peel will turn black, but the meat will remain firm and white for several days.

prepare: Bananas are usually eaten fresh, requiring no preparation.

cook: Dry, bake, fry, boil, steam, or sauté to add sweet flavor to both savory and sweet dishes.

Pineapples

select: A fresh pineapple should have firm green leaves on its top, and the body should be firm.

store: Pineapple will not become sweeter once picked, but will soften if left at room temperature for a few days. It should be refrigerated and used as soon as possible. Cut pineapple will last longer if placed in a tightly covered container and refrigerated or frozen.

prepare: To peel a pineapple, slice off the bottom and the green top. Stand the pineapple on one cut end, and slice off the skin, cutting just below the surface in wide vertical strips, leaving the small brown eyes. Remove the eyes by cutting diagonally around the fruit, following the pattern of the eyes and making shallow, narrow furrows, cutting away as little of the flesh as possible. Slice the pineapple into rings, and use a round cookie cutter or knife to remove the core.

cook: Pineapple is used in desserts, salads, and as a marinade and garnish for meats and seafood.

Strawberries

select: Choose brightly colored berries that still have their green caps attached.

store: Store in a moisture-proof container in the refrigerator for 3 to 4 days.

prepare: Do not wash or remove the hulls until you're ready to use the strawberries. It's best not to overwhelm the fresh flavor of strawberries. Try a mousse or a simple, sweet soup—or toss the berries with fresh salad greens.

Artichokes

select: Look for heavy, compact artichokes that have deep green, tight leaves.

store: Store artichokes in a plastic bag in the refrigerator up to 1 week.

prepare: Hold artichokes by the stem, and plunge them up and down in cold water. Cut off stems, and trim about $1/2$ inch from the top. Remove any loose bottom leaves, and trim approximately $1/4$-inch off the top of each outer leaf.

cook: Artichokes can be grilled, steamed, roasted, fried, or sautéed. When cooking, use stainless steel cookware and add a little lemon juice to the water to keep the leaves from darkening.

Arugula

select: Leaves should be bright green and crisp; stems shouldn't be withered or slimy.

store: Wrap a moist paper towel around the bunch, and store it up to 2 days. Dirt particles cling tightly to the leaves, so wash them well, and spin them dry just before using.

prepare: Make sure to remove any wilted leaves. Arugula is most commonly used as a salad green. It can also be wilted like spinach.

Asparagus

select: Look for asparagus with uniform color, smooth skin, and a dry, compact tip.

store: It's okay to wrap them in damp paper towels for several days; to extend their life, refrigerate stalks, tips up, in a cup of shallow water. Don't freeze fresh asparagus.

prepare: Snap fibrous ends from asparagus spears. Cook asparagus as is, or peel the skin with a vegetable peeler to make the stalks more tender.

cook: Broil, steam, grill, roast, or sauté for a few minutes until crisp-tender.

Baby leeks

select: Choose leeks with clean, white bulbs and firm, tightly rolled dark green tops.

store: Refrigerate leeks in a plastic bag up to 5 days.

prepare: Because leeks grow partly underground, they are often very dirty. To clean, trim off the roots and the tough tops of the green leaves. Then cut the leek stalk in half, and rinse well.

cook: Leeks can be cooked whole or chopped and sliced for salads, soups, or other dishes.

Fava beans
select: Look for long, plump, heavy pods that are bright green and unblemished.

store: Keep the pods in a bag in the refrigerator up to a week; store peeled beans 1 to 2 days. You can freeze blanched, peeled beans for a couple of months.

prepare: Open the pods and remove the beans. Boil briefly, then remove the tough outer skin.

cook: Once blanched and peeled, they add crunch to any dish. If you prefer a softer texture, sauté or cook the blanched beans in boiling water until tender.

Green onions
select: Look for healthy dark green tops on the onions. Dry, wilted, or slimy tops are signs of age.

store: Wrap green onions in plastic and refrigerate up to 3 weeks, depending on the variety.

prepare: Cut off root ends and any limp or damaged parts of the green tops. Remove the outer layers of skin before you slice or chop.

cook: Green onions can be eaten raw, sautéed, baked, blanched, grilled, or used as a garnish.

Green peas
select: Look for crisp, medium-size bright green pods; avoid full, oversized pods, which tend to hold starchy paste.

store: Shell and chill green peas as soon as possible. If you can't cook and eat fresh peas within 2 or 3 days, blanch and freeze them up to 2 months.

prepare: Green peas will open like a zipper when pressure is applied to the middle of the pod.

cook: Boil, steam, or braise peas just until tender.

Lettuce
select: Look for lettuce that's unbruised, unwilted, and has bright color.

store: Refrigerate clean lettuce in a plastic bag or an airtight container up to 5 days.

prepare: Since leaves can be dirty as well as delicate, wash them gently in cool water, and then dry thoroughly. A salad spinner can be used to dry greens, or you can shake them free of excess moisture and blot dry with paper towels. Dressings cling better to dry leaves.

Rhubarb
select: Choose firm, crisp, medium-size stalks.

store: Rhubarb is highly perishable, so it should be refrigerated in a plastic bag up to 3 days. It can also be blanched and frozen in freezer containers for up to 6 months.

prepare: Wash and trim the stems; remove and discard all leaves, as they are poisonous.

cook: Rhubarb is usually cooked with a generous amount of sugar to balance its tartness. It makes delicious sauces, jams, and desserts.

Snap beans
select: Look for small, tender, crisp pod beans with bright color. If they're fresh, you'll hear the snap when you bend pod beans.

store: Wash fresh beans before storing them in the refrigerator in plastic bags up to 3 or 4 days.

prepare: Before you cook snap beans, wash them thoroughly, and cut off the tips.

cook: When steamed, sautéed, or simmered, this vegetable makes a popular side dish.

Snow peas
select: Once picked, the sugar in snow peas quickly converts to starch, so cook them soon. You can refrigerate them in a plastic bag for a day or so before they begin to lose flavor.

store: Keep the pods in a bag in the refrigerator up to a week; store peeled beans only a day or 2. You can freeze blanched, peeled beans for a couple of months.

prepare: Snow peas are sweet and tender enough to be eaten raw or cooked whole, although it's best to pinch off the tip ends and remove any strings just before using.

cook: Snow peas are easy to cook. Drop them into boiling water and cook about 30 seconds or steam over boiling water less than a minute. They can also be stir-fried by themselves or tossed into a stir-fry recipe; add them at the last minute, and cook just until they turn bright green.

Spinach
select: Select spinach bunches with crisp leaves; avoid limp bunches with yellowing leaves. Spinach is available year-round, but its peak local season is May to August.

store: If unwashed, wash in cold water, and pat dry. Chill the leaves in a plastic bag lined with damp paper towels up to 3 days.

prepare: Spinach is usually very gritty, so make sure that it's thoroughly washed.

cook: Spinach leaves can be served cooked, as in spanakopita, or served raw in salads.

Sugar snap peas

select: Choose sugar snap peas that are firm, plump, and bright green with no yellowing in color. Sugar snaps are available during spring and fall months.

store: Keep sugar snaps refrigerated in a plastic bag up to 3 or 4 days.

prepare: Sugar snaps do not require shelling or stringing. You can remove the cap end, if desired.

cook: Sugar snap peas can be served raw or briefly cooked. Whether you serve them warm or chilled, they are best blanched first.

Sweet onions

select: Look for sweet onions that are light golden brown in color with a shiny tissue-thin skin and firm, tight, dry necks.

store: To extend the life of sweet onions, store them so that they aren't touching each other; some cooks hang them in old pantyhose with knots tied between each onion.

prepare: Cut through the stem end, peel back the papery skin, and cut the onion down the middle lengthwise. Place each half, cut side down, on a cutting board, and make several parallel horizontal cuts almost to the root end. Then make several parallel vertical cuts through the onion layers, but again, not cutting through the root end. Finally, cut across the grain to make chopped pieces.

cook: Sweet onions can be grilled, sautéed, caramelized, baked, cooked, broiled, or eaten raw.

Summer

Blackberries

select: Select plump berries with hulls detached. If hulls are still intact, the berries were picked too early.

store: Fresh blackberries are best stored in the refrigerator for up to a week. Choose a wide, shallow bowl to store berries, and cover with plastic wrap to keep them from drying out.

prepare: Just before you use blackberries, rinse them under cold water. For the best flavor, allow the berries to come to room temperature.

cook: Blackberries can be eaten out of hand, in desserts, or topped with sweetened whipped cream. When pureeing blackberries, press them through a sieve to remove the seeds and pulp.

Blueberries

select: Pick plump, juicy berries with blooms that have no trace of mold or discoloration. Look for firm, uniformly sized berries with deep color and no hulls or stems.

store: If eating blueberries within 24 hours of picking, store them at room temperature; otherwise, keep them refrigerated in a moisture-proof container up to 3 days.

prepare: Wash berries just before using them.

cook: Blueberries can be eaten out of hand, in pies, pancakes, salads, jams, and jellies.

Cantaloupes

select: Pick a cantaloupe with a soft stem end. Look for a light yellow ridged or smooth outer shell. Avoid cantaloupe with a green cast.

store: Store unripe cantaloupes at room temperature and ripe cantaloupes in the refrigerator for 1 to 2 days.

prepare: Wash cantaloupe in warm soapy water before cutting to get rid of any impurity on the rind that might be carried from the knife blade to the flesh. Remove all seeds and strings. Cantaloupe can be served many ways, including in chutneys, salads, and beverages.

Cherries

select: Choose cherries with firm, smooth, unblemished skins with stems still attached.

store: Fresh cherries should be eaten as soon as possible; they can be covered and refrigerated up to 4 days. After opening canned cherries, store them in an airtight container in the refrigerator up to a week. Maraschino cherries last up to 6 months in the refrigerator.

prepare: The quickest way to pit fresh cherries is with a cherry pitter. If you don't have one, try this: Push the cherry firmly down onto the pointed end of a pastry bag tip, or push a drinking straw through the bottom of the cherry, forcing the pit up and out through the stem end.

cook: Sweet cherries can be eaten out of hand; sour cherries are great in desserts and sauces.

Honeydew melons

select: Fresh, ripe honeydews should have a soft, velvety texture and be heavy for their size.

store: Ripe honeydews will keep up to 5 days in the refrigerator or in a cool, dark place. Seal cut honeydew in plastic wrap or an airtight container; it readily absorbs the odors and flavors of other foods.

prepare: Wash honeydew before cutting. Cut the melon in half, and scoop out the seeds. You can serve honeydew alone, or mix it with other fresh fruits for a salad. Honeydew can be pureed and made into a cold soup or used in a smoothie.

Nectarines

select: Nectarines should be plump, rich in color, and have a softening along the seam.

store: Speed the nectarines' ripening by placing them in a paper bag for several days at room temperature. Once ripened, store nectarines in the refrigerator, and use within 2 or 3 days.

prepare: Nectarines can be eaten out of hand or used in a variety of salads and desserts.

cook: Nectarines can be grilled or used in dishes including pork, chicken, and fish.

Peaches

select: Look for peaches that are firm, with a taut, unblemished skin and no signs of bruising or wrinkles. If you smell peaches when you walk up to the stand, you know they are ripe.

store: Ripen peaches at room temperature. If ripe, refrigerate them; they'll keep for a few days.

prepare: Wash, peel, if desired, and slice peaches before eating, or prepare according to recipe directions.

cook: Peaches work with both sweet and savory dishes. Cook with sugar on the stove until thickened for a delicious jam. Sauté, grill, or roast them to serve with duck, chicken, or pork.

Plums

select: Choose plums that have a little give when you squeeze them and a sweet-smelling aroma.

store: Firm plums can be stored at room temperature until they become slightly soft. Refrigerate ripe plums in a plastic bag up to 4 or 5 days.

prepare: Wash plums before you eat them. Try slicing a plum, and adding it to a salad or slaw.

cook: Plums can be used for fruit compotes, desserts, jams, jellies, sauces, snacks, and tarts.

Raspberries

select: Fresh, ripe raspberries should be plump and tender, but not mushy. Raspberries are sold in clear packaging, so make sure to check all sides for signs of poor quality.

store: Store in an airtight container in the refrigerator for 2 to 3 days.

prepare: Rinse raspberries lightly under cold water just before using them.

cook: Add raspberries to pancakes or waffles, or make them into jellies and jams.

Watermelons

select: Choose a firm, symmetrical, unblemished watermelon with a dull rind, without cracks or soft spots, that barely yields to pressure.

store: Store uncut at room temperature up to 1 week. Refrigerate 8 to 10 hours to serve chilled.

prepare: Wash and dry the rind before cutting to prevent bacterial contamination. Once sliced, cover with plastic wrap; refrigerate up to 4 days.

cook: Use watermelon to make glazes or sauces. It can also be grilled and stir-fried or eaten chilled and uncooked.

Carrots

select: Choose carrots that are firm and brightly colored, avoiding ones that are cracked. If the leafy tops are attached, make sure they are not wilted.

store: Remove tops if attached; place carrots in plastic bags, and refrigerate up to 2 weeks.

prepare: Wash and cut carrots into sticks for dipping and eating, or shred them to add to salads or slaws.

cook: You can steam, braise, sauté, bake, or microwave carrots. Add them to soups and stews, or serve them as a side dish.

Celery

select: Choose celery that is bright in color, firm, and crisp. Avoid stalks with wilted leaves.

store: Store celery in a plastic bag in the refrigerator, leaving the ribs attached to the stalk until ready to use. It will typically keep up to a couple of weeks.

prepare: To restore crispness to fresh celery, trim ribs and soak them in ice water 15 minutes.

cook: Celery is a popular ingredient in soups and stews. It is also commonly used in stuffing recipes, stir-fries, and salad dressings. Cut into strips for dipping.

Collards

select: Young collards with small leaves are more tender and less bitter. Avoid collards with large leathery leaves that are withered or that have yellow spots.

store: Wash collards, and pat dry. Place them in a plastic bag, and refrigerate up to 5 days.

prepare: Make sure you wash collard green leaves by hand, once in warm water and three times in cold water, to get rid of all the grit. Like all greens, collards cook down considerably. A good rule of thumb is that 1 lb. of raw greens yields 1½ cups cooked.

cook: Collards are traditionally cooked in a pork-seasoned broth to tame bitter flavors.

Corn

select: A fresh husk is the number one thing to look for. Deep brown silk tips or ends mean it's ripe, but the whole silk shouldn't be dried up. Open the tip of the husk to see if the kernels are all the way to the end of the ear. The kernels should be plump and milky when pinched.

store: The sugars in corn begin to turn to starch as soon as it's harvested, so plan to eat it as soon as possible. You can store it in its husk in the refrigerator up to a day.

prepare: Sweet summer corn requires minimal preparation and cooking.

cook: Place husked ears in a pot of cold water; bring water to a boil. Once the water boils, remove from heat, and let stand 1 minute before serving. Serve it on the cob, or cut the kernels off to use in soups, salads, succotash, salsas, and other dishes.

Cucumbers

select: Choose cucumbers with a deep green color. Avoid soft patches or shriveled ends.

store: Refrigerate cucumbers for up to 2 weeks. Use pickling cucumbers soon after picking.

prepare: If you don't peel your cucumbers, make sure you wash the waxy finish off before using.

cook: Cucumbers are best eaten raw and are traditionally used as a salad ingredient or on vegetable trays. They can also be battered and fried.

Green beans

select: Look for small, tender, crisp pod beans with bright color that snap when you bend them.

store: Fresh beans should be washed before being stored in the refrigerator in plastic bags for up to 3 or 4 days.

prepare: Although they are generally cooked, green beans can be eaten raw. Just rinse them and snap them into bite-size pieces.

cook: To retain nutrients, cook green beans a minimal amount of time. They should keep their bright color when cooked. Steaming or stir-frying works best.

Lima beans

select: Fresh limas are available from June to September and are usually sold in their pods.

store: Store dried beans at room temperature in tightly covered containers up to 1 year, or freeze up to 2 years.

prepare: Shell fresh limas before eating them. Dried beans require soaking before cooking.

cook: Limas can be used as a side dish or an ingredient in soups, or cooked and cooled for salads.

Okra

select: Choose tender, bright green pods with no signs of damage.

store: Store okra in a plastic bag in the refrigerator up to 3 days.

prepare: Make sure to rinse and pat okra dry before using. Unless you want to use okra as a thickener, don't cut the pods; just remove the tip of the stem.

cook: Okra can be fried, steamed, or grilled.

Peas

select: Fresh peas should have a good green color.

store: Store fresh peas refrigerated in a plastic bag.

prepare: The sugar in fresh peas quickly converts to starch, so it's important that they be prepared and eaten as soon as possible after picking, usually within 2 to 3 days.

cook: Peas do not require long cooking times because of their natural tenderness.

Summer squash

select: Choose small, firm squash with bright-colored, blemish-free skins.

store: Refrigerate squash in plastic bags up to 5 days before cooking.

prepare: Summer squash is great for blending with other ingredients or in simple preparations highlighting the taste of fresh herbs. Delicate yellow squash is perfect in chilled soups.

cook: Because it has a high water content, summer squash doesn't require much cooking.

Tomatoes

select: Smell them—a good tomato should smell like a tomato, especially at the stem end.

store: Place tomatoes at room temperature in a single layer, shoulder side up, and out of direct sunlight. To store ripe tomatoes for any extended period, keep them between 55° and 65°.

prepare: If you want to seed a tomato, core it, and then cut it in half crosswise. Use your thumbs to push the seeds out of the tomato halves. Seed tomatoes when you don't want much juice.

cook: Tomatoes can be stewed or crushed for use in casseroles, chili, and many Italian dishes.

Basil
select: Look for leaves that show no signs of wilting. Colors vary from shades of green to purple.

store: Store basil in a plastic bag in the refrigerator.

prepare: Slice basil by rolling up a small bunch of leaves and snipping it into shreds with kitchen shears. To chop it, snip the shreds crosswise.

cook: Use basil in salads, pestos, pasta dishes, pizza, and meat and poultry dishes.

Cilantro
select: When choosing cilantro, make sure you see no signs of wilting on the leaves.

store: Store in the refrigerator in a plastic bag up to 1 week.

prepare: Be sure to wash cilantro thoroughly after purchasing to remove any bits of sand.

cook: Cilantro is popular in Mexican, Asian, and Caribbean cuisines. Adding a tablespoon jazzes up a dish and offers a good bit of vitamin A.

Lavender
select: When choosing fresh lavender, look for herbs that show no signs of wilting.

store: Treat fresh herbs like a bouquet of flowers. Douse the leaves with cool water, and wrap the stems in a damp paper towel. Place the towel-wrapped herbs in a zip-top plastic freezer bag, remove as much air as possible from the bag, and refrigerate up to 1 week.

prepare: To chop fresh lavender, stuff the leaves into a glass measuring cup, and insert kitchen shears or scissors; snip in cup, rotating shears with each snip.

cook: Use lavender flowers and their leaves in desserts, marinades, and sauces.

Oregano
select: Choose fresh oregano that is vibrant green in color with firm stems. It should be free from dark spots or yellowing.

store: Keep fresh oregano in the refrigerator wrapped in a slightly damp paper towel. You can also freeze oregano, either whole or chopped, in airtight containers.

prepare: Oregano should be added toward the end of the cooking process since heat can easily cause a loss of its delicate flavor.

cook: Add to meat, fish, eggs, fresh and cooked tomatoes, vegetables, beans, and marinades.

Autumn

Figs
select: Don't judge by looks alone. A shrunken and wrinkled fig may actually be a better choice. Small cracks won't affect the flavor. Ripe figs should be heavy for their size.

store: Fresh figs are extremely perishable; handle them gently. Use them soon after purchasing, or store them in the refrigerator in a single layer no more than 2 or 3 days.

prepare: Fresh figs are best when simply prepared to enhance their natural sweetness.

cook: Fresh figs are most commonly used in desserts. Use figs in recipes including chutneys, sauces, and salads. They are also a flavorful companion for braised meats and poultry.

Grapes
select: Look for grapes that are plump and securely attached to their stem. Avoid grapes that are withered, soft, or bruised.

store: Store grapes, unwashed, in plastic bags in the refrigerator up to a week.

prepare: Wash grapes before eating.

cook: Use grapes to make delicious jellies and jams, add to salads or yogurt, or use as a garnish.

Pears
select: Apply light thumb pressure near the pear's stem. If it is ripe, there will be a slight give.

store: If pears aren't quite ripe, place them on a kitchen counter in a brown paper bag. Once ripened, fresh pears will keep for several days in the refrigerator. Don't store them in plastic bags.

prepare: To core a pear, cut it in half lengthwise, and scoop out the core with a melon baller or grapefruit spoon. Toss cut pears with a little citrus or pineapple juice to prevent discoloring.

cook: Use ripe pears in desserts, pancakes, and meat dishes. The best pears for cooking are varieties such as Bosc, Comice, Seckel, and red and green Anjous.

Persimmons

select: Choose persimmons that are medium to large in size and uniform in color. Avoid fruit that has cracks or signs of decay.

store: Always allow persimmons to ripen at room temperature; the Hachiya will be soft to the touch when ripe, but the Fuyu will be firm. Once ripened, refrigerate persimmons, and use as soon as possible, or place them in an airtight container whole and freeze up to 3 months.

prepare: Fuyu persimmons can be eaten raw as a snack, but make sure that they are ripe, as unripe persimmons are sour.

cook: Add persimmons to quick breads or desserts. They also make tasty jams and jellies.

Bell peppers

select: Bell peppers are at their best from July through September. Look for firm, nicely colored fruit that is fragrant at the stem end. Avoid peppers that are damp, because they can mold.

store: Store peppers in a plastic bag in the refrigerator up to 1 week. They can also be sliced or chopped and frozen in a freezer bag up to 6 months.

prepare: Be sure to wash peppers just before using.

cook: Bell peppers can be roasted, stuffed, stir-fried, or used in casseroles and salads.

Broccoli

select: Look for firm stalks with tightly bunched crowns. If the heads show signs of buds beginning to turn yellow, the broccoli is over the hill.

store: Refrigerate fresh broccoli in a plastic bag up to 4 days. To revive broccoli, trim $1/2$ inch from the base of the stalk and set the stalk in a glass of cold water in the refrigerator overnight.

prepare: When serving broccoli raw, trim it down into florets.

cook: Broccoli can be steamed, stir-fried, or cooked in the microwave. It is great on vegetable trays with dip or in green salads.

Cabbage

select: Choose heads that are compact and heavy for their size. The outer leaves should be without defect and have good green or red color.

store: Refrigerate cabbage, wrapped in plastic wrap, up to 1 week. Don't cut or shred it until ready to use to maximize freshness, color, and nutrients.

prepare: Always wash the cabbage head before use. To shred cabbage quickly, quarter it, cut away the core, and thinly slice the quarters into shreds.

cook: Cabbage can be steamed, boiled, roasted, stir-fried, or used in casseroles, soups, and stews.

Cauliflower

select: Cauliflower heads should be tightly packed. Avoid heads that have browning on them.

store: Wrap fresh cauliflower in plastic wrap, and refrigerate for 3 to 5 days. Once cooked, it can be refrigerated for 1 to 3 days.

prepare: Cauliflower should be washed and removed from the stem before using. Cut it into bite-size florets, which are great for dipping or eating in salads.

cook: Cauliflower can be boiled, baked, and sautéed; the whole cauliflower head may be cooked in one piece and topped with sauce.

Eggplant

select: Choose a firm, smooth-skinned eggplant, avoiding ones with soft or brown spots.

store: Refrigerate fresh, uncut eggplant up to 2 days.

prepare: The eggplant's skin should be washed thoroughly before preparing. Because eggplant flesh discolors rapidly, cut it just before using. The cut flesh can be brushed with lemon juice or dipped in a mixture of lemon juice and water to prevent browning.

cook: Eggplant can be baked, broiled, fried, or grilled.

Leeks

select: Buy leeks with crisp leaves and blemish-free stalks.

store: Keep leeks tightly wrapped in the refrigerator up to 5 days.

prepare: Cut the bulb in half lengthwise, and wash thoroughly, removing any soil or grit. Trim the root and leaf ends, discarding tough and withered leaves.

cook: Use leeks in quiches, risottos, pilafs, soups, and stews. When preparing leeks, be attentive; they overcook easily. They're ready when the base can be pierced with a knife.

Mushrooms

select: When buying fresh mushrooms, choose those that are smooth and have a dry top.

store: Refrigerate fresh mushrooms, unwashed, for no more than 3 days; they're best kept in a paper or cloth bag that allows them to breathe. Do not store mushrooms in plastic.

prepare: Clean fresh mushrooms with a mushroom brush or damp paper towel just before using. Never clean fresh mushrooms by soaking them in water. You can give them a quick rinse and pat them dry when you're about to use them.

cook: Sauté, microwave, roast, grill, broil, or use mushrooms for pizza toppings.

Pumpkins

select: Look for pumpkins that are small, about 5 to 8 lb., with tough skin. They are prized for their concentrated flavor and sweetness.

store: Store in the refrigerator up to 3 months, or in a cool, dry place up to 1 month. Once cut, wrap pumpkins tightly in plastic, refrigerate, and use within 3 or 4 days.

prepare: If you've ever carved a jack-o'-lantern, you know how to tackle a fresh pumpkin. Use your hand or a spoon to remove the seeds and stringy flesh.

cook: Go beyond traditional pumpkin dishes; quarter, steam, and mash the flesh, mixing it with black pepper or brown sugar to serve as a side dish. For a healthy snack, roast the seeds.

Red potatoes

select: When buying potatoes, choose those that are firm and blemish-free. Avoid potatoes with soft spots or those that have a green cast to the skin.

store: Store potatoes for 2 weeks in a cool, dry, dark, well-ventilated place. New potatoes should be used within 2 or 3 days of purchase.

prepare: Make sure you thoroughly wash raw potatoes before cooking to remove any dirt.

cook: Red potatoes are great for making potato salad or for pan roasting.

Shallots

select: Choose shallots that are firm to the touch with a dry, papery, thin skin.

store: Store shallots in a cool, dry place for up to a month.

prepare: Peel and slice or chop shallots before you use them in cooking.

cook: Use shallots in place of onions.

Sweet potatoes

select: Look for small to medium-size potatoes with few bruises and smooth skin.

store: Store sweet potatoes in a cool, dry, dark place. If the temperature is right (about 55°), you can keep them 3 to 4 weeks. Otherwise, use them within a week. Do not refrigerate.

prepare: Sweet potatoes can be cooked with the skin on or peeled before cooking.

cook: This versatile vegetable is best for mashing or tossing into soups and stews but can be boiled, baked, roasted, and sautéed.

Yukon gold potatoes

select: Choose potatoes that are firm and blemish-free without any soft spots.

store: Store potatoes for up to 2 weeks in a cool, dry, dark, well-ventilated place.

prepare: To prepare raw potatoes for cooking, wash them thoroughly to remove any dirt.

cook: Yukon potatoes can be baked, boiled, sautéed, or fried.

Bay leaves

select: You can use fresh or dried bay leaves in your dishes. Fresh bay leaves are less available.

store: Store dried bay leaves in an airtight container in a cool, dark place up to 1 year.

prepare: If using fresh bay leaves, be sure to wash them before cooking.

cook: Use fresh or dried bay leaves in soups and stews. Discard whole leaves before serving food.

Rosemary

select: Buy rosemary dried or fresh at your local market. You could also buy a rosemary plant and keep it in your kitchen.

store: Keep fresh rosemary in plastic bags in the refrigerator. Store dry rosemary sprigs in an airtight container, or freeze in a zip-top plastic freezer bag.

prepare: To harvest rosemary (from your home plant), strip the leaves from the stem.

cook: Use the strong-flavored leaves sparingly. Rosemary adds a wonderful accent to soups, meats, stews, breads, and vegetables.

Sage

select: Sage is available either fresh or in three dried forms: ground, coarsely crumbled, or rubbed (finely chopped).

store: Keep fresh sage leaves in a plastic bag in the refrigerator. Use within 4 to 5 days. Freeze fresh sage leaves in a zip-top plastic freezer bag for up to a year.

prepare: Trim the ends of the stems and wrap the leaves in paper towels.

cook: Sage is best known for use in holiday dressings. It also flavors sausage well. Sage leaves are soft and pliable, which makes them easy to tuck under poultry skin before roasting.

Tarragon

select: In general, herbs should be fresh looking, crisp, and brightly colored.

store: Keep tarragon in a plastic bag with damp paper towels, and refrigerate for 1 to 2 days.

prepare: Tarragon's leaves bruise easily, so be gentle when chopping them.

cook: This leafy herb plays a classic role in Béarnaise sauce. It also adds flavor to soups, poultry, seafood, vegetables, and egg dishes. It's often used to make herb butter or vinegar.

Winter

Grapefruit

select: The heavier the grapefruit, the juicier it will be.

store: Grapefruits have a long shelf life and can be kept in the refrigerator for 6 to 8 weeks.

prepare: Grapefruit is most often eaten raw. It can be peeled and sectioned like oranges and added to fruit salad. Or for breakfast, cut a grapefruit in half, and eat it with a spoon.

Kumquats

select: Look for kumquats with bright orange skin. Avoid any citrus with signs of decay.

store: Keep kumquats at room temperature up to 1 week or refrigerated in a plastic bag for 3 to 4 weeks.

prepare: Kumquats can be sliced to serve in salads or used as a garnish.

cook: Try candying or pickling whole kumquats for a delicious treat, or use them to make preserves or marmalades.

Navel oranges

select: Choose navel oranges that have smooth skins and are not moldy. Don't worry about brown patches on the skin; this does not indicate poor quality.

store: Store navel oranges at room temperature up to a week or refrigerate up to 3 weeks.

prepare: To section an orange, peel it with a paring knife. Be sure to remove the bitter white pith. Hold the orange over a bowl to catch the juices, and slice between the membranes and one side of one segment of the orange. Lift the segment out with the knife blade. For the best flavor, use navel oranges raw. If they are cooked, cook them only briefly.

Beets

select: Look for small to medium-size well-shaped beets with smooth skins. Very large beets may be tough. If the leaves are attached, they should be crisp and bright green.

store: A beet's green leaves leach nutrients from the root, so immediately trim them to about an inch. Because the greens are highly perishable, you should use them within a day. Store beets in plastic bags in the refrigerator up to 2 weeks; gently wash before use.

prepare: Because the juice can stain your hands, wear disposable latex gloves.

cook: Beets hold up well when julienned raw, roasted, baked, or broiled, and pair well with orange juice, vinegar, and wine. They are often used in salads, pickles, and the soup known as borscht.

Fennel

select: Look for small, heavy, white fennel bulbs that are firm and free of cracks, browning, or moist areas. Stalks should be crisp with feathery, bright green fronds.

store: Store fresh fennel in a plastic bag in the refrigerator up to 5 days. Fennel seeds should be stored in a cool, dark place up to 6 months.

prepare: Before using fennel, trim the stalks about an inch above the bulb.

cook: Fennel is often added to soups and stews, and its licorice flavor becomes milder when cooked. Fennel is a good complement to seafood and poultry recipes.

Parsnips

select: Because parsnips are a root vegetable, some dirt may still be on the vegetable; they should be mostly clean. Look for firm, medium-size vegetables with uniformly beige skin.

store: Keep parsnips refrigerated in a plastic bag up to 1 month.

prepare: Wash parsnips before cooking. You can peel them as you would a carrot.

cook: Parsnips are suitable for baking, boiling, sautéing, roasting, or steaming and are often boiled and mashed like potatoes. They are also wonderful roasted; it brings out their sweetness.

Rutabagas

select: Rutabagas should be heavy for their size; lightweight ones tend to have a woody flavor.

store: Store rutabagas sealed in a plastic bag in the refrigerator up to a month.

prepare: Rutabagas are coated with clear paraffin wax to hold in moisture, so make sure you wash and peel them before cooking.

cook: Rutabagas are delicious peeled and cooked as a turnip, in a small amount of water, sometimes with a little added sugar, salt, or herbs.

Turnips

select: If you prefer a sweeter tasting turnip, look for small- to medium-size vegetables.

store: Turnip roots can be refrigerated in a plastic bag for 1 to 2 weeks. Wash greens in cold water, and pat dry; store in a plastic bag lined with moist paper towels in the refrigerator up to 3 days.

prepare: Wash and peel turnip roots before cooking them.

cook: Turnip roots can be boiled and mashed; roasted and pureed or cubed and tossed with butter; or used raw in salads. Turnip greens can be boiled, steamed, sautéed, or stir-fried.

Winter squash

select: The tastiest winter squash are solid and heavy, with stems that are full, firm, and have a corky feel. The skin of the squash should be deep colored with a nonshiny finish.

store: You don't have to refrigerate winter squash; keep it in a paper bag in a cool, dark place (about 50°) for about a month. Don't store winter squash in plastic bags for more than 3 days, because the plastic traps moisture and causes the squash to rot.

prepare: Winter squash are almost impossible to overcook. They can be boiled, baked, roasted, simmered, steamed, microwaved, or sautéed.

cook: To microwave a whole squash, pierce the rind in several places so it won't explode.

Chives

select: Chives should be fresh looking, crisp, and brightly colored. Avoid herbs that have dry patches, are wilted, or look slimy.

store: Store chives in a plastic bag in the refrigerator up to 1 week.

prepare: Fresh chives can be snipped with kitchen shears to the desired length.

cook: Chives add a mild onion or garlic flavor and are used in cooked dishes and cold salads.

Parsley

select: Fresh and dried parsley is widely available; fresh is sold in bunches in the produce department. Look for crisp, brightly colored parsley, avoiding any wilted or slimy leaves.

store: Wash parsley and shake off excess moisture. Wrap in damp paper towels; chill in a plastic bag up to 1 week.

prepare: If parsley begins to wilt, snip the lower stems and place the bunch in a glass of cold water; loosely cover leaves with a plastic bag, and chill. It will perk up in no time.

cook: Italian flat-leaf parsley offers a fresh flavor to stews, bean dishes, and salads.

Thyme

select: Thyme leaves should look fresh and crisp and be a vibrant green-gray in color.

store: Keep fresh thyme in a plastic bag lined with a damp paper towel in the refrigerator for up to a week.

prepare: Thyme leaves are small and often don't require chopping. Strip the leaves from their stems just before using.

cook: Thyme's earthiness is welcome with pork, lamb, duck, or goose, and it's much beloved in Cajun and Creole cooking. It's also the primary component of Caribbean jerk seasonings.

Metric Equivalents

The recipes that appear in this cookbook use the standard U.S. method for measuring liquid and dry or solid ingredients (teaspoons, tablespoons, and cups). The information in the following charts is provided to help cooks outside the United States successfully use these recipes. All equivalents are approximate.

Metric Equivalents for Different Types of Ingredients

A standard cup measure of a dry or solid ingredient will vary in weight depending on the type of ingredient. A standard cup of liquid is the same volume for any type of liquid. Use the following chart when converting standard cup measures to grams (weight) or milliliters (volume).

Standard Cup	Fine Powder (ex. flour)	Grain (ex. rice)	Granular (ex. sugar)	Liquid Solids (ex. butter)	Liquid (ex. milk)
1	140 g	150 g	190 g	200 g	240 ml
¾	105 g	113 g	143 g	150 g	180 ml
⅔	93 g	100 g	125 g	133 g	160 ml
½	70 g	75 g	95 g	100 g	120 ml
⅓	47 g	50 g	63 g	67 g	80 ml
¼	35 g	38 g	48 g	50 g	60 ml
⅛	18 g	19 g	24 g	25 g	30 ml

Useful Equivalents for Liquid Ingredients by Volume

¼ tsp						=	1 ml		
½ tsp						=	2 ml		
1 tsp						=	5 ml		
3 tsp	=	1 Tbsp			=	½ fl oz	=	15 ml	
		2 Tbsp	=	⅛ cup	=	1 fl oz	=	30 ml	
		4 Tbsp	=	¼ cup	=	2 fl oz	=	60 ml	
		5⅓ Tbsp	=	⅓ cup	=	3 fl oz	=	80 ml	
		8 Tbsp	=	½ cup	=	4 fl oz	=	120 ml	
		10⅔ Tbsp	=	⅔ cup	=	5 fl oz	=	160 ml	
		12 Tbsp	=	¾ cup	=	6 fl oz	=	180 ml	
		16 Tbsp	=	1 cup	=	8 fl oz	=	240 ml	
		1 pt	=	2 cups	=	16 fl oz	=	480 ml	
		1 qt	=	4 cups	=	32 fl oz	=	960 ml	
						33 fl oz	=	1000 ml	= 1 l

Useful Equivalents for Dry Ingredients by Weight

(To convert ounces to grams, multiply the number of ounces by 30.)

1 oz	=	¹⁄₁₆ lb	=	30 g
4 oz	=	¼ lb	=	120 g
8 oz	=	½ lb	=	240 g
12 oz	=	¾ lb	=	360 g
16 oz	=	1 lb	=	480 g

Useful Equivalents for Length

(To convert inches to centimeters, multiply the number of inches by 2.5.)

1 in					=	2.5 cm	
6 in	=	½ ft			=	15 cm	
12 in	=	1 ft			=	30 cm	
36 in	=	3 ft	=	1 yd	=	90 cm	
40 in					=	100 cm	= 1 m

Useful Equivalents for Cooking/Oven Temperatures

	Fahrenheit	Celsius	Gas Mark
Freeze water	32° F	0° C	
Room temperature	68° F	20° C	
Boil water	212° F	100° C	
Bake	325° F	160° C	3
	350° F	180° C	4
	375° F	190° C	5
	400° F	200° C	6
	425° F	220° C	7
	450° F	230° C	8
Broil			Grill

Subject Index

Recipe Index